STUDY GUIDE

Psychological Science

SECOND EDITION

Michael S. Gazzaniga • *Todd F. Heatherton*

Brett L. Beck and
Eileen Astor-Stetson
BLOOMSBURG UNIVERSITY

 W • W • NORTON & COMPANY • NEW YORK • LONDON

Printed in the United States of America

Second Edition

Composition and layout by R. Flechner Graphics

ISBN 0-393-92540-4

W. W. Norton & Company, Inc., 500 Fifth Avenue, New York, NY 10110
www.wwnorton.com

W. W. Norton & Company Ltd., Castle House, 75/76 Wells Street, London W1T 3QT

1 2 3 4 5 6 7 8 9 0

CONTENTS

CHAPTER 1 | Introduction to Psychological Science

GUIDE TO THE READING

Gazzaniga and Heatherton introduce their book by first defining psychological science as including the study of mind, brain, and behavior. They then present four major themes in psychological science today. These themes provide a structure guiding the ways in which psychological scientists develop theories and research. A history of the origins of psychological science follows. This section discusses the roots of psychological science in early philosophy, the influence of biological theories, and the beginnings of psychology. The application of psychological science is then presented, including how psychological science serves as a base for psychological therapy and how information gained through psychological research influences other fields. The section ends by emphasizing that because psychology is a science it requires critical thinking.

What Are the Themes of Psychological Science?

Four basic themes are presented that help to define psychological science. The first is that research in psychology resulted in accumulated knowledge. This means that knowledge gained from early researchers served as a foundation for current scientists. This accumulated knowledge resulted in the basic principles of psychology. These principles are the focus of this book.

The second theme is the biological revolution. Although you may not realize it, there is currently a revolution occurring in science. Changes in what we know about brain chemicals, genes, and techniques to measure brain functions have had a profound influence on psychological science. For example, by watching how the brain works we can now see not just which structures are involved in memory but which are involved in memory for words as opposed to memory of pictures.

The third theme focuses on evolution. According to evolutionary theory, some members of a species have adaptive traits, while other members do not. The adaptive traits are those that allow an individual to survive to reproduce. These adaptive traits are then passed on to offspring. Psychological science assumes that humans have been evolving, and so many human behaviors must have adaptive significance. For example, social behaviors such as joining groups, or cognitive abilities such as memory for location of food, may be important for survival. In addition to discussing biological adaptation, the authors also discuss the importance of cultural evolution. A culture defines the beliefs, values, and rules of a group of people. Culture, therefore, has a huge impact on the individual's worldview and daily life. To understand human mind, brain, and behavior, we must consider both biology and culture.

The fourth theme is that several categories of analysis can be used to study psychological science: social, psychological, and biological. For example, some psychological scientists may study brain chemistry, reflecting a biological approach. Others may study how people act in groups, reflecting a social approach. Still others may study individuals' thinking, reflecting a psychological approach.

What Are the Origins of Psychological Science?

Psychological science addresses issues that were first discussed by philosophers long before the field of psychology even existed. One major issue is the nature–nurture debate. Since the time of the ancient Greeks, there has been a debate over the degree to which an individual's traits are the result of genes (nature) or the result of the environment (nurture).

A second question involves the mind–body problem. A common belief through history was that the mind and body are distinct: This is a view known as dualism. If the mind and body are independent, how can the mind be studied? The French philosopher René Descartes proposed that although they are distinct, the mind and body are connected and interact with each other.

In the nineteenth century a third major influence on psychological science was introduced by Charles Darwin: evolutionary theory and natural selection. Natural selection is the basis of the idea of "survival of the fittest." Organisms that have adaptive traits live long enough to pass those traits on to offspring, who in turn will continue to pass the traits on.

How Did the Foundations of Psychological Science Develop?

The foundations of psychological science started in the nineteenth century with both philosophy and biology. Philosopher John Stuart Mill proposed that psychology should become a science based on experimentation. Biologists developed methods to measure psychological functions such as sensation and perception.

Experimental psychology developed from this foundation. Wilhelm Wundt established the first psychological laboratory. His student, Titchener, developed the first perspective in psychology, structuralism. This is the view that conscious experience can be broken down into its parts.

William James criticized Titchener's approach. Instead of focusing on components of consciousness, he focused on what the mind is used for and how it works. His perspective became known as functionalism. Another alternative to structuralism was the Gestalt movement, which emphasized that perception is more than the sum of its parts. At the end of the nineteenth century a view was presented that there was more to mental life than the individual was aware of: Freud presented his ideas on the unconscious.

While Freud was discussing parts of the mind that could not be directly observed, John Watson eliminated study of the mind altogether. He developed behaviorism: He proposed that psychologists study only what was observable. This was the dominant perspective in psychology until the 1960s, when a cognitive revolution changed the focus to how people think and reason. There was also increased research on how people behave in social contexts. Today we can see the influence of the development of psychological science not only on research but also on therapy. The ways in which psychological disorders are treated are clearly based on advances in research.

How Can We Apply Psychological Science?

Psychological science includes a number of subfields. These subfields may approach psychological science from varying levels of analysis. For example, cognitive psychologists may focus on thinking, whereas physiological psychologists study biological bases for behavior. Examining behavior from multiple levels allows more insight than doing so from any single level. Throughout the text, information will be critically examined from the three levels of analysis.

Psychological scientists do not simply accept findings but critically evaluate evidence. The information gained from psychological science may be used in many different disciplines. Regardless of approach, psychological science emphasizes critical thinking. For example, psychological practitioners use the information gained through psychological science to help people in their daily living. Today's therapies are based on scientific advances in the study of behavior, cognition, and biology. Information from psychological science also influences professions outside psychology. Physicians, lawyers, and advertisers all use information from psychological science, which is based on critical evaluation.

FILL-IN-THE-BLANK QUESTIONS

1. Dr. Garcia studies college students' thoughts and feelings. Of the three components of psychological science, Dr. Garcia is most clearly interested in the _____.

2. An observable action or response is a _____.

3. Dr. Smith studies how an animal's behavior allows that animal to survive. Dr. Smith most clearly is influenced by what theory? _____

4. A revolution in _____ is having a great effect on psychological science.

5. Schizophrenia is apparently related to an imbalance of chemicals in the brain. It therefore involves a problem with _____.

6. The basic genetic code for the human body is called the _____.

7. Characteristics that increase the chance of reproduction or survival are said to be _____.

8. The finding that evolutionary theory can be applied to aggression, lying, or cheating shows it is relevant to _____ behavior.

9. Janice, Henry, and Chavonne live in the same society, speak the same language, and share the same beliefs and values. They are living in the same _____.

10. Research on culture indicates that Westerners tend to be analytic, whereas Easterners tend to be _____.

11. Dr. Littlejohn studies how the chemicals in the brains of people with schizophrenia differ from those in the brains of people without mental disorders. Dr. Littlejohn is using which category of analysis to study psychological science? _____

12. Dr. Hernandez is interested in how a society's views on weight influence perception of beauty. Dr. Hernandez is using which category of analysis to study psychological science? _____

13. Daron was in a study that looked at his ability to recall words and pictures. This study was focused on which level of analysis in psychological science? _____

14. Dr. Fellman takes pictures of brain activity as people solve problems. He is studying psychological science at what level of analysis? _____

15. Tanika and Joe were arguing about whether people are more influenced by their genes or by the way in which they are treated. Tanika and Joe's discussion reflects which controversy? _____

16. The belief that the mind and body are separate yet intertwined reflects what theory? _____

17. Which philosopher first suggested that the mind and body though separate were connected? _____

18. Which theorist developed evolutionary theory? _____

19. John Stuart Mill proposed that psychology is separate from philosophy and focus on _____ and _____.

20. Tobi is doing an experiment where she hopes to break thoughts down into their components. Tobi's experiment is most similar to which psychological perspective? _____

21. Jim was in an experiment where he was shown a color and then had to say all the thoughts he had while contemplating this color. The method of the experiment Jim was in is called _____.

22. _____ believed that thought was ever-changing and could not be frozen in time.

23. Who was the first woman to set up a psychological laboratory? _____

24. Dr. Small believes that her patients are influenced by thoughts and desires of which they are not aware. Dr. Small believes they are influenced by the _____.

25. When you look at four lines of equal size connected at right angles, you see a square, not four individual lines.

This perception would be predicted by which approach to psychology? _____

26. The psychological perspective that focuses on the unconscious is called _____.

27. Steve studies how stimuli in the environment influence the responses of animals. Steve takes which approach to psychology? _____

28. Which theorist developed field theory to study how biology, habits, and beliefs all influence behavior? _____

29. Dr. Wright is a psychologist who helps athletes stay focused and remain calm during a game. Dr. Wright practices which area of psychology? _____

30. When you think skeptically and systematically evaluate information you are practicing _____.

MULTIPLE-CHOICE QUESTIONS

1. Janice is interested in studying thoughts and feelings. Therefore, the aspect of psychological science that she is most clearly focusing on is the
   a. mind.
   b. brain.
   c. behavior.
   d. nonconscious.

2. Early researchers of memory found that it is easier to recognize previously learned information than it is to recall the same information. New research has found that although this is often true, there are times when it is not the case. The development of new research based on findings from older research demonstrates which theme of psychology?
   a. There is currently a biological revolution.
   b. Principles of psychology are cumulative.
   c. Brain chemistry affects memory.
   d. Memory has adaptive value.

3. Some animals shed their fur in the summer when it is warm and become furrier in the winter when it is cold. This characteristic is an example of
   a. the effects of dopamine.
   b. dualism.
   c. the genome.
   d. adaptation.

4. Joe loves his sweets! Candy, cookies, and the like are his favorite foods. Unfortunately, Joe is starting to put on weight. Based on the information on adaptive behavior, Joe's overeating of high-calorie foods may indicate that

a. a human trait that was once adaptive is no longer adaptive.
b. Joe is an example of where evolution did not work.
c. psychological science cannot predict this kind of behavior.
d. cultural variables do *not* influence adaptation.

5. One outgrowth of humans living together in complex groups is the development of
a. anterior socialization.
b. monism.
c. culture.
d. Gestaltism.

6. Which of the following individuals is most likely to be from a Western culture?
a. Grace, who is interested in using logical arguments during debates.
b. Sue, who lives within an extended family.
c. Mary, who does *not* think much about her strengths and weaknesses.
d. Trisha, who lives in a collectivist society.

7. Who of the following is studying psychological science from a cultural level? The researcher who
a. studies how memory influences school performance.
b. studies differences in dopamine levels in depressed and nondepressed individuals.
c. observes the behaviors of two colonies of rats during mating.
d. observes how parents teach their children to behave in restaurants.

8. Who of the following is studying psychological science within the biological category? The researcher who
a. observes how quickly hungry rats will run to food.
b. studies the effects of cocaine on brain chemistry.
c. studies differences in Chinese and American teenagers' relationships with their grandparents.
d. compares how Chinese teens flirt to how American teens flirt.

9. Some children reach puberty younger than other children. If a researcher believes that the main cause for this is inborn, inherited differences, the researcher is studying the differences from what perspective?
a. Cultural.
b. Individual.
c. Brain systems.
d. Genetic.

10. Sy believes that if people are bad it's because they were born that way. June disagrees: She feels that it is treatment that makes someone turn out bad. Their disagreement reflects
a. James's ideas on stream of consciousness.

b. different levels of extroversion.
c. differences in their abilities to introspect.
d. the nature–nurture debate.

11. Carol believes that you can study bodily processes but you cannot study the mind. Her view reflects
a. monism.
b. dualism.
c. the nature–nurture debate.
d. the limitations of adaptation.

12. Stuart believes that he has a soul that is distinct from his body. He is interested, however, in just what is the relationship between them. Stuart's interests reflect
a. the neuroscience–cognition debate.
b. the mind–body problem.
c. the application of Darwin's theory to psychology.
d. the basic question of behaviorism.

13. John Stuart Mill proposed that psychology should become distinct from philosophy by focusing on
a. theory and speculation.
b. the functioning of nerve energies.
c. observation and experimentation.
d. functionalism and structuralism.

14. Frank works at a carnival where he tells people their personality by feeling the bumps on their heads. Frank is practicing
a. a well-proven method of learning about people.
b. structural introspection.
c. phrenology.
d. psychoanalysis.

15. Which researcher is credited with opening the first psychological laboratory?
a. Wundt.
b. James.
c. Freud.
d. Cattel.

16. If you believe that the mind is not made of discrete elements, but rather is flowing, changing, and continuous, your beliefs are most similar to those of
a. Wundt.
b. Titchner.
c. James.
d. Watson.

17. Which of the following is true of Mary Calkins, one of America's early psychologists?
a. She never worked as a professor, but instead helped her husband earn his degree.
b. She was denied a degree by Harvard despite her outstanding performance.
c. She was the first American to earn a Ph.D. in psychology.

d. She was asked to leave the practice of psychology by the American Psychological Association.

18. The approach to psychology that emphasizes the adaptive value of the mind is
    a. social psychology.
    b. structuralism.
    c. introspection.
    d. functionalism.

19. Tony had a dream about a duck flying away with his penis. Tony's therapist believes the dream is not really about ducks, but is about some conflict in Tony's mind of which he is not aware. Tony's therapist is taking an approach similar to
    a. James.
    b. Watson.
    c. Levine.
    d. Freud.

20. The approach that Tony's therapist is taking is called
    a. psychoanalysis.
    b. structuralism.
    c. behaviorism.
    d. cognitivism.

21. Dr. Cohen believes that the study of psychology should be limited to stimuli that can be measured and responses that can be observed. This approach is
    a. psychoanalysis.
    b. structuralism.
    c. behaviorism.
    d. cognitivism.

22. The cognitive revolution focused research in psychology on such things as
    a. how consequences influence rats' behaviors.
    b. thinking and decision making.
    c. neuroanatomical structures.
    d. the building blocks of thought.

23. After studying psychology, Dr. Smith became a therapist who treats adolescents. Dr. Smith is a
    a. psychological scientist.
    b. biological scientist.
    c. social practitioner.
    d. psychological practitioner.

24. Which of the following is most true of the relationship between psychological science and psychological practice today?
    a. Psychological scientists and psychological practitioners have little in common.
    b. Psychological science has little relevance for practice.
    c. Psychological therapy is increasingly based on psychological science.

d. Psychological scientists and psychological practitioners are generally interested in unrelated areas.

25. Psychological science is based on critical thinking. This means that psychological scientists
    a. evaluate information before they accept it.
    b. do not believe anything that they did not discover themselves.
    c. do not have any kind of faith.
    d. accept without question any information that is given to them by an authority.

MATCHING QUESTIONS

Fill in the letter from Column B corresponding to the name or term that is most associated with the description presented in Column A.

COLUMN A

___ 1. Developed structuralism.
___ 2. Refers to observable action.
___ 3. The beliefs, values, and norms of a group.
___ 4. Theory that the mind and body are separate.
___ 5. Mental processes below the level of awareness.
___ 6. The basic genetic code for the human body.
___ 7. Traits or skills that increase the chances of survival.
___ 8. A technique requiring people to report the content of their thoughts.
___ 9. Opened the first psychological laboratory.
___ 10. Level that studies personality traits.
___ 11. Level that studies group influence.
___ 12. Theory based on the idea that the whole of experience is more than the sum of its parts.
___ 13. Was a founder of social psychology.
___ 14. The ability to think skeptically.
___ 15. Mental activity such as thoughts and feelings.

COLUMN B

A. Human genome
B. The mind
C. Dualism
D. Critical thinking
E. Titchner
F. Social
G. Behavior
H. Gestalt
I. Individual
J. Introspection
K. Lewin
L. Culture
M. Unconscious
N. Adaptations
O. Wundt

THOUGHT QUESTIONS

1. What are the three categories of analysis? What are the levels within each?

2. Describe psychoanalysis and behaviorism. How did they change the study of "mind"?

3. What are psychological scientists and psychological practitioners? How are they related?

APPLICATIONS

Thinking Critically about Psychological Science and the Media

Psychological practitioners and psychological scientists are presented in the media. They can be seen in a variety of contexts. Some are characters on television programs or in films. Others are experts interviewed on television, the radio, or in newspapers or magazines. However, do the media accurately represent psychological scientists and practitioners? This exercise involves thinking critically about the media's presentation of psychological scientists and practitioners. Make a list of the areas in which psychologists work that are cited in the text. Which of these do you see presented on TV in comedies or dramas? Which professions do you see on TV news shows or talk shows? Which do you see cited in magazines or newspapers? Do you think the media present a balanced view of what psychological science is? Why or why not?

Application of Levels of Analysis: Alzheimer's Disease

Alzheimer's disease is a terrible disorder where slow destruction of the brain results in dementia. Dementia refers to a loss of cognitive ability. People with Alzheimer's disease develop problems with memory, reasoning, and language. They also have increasing problems with behavior and anxiety. What causes Alzheimer's disease is not clear. There may be a genetic component, at least in some cases. Some researchers think that toxins from the environment may also cause the disease. It often is very difficult for family members to cope with the disease. It is painful to watch a loved one decline. It may also be hard to care for the afflicted person.

Clearly, to best understand and treat Alzheimer's disease, an approach that incorporates multiple levels of analysis is needed. Diagnosis involves both a biological approach, with evaluation of brain functioning, and a psychological approach, which evaluates cognitive ability. Treatment often involves medication, which is biological. It may also include teaching the individual strategies to make up for memory loss, which is psychological. Just as important as these, treatment may also include support for family members, which reflects the social level of analysis.

For more information on Alzheimer's disease, see www.alz.org.

PBS presented an excellent program, *The Forgetting*, on Alzheimer's disease. For information see www.pbs.org/theforgetting/.

WEB SITES

Careers in Psychology

www.apa.org/students/brochure/
www.apa.org/science/nonacad.html
www.rider.edu/users/suler/gradschl.html

History of Psychology

www.psychclassics.yorku.ca
www.allpsych.com

ANSWER KEY

Fill-in-the-Blank Questions

1. Mind
2. Behavior
3. Evolution
4. Biology
5. Brain chemistry
6. Human genome
7. Adaptive
8. Social
9. Culture
10. Holistic
11. Biological
12. Social
13. Individual
14. Brain systems
15. Nature–nurture
16. Dualism
17. Descartes
18. Darwin
19. Observation and experimentation
20. Structuralism
21. Introspection
22. William James
23. Mary Calkins
24. Unconscious
25. Gestalt
26. Psychoanalysis
27. Behaviorism
28. Kurt Lewin
29. Sports psychology
30. Critical thinking

Multiple-Choice Questions

1. a. "Mind" includes mental activities such as thoughts and feelings.

   Incorrect answers:
   b. Brain—includes nerve cells and chemicals.
   c. Behavior—is defined as observable actions.

d. Nonconscious—is not discussed in this chapter, and includes bodily processes of which one is unaware such as blood flow.

2. b. Over time knowledge has accumulated about mind, brain, and behavior. New knowledge is influenced by this accumulation.

   Incorrect answers:
   a. The biological revolution refers to the increased understanding of how biology relates to mental activity that has occurred over the last 20 years.
   c. The study of brain chemistry, the neurotransmitters that communicate messages between cell, is a part of the biological revolution.
   d. The adaptive value of memory means that memory allows people to survive in their environment.

3. d. Adaptation refers to the ability of animals to change in response to the environment to increase their chances of survival.

   Incorrect answers:
   a. Dopamine is a neurotransmitter that influences communication between brain cells.
   b. Dualism is the theory that the mind and body are separate.
   c. The genome is the genetic code for an organism.

4. a. Preference for sweet or fatty foods helped survival when food was scarce and it was difficult for humans to find calories. Now that food is plentiful in our culture, this preference can be a problem, leading to obesity.

   Incorrect answers:
   b. Joe's preference is predicted from evolutionary theory.
   c. Psychological science can predict the behavior from the theory of evolution.
   d. Culture does have an effect on adaptive behavior.

5. c. Culture refers to the norms and beliefs of a group of people and appears to have developed from living together in complex groups.

   Incorrect answers:
   a. Anterior socialization is not a concept.
   b. Monism, which is not discussed in this chapter, refers to the mind and body as unitary.
   d. The Gestalt school of psychology saw perception as more than the sum of its parts.

6. a. Individuals in Western cultures tend to be more analytic and more likely to use logic to explain behaviors, whereas individuals in Eastern cultures tend to be more holistic.

   Incorrect answers:
   b. Western culture is not more likely to promote living in an extended family.
   c. Westerners are more likely to evaluate their own strengths and weaknesses.
   d. Eastern cultures are more likely to be collectivist.

7. d. The cultural level includes the norms and values of a society—for example, how people are expected to act in varying situations.

   Incorrect answers:
   a. The study of memory reflects the level of perception and cognition.
   b. Research on levels of dopamine, a neurotransmitter, exemplifies the neurochemical level.
   c. Observation of rats' behavior falls under the behavioral level.

8. b. The biological category, neurochemical level, would include studying the effects of cocaine on brain chemistry.

   Incorrect answers:
   a. Studying the speed with which rats run to food is an example of the behavioral level.
   c. The social category, cultural level, would include studying differences in American and Chinese teenagers' family relationships.
   d. The social category, cultural level, would include studying differences between American and Chinese teenagers' flirting.

9. d. Genes direct the inherited, inborn characteristics of individuals.

   Incorrect answers:
   a. Culture focuses on the norms and beliefs of a group.
   b. The individual perspective focuses on people's traits.
   c. The brain systems level studies the structure of the brain.

10. d. The nature–nurture debate focuses on the degree to which one's genes (nature) influence one's traits as opposed to the degree to which environmental factors (nurture) influence those traits.

    Incorrect answers:
    a. James believed consciousness could not be broken down into parts; rather it was like a stream, continuous and changing. This is not relevant for this question.
    b. Extroversion is a personal trait given as an example of the individual level of analysis.
    c. Introspection was a technique used by Wundt

where people reported on the contents of their thoughts.

11. b. Dualism refers to the theory that the mind and body are separate.

Incorrect answers:
a. Monism is not discussed in this chapter. It refers to the idea that the mind and body are a unit.
c. The nature–nurture debate focuses on the degree to which human traits are the result of genes as opposed to the result of environmental influences.
d. Adaptation refers to the ability of organisms to change in response to the environment to maximize their chances of survival. It is not relevant to this question.

12. b. The mind–body problem addresses whether the mind and body are distinct or whether the mind is the experiencing of the functions of the brain.

Incorrect answers:
a. There is no official neuroscience–cognition debate.
c. The mind–body problem is a question from philosophy; it did not grow out of Darwin's theory of evolution.
d. Behaviorism focused on stimuli and responses; it did not study the mind.

13. c. John Stuart Mill proposed that psychology separate itself from philosophy by focusing on observation and experimentation. This formed one of the foundations of psychological science.

Incorrect answers:
a. Philosophy included theory and speculation; Mill suggested psychology go beyond this.
b. Research on nerve energies also served as a foundation for psychological science, but it was introduced by biologists, not by Mill.
d. Functionalism and structuralism were early perspectives on psychology. These included observation and experimentation as suggested by Mill.

14. c. Phrenology was an early attempt to measure personality and mental ability by examining bumps on individual's skulls.

Incorrect answers:
a. It was not possible to test the validity of phrenology scientifically.
b. Structural introspection is not a concept. Structuralism is a perspective focusing on breaking consciousness to its components. Introspection is a method of doing this.
d. Psychoanalysis was the perspective developed by Freud, who proposed that individuals are influenced by mental processes of which they are unaware.

15. a. Wundt is credited with opening the first psychological laboratory in Leipzig, Germany in 1879.

Incorrect answers:
b. James, an early American psychologist, developed functionalism. This perspective is concerned with the purpose, or function, of the mind.
c. Freud was the developer of psychoanalysis.
d. Cattel did research on intelligence. His work is discussed in Chapter 8.

16. c. James believed consciousness could not be broken down into parts; rather it was like a stream, continuous and changing. He therefore referred to the "stream of consciousness."

Incorrect answers:
a. Wundt studied what are the building blocks of the mind.
b. Titchner, a student of Wundt, developed structuralism. This perspective focused on breaking down consciousness into its components.
d. Watson developed behaviorism. Behaviorism limited the study of psychology to stimuli and responses. It did not include conscious experience.

17. b. Although she was an excellent student and completed her training, Harvard refused to grant Mary Calkins a degree because she was a woman.

Incorrect answers:
a. Calkin was a professor at Wellesley College.
c. Calkin was never awarded the Ph.D.
d. Calkin was the first woman president of the American Psychological Association.

18. d. Functionalism is concerned with the purpose, or adaptive function of the mind and behavior.

Incorrect answers:
a. Social psychology, pioneered in part by Kurt Lewin, looks at the relationship between individuals and social situations.
b. Structuralism focused on breaking down consciousness into its components.
c. Introspection was a method used by Wundt where people reported on the contents of their thoughts.

19. d. Freud believed that the mind included unconscious forces that influenced behavior. One way to uncover these forces was through dream interpretation.

Incorrect answers:
a. James's approach, functionalism, focused on the function of the mind, not on unconscious forces.
b. Watson's approach, behaviorism, did not include study of the mind but focused only on stimuli and responses.
c. Levine was not a theorist discussed in this chapter.

20. a. The name of Freud's perspective is psychoanalysis.

Incorrect answers:
b. Structuralism focused on breaking down consciousness to its elements.
c. Behaviorism did not include study of the mind at all.
d. Cognitivism was not a perspective discussed in the chapter.

21. c. Behaviorism limits the study of psychology to stimuli and responses.

Incorrect answers:
a. Psychoanalysis is the perspective developed by Freud. It focuses on the role of unconscious forces in influencing behavior.
b. Structuralism focused on breaking down consciousness to its elements.
d. Cognitivism was not a perspective discussed in the chapter.

22. b. The cognitive revolution shifted focus away from just stimuli and responses onto mental activities such as thinking and decision making.

Incorrect answers:
a. Behaviorism focuses on the effects of consequences on behavior and often includes animals in experiments.
c. The study of neuroanatomical structures was influenced by the current biological revolution and the techniques recently developed to study the brain.
d. The building blocks of thought were studied by early psychologists interested in structuralism.

23. d. Psychological practitioners apply the findings from psychological science to help people with their lives.

Incorrect answers:
a. A psychological scientist does research on the brain, mind, and behavior.
b. A biological scientist would be trained in biology to do research in that discipline.
c. "Social practitioner" is not a term in this chapter.

24. c. The text discusses the increasing relationship between psychological therapy and psychological science. Now, more than ever, advances in psychological science impact psychological therapies.

Incorrect answers:
a. Because both psychological therapists and psychological scientists study psychology, they have much in common.
b. Because advances in psychological science impact psychological therapy, science is relevant to practice.
d. Psychological scientists and psychological practitioners share common focuses.

25. a. One of the bases of critical thinking is questioning and evaluating information before it is accepted as fact.

Incorrect answers:
b. Scientists accept the findings of others after critically evaluating the information.
c. Faith is not a relevant concept here.
d. Critical thinking implies that no information is accepted without question.

Matching Questions

1. E Titchner
2. G Behavior
3. L Culture
4. C Dualism
5. M Unconscious
6. A Human genome
7. N Adaptations
8. J Introspection
9. O Wundt
10. I Individual
11. F Social
12. H Gestalt
13. K Lewin
14. D Critical thinking
15. B The mind

Thought Questions

1. The three categories are social, psychological, and biological. The social category includes the cultural level and the social level. The psychological category includes the individual level, the level of perception and cognition, and the behavioral level. The biological category includes the level of brain systems, the neurochemical level, and the genetic level.

2. Psychoanalysis was developed by Freud. Freud proposed that the mind includes mental processes that are below the level of awareness. He expanded understanding of the mind by including the unconscious. Behaviorism was developed by Watson. Watson proposed that psychology study only observable stimuli and responses. He changed the study of the mind by not including it in psychology at all.

3. Psychological scientists research the interrelationships between the mind, the brain, and behavior. Psychological practitioners use these research findings to help people in their daily lives. Increasingly, psychological practice is influenced by the findings of psychological science. For example, research on behavior, cognition, and biology have all impacted the therapies used by psychological practitioners.

CHAPTER 2 | Research Methodology

In the first chapter the authors emphasized that the basis of scientific inquiry must be critical thinking. Critical thinking means that scientists must systematically evaluate evidence, rather than rely on subjective beliefs. In this chapter the authors first discuss what scientific inquiry is, focusing on objectively answering scientific questions. The authors then describe the different types of psychological studies, including experiments, correlational designs, and descriptive studies. Varying methods of data collection are presented. The different methods of data collection reflect the levels of analysis described in Chapter 1. Scientists employ the method most appropriate for the level of analysis of their research. Both the strengths of each method and its limitations are discussed. Following description of the methods, the authors discuss ethical issues to be considered before performing research with humans or animals. The authors conclude the chapter with a discussion of how data are analyzed and evaluated. That is, how do we interpret data? And how do we judge whether data are good and believable?

What Is Scientific Inquiry?

To learn about the mind, brain, and behavior, psychologists gather data using scientific techniques. When investigating a question, scientists do so systematically by employing the scientific method. The scientific method has four basic goals: description, prediction, causal control, and explanation. Description is based on systematic observation of a behavior. Predictions can then be made based on observations of when two events occur together. Causal control, or determining whether there is a cause and effect relationship between variables, can be assessed by systematically varying a situation. Explanation involves understanding why an event occurred. Scientific inquiry takes an empirical approach. It is based on observation and measurement. Because it is objective, other researchers should be able to replicate the research—that is, repeat the experiment and find the same results.

The empirical process includes three elements: theories, hypotheses, and research. A theory is an idea of how something works; it includes interconnected ideas that explain observations and make predictions about the future. A hypothesis tests the theory; it is a specific statement of what should occur if the theory is correct. Research is the systematic collection of data, or information, to test the hypothesis. Good theories result in testable hypotheses.

What Are the Types of Studies in Psychological Research?

The authors present three main types of designs: experimental, correlational, and descriptive. All are used to assess the relationships between variables. A variable can be anything that is measurable and comes in different degrees or amounts. Variables must be operationally defined—that is, defined in a way that can be measured.

The first method discussed by the authors is the experiment. In an experiment there are two kinds of variables: the independent variable, which the researcher manipulates; and the dependent variable, which is measured. The purpose of the experiment is to see if the independent variable causes a change in the dependent variable. To make a causal conclusion, the researcher must have rigorous control. The researcher attempts to ensure that the independent variable and not some other factor, a confound, is influencing the dependent variable.

The second method discussed is the correlational design. Correlational studies assess how variables are related in the real world. Correlational studies do not show causal relationships. With a correlational study, one may observe that two variables occur together. However, observing that two variables occur together does not necessarily mean that one caused the other.

The third type of study is the descriptive study. Descriptive studies, or observational studies, involve systematically noting a behavior. Two types of descriptive studies include naturalistic observation, where an observer just watches the behavior, and participant observation, where the observer becomes involved in the situation.

What Are the Data Collection Methods of Psychological Science?

A method to collect data is selected after the researcher has decided on a type of study. The method the researcher selects must be appropriate for the level of analysis reflected by the research question. Five types of data collection methods are presented: observational techniques, self-report methods, case studies, response performance measures, and psychophysiological assessments.

The observational technique involves recording overt behaviors. Several problems may occur with this method. Animals may change their behaviors if they are aware they are being watched, a problem known as reactivity. Observer bias, when researchers' expectations may influence what they see, can also be a problem. Finally, experimenter expectancy, when observer expectations cause the observed behavior to change, can be an issue.

Self-report methods ask people about their thoughts, actions, feelings, and so on. Surveys, questionnaires, and interviews are all self-report methods. These methods efficiently gather a lot of information from many people. However, people may not pay attention to each question on a long survey. They may also report the answers they think are appropriate, evidencing socially desirable responding. Wording on surveys must also be especially precise if the survey is to be given to more than one cultural group.

Case studies are detailed descriptions of a single individual. Case studies of individuals with brain damage have provided useful information about the relationship between psychological functions and brain parts. However, because case studies are subjective, one must be careful before drawing conclusions from them.

Cognitive and perceptual processes are assessed indirectly through response performance measures. There are three basic types of response performance measures: reaction time, or how quickly one responds; response accuracy, or how correctly one responds; and stimulus judgments, which include comparing stimuli. The benefit of the response performance measures is they are simple and provide a quantitative measure of perceptual or cognitive processes.

Psychophysiological assessments directly measure body and brain processes. Electrophysiology is a method that measures electrical activity in the brain. Brain imaging techniques, such as PET and fMRI, assess changes in blood flow in the brain. These techniques allow researchers to directly see the relation between psychological process and brain activity.

The authors end this section with a discussion of ethical issues that must be considered when performing research with human or animal participants. Ethics must be considered in any research. Regardless of whether the research is with humans or with animal, the benefits of the research must outweigh the costs.

How Are Data Analyzed and Evaluated?

This section discusses how to determine whether data are good and how to statistically analyze data. For data to be good, they must be reliable, valid, and accurate. *Reliability* refers to stability or consistency. Data are *valid* when they provide clear information on the hypothesis. Data are *accurate* when they are free from error.

There are a number of different ways to analyze data. Descriptive statistics summarize overall findings. These include measuring central tendency, or what is a typical response. The measures of central tendency include the mean, or average score; the median, or score that is halfway between the highest and lowest values in a set; and the mode, or most common score. Another descriptive statistic is a correlation. Correlations indicate the strength of the relationship between two variables. They can be positive or negative. Positive correlations mean the two variables change in the same way; that is, as one increases the other also increases (or as one decreases the other also decreases). Negative correlations indicate that as one variable increases the other decreases. The strength of the correlation indicates the degree to which one variable predicts the other. The closer the correlation is to +1.0 or −1.0, the stronger the correlation. Inferential statistics are used to determine whether differences between groups are probably due to the influence of one variable on another as opposed to being the result of chance.

The chapter concludes with the reminder that for any research to be useful it must be based on critical evaluation, which is based on critical thinking. The authors present a critical analysis of an article in *The New York Times* that described a research study. Critical readers of the article would note that the conclusions drawn by the *Times* were not justified by what was reported.

FILL−IN-THE-BLANK QUESTIONS

1. _____ is an objective examination of the natural world.

2. A scientist who has developed a specific prediction of what should be observed if a theory is correct has developed a _____.

3. A model of interconnected ideas and concepts that explain what is observed and make predictions about future events is a _____.

4. A scientific process that involves the systematic and careful collection of data is _____.

5. _____ are objective observations or measures.

6. _____ is the unexpected stumbling upon something important.

7. A scientist investigated the effects of alcohol on driving ability. Alcohol and driving ability are both _____.

8. In an experiment, the _____ is affected by the independent variable.

9. An _____ is a method by which researchers quantify variables to measure them.

10. Anything that affects a dependent variable that may unintentionally vary between the different experimental conditions of a study is a _____.

11. _____ is a passive descriptive study in which observers do not change or alter ongoing behavior.

12. A psychologist who joined a cult to observe the behavior of cult members engaged in what kind of descriptive study? _____.

13. _____ techniques involve systematic assessment of overt behavior.

14. Tanika was being observed as part of a research study. However, because she was being observed she started to behave differently than she typically acts. The change in her behavior because of being observed is called _____.

15. For a research project, Janice was observing boys and girls play. However, her expectations about differences in boys and girls caused systematic errors in her observation. This is known as _____.

16. Ray filled out a questionnaire about his attitudes to drugs. This is an example of the _____ method of data collection.

17. If a person's response to a survey is not true, but rather is socially acceptable or "faking good," this may be an example of _____.

18. A _____ involves the intensive examination of one person.

19. _____ is the quantification of performance behavior that measures the speed of a response.

20. _____ is a method of data collection that measures electrical activity in the brain.

21. PET scans and fMRI are both examples of _____ methods.

22. _____ provides a record of overall brain activity.

23. The board that evaluates proposed research to ensure that it meets the accepted ethical standards of science is the _____.

24. _____ means either misleading participants about the goal of a study or not fully revealing what will take place.

25. _____ is the extent to which the data collected address the research hypothesis in a way they were intended.

26. _____ is the extent to which a measure is stable and consistent.

27. _____ is the extent to which an experimental measure is free from error.

28. The arithmetic average of a set of numbers is the _____.

29. On a math test the most frequent score was 80%; 80%, therefore, was the _____.

30. The statistical procedure that provides a numerical value indicating the strength and direction of the relationship between two variables is a _____.

MULTIPLE-CHOICE QUESTIONS

1. Dr. Hernandez did an experiment where she gave half her participants alcohol and half the participants no alcohol. She then measured how long each participant could balance on one leg. The participants who received no alcohol are
   a. irrelevant to the experiment.
   b. the experimental group.
   c. the independent variable.
   d. the control group.

2. Dr. Smith replicated Dr. Hernandez's study. This means
   a. Dr. Smith repeated Dr. Hernandez's experiment and found the same results.
   b. Dr. Smith systematically criticized Dr. Hernandez's experiment.
   c. Dr. Smith collected data while Dr. Hernandez did not.
   d. Dr. Smith used the scientific method while Dr. Hernandez did not.

3. After extensive reading in psychology, Chavonne decided to test the idea that males will perform more poorly on memory for grocery lists than will females. The specific idea that she is testing is called a
   a. data set.
   b. hypothesis.
   c. theory.
   d. variable.

4. Freud believed that dreams represented people's wishes. The problem with this idea was that
   a. it was not true—dreams are unrelated to wish fulfillment.
   b. it was not based on a theory.
   c. it was not a variable.
   d. it was not testable.

5. Louis did an experiment where he gave one group of students alcohol and another group no alcohol. He then compared how quickly they memorized a list of words. What was the dependent variable in this experiment?
   a. The amount of alcohol.
   b. The age of the students.
   c. The time it took to memorize the words.
   d. The number of words recalled by each group.

6. Janet wanted to compare the effects of playing video games on children's aggressive behaviors. She had one group of children play violent games while another group played nonviolent games. She then counted the number of aggressive behaviors performed by the two groups. Why would she make sure that the same number of boys and girls were in each group?
   a. Gender may be a confound.
   b. Observational techniques may be a problem.
   c. She needs to control the independent variable.
   d. She needs to control the dependent variable.

7. When doing her experiment, Janet needed to operationally define "aggressive behavior." Which of the following might be her operational definition?
   a. Being mean to someone.
   b. Number of times one child hit another.
   c. Number of times one child was unkind to another.
   d. Being inconsiderate of another child's feelings.

8. Joe, who works in urban planning, found that the more dogs there were in a city, the more fire hydrants there were, too. He knew he could not conclude that having more dogs caused an increase in fire hydrants. Rather, some other factor probably caused both the increase in dogs and the increase in hydrants. This reflects
   a. the third variable problem.
   b. the limitations of an experiment.
   c. the ability to make a causal statement from a correlational study.
   d. the limits of random assignment.

9. Dr. Brown studied monkeys by observing their behavior in the wild. Dr. Brown's research is an example of a(n)
   a. reaction time study.
   b. case study.
   c. experiment.
   d. descriptive study.

10. Dr. Wright studies rats by videotaping their behavior in garbage dumps. The rats are not aware of the video recorder and so it has no effect on their behavior. Dr. Wright's research is an example of
    a. participant observation.
    b. naturalistic observation.
    c. case study research.
    d. response performance research.

11. Dr. Bert tried to do an observational study of how students act at parties. However, he noticed that when he attended a party, the students tended to be very quiet and just stare at him. He decided that they were not acting naturally. The fact the students were not acting naturally demonstrates the
    a. Hawthorne effect.
    b. third variable problem.
    c. directionality problem.
    d. causation problem.

12. Sam was observing sharing behavior in 3- and 5-year-old children. Because he was sure the 5-year-olds would share more, he tended to overlook sharing in the younger children, which led to errors in his observation. Sam was suffering from
    a. self-report method bias.
    b. directionality problems.
    c. observer bias.
    d. reactivity.

13. Fran filled out a survey on her self-esteem. This is an example of which research method?
    a. Observational.
    b. Response performance.
    c. Self-report.
    d. Psychophysiological.

14. When her mom asked Michelle how much she liked her political science professor, Michelle said "The prof is OK." Michelle did not say what she really thought—the professor was *really* good-looking. Michelle did not think her mother wanted to hear that. Michelle's response reflects
    a. a response set.
    b. socially desirable responding.
    c. experimenter expectancy effects.
    d. participant observation effects.

15. People from which culture are *least* likely to say positive things about themselves?
    a. Korea.
    b. The United States.
    c. France.
    d. Germany.

16. Dr. Ramirez did research that involved a detailed examination of a patient who suffered brain damage from a car accident. Dr. Ramirez's study is an example of a
    a. response performance study.
    b. reaction time study.
    c. case study.
    d. correlational study.

17. Sarah was in a study where the experimenter measured how quickly she could judge whether a group of letters made up a word. What was the experimenter measuring?
    a. Reaction time.
    b. Response accuracy.
    c. Reliability.
    d. Electrophysiology.

18. According to recent research, adolescent killers may differ from adult killers in which way?
    a. They were abused as children.
    b. They have more dopamine in their brains.
    c. They have immature frontal lobes.
    d. They have lower intelligence.

19. Which of the following provides a record of overall brain activity? A(n)
    a. PET scan.
    b. MRI.
    c. fMRI.
    d. EEG.

20. A PET scan is an example of a(n)
    a. electrophysiological measure.
    b. brain imaging technique.
    c. reaction time technique.
    d. EEG technique.

21. Dr. Smith designed a study to investigate memory in college students. Before she could do the study she first had to get approval from which group?
    a. The school board.
    b. The Institutional Review Board.
    c. The American Psychological Association.
    d. The American Psychological Society.

22. When scientists manipulate chemicals in the brains of animals and note the effects on the animals' behavior, the scientists are studying psychology at which level of analysis?
    a. Cognitive.
    b. Social.
    c. Individual.
    d. Neurochemical.

23. Before Alicia participated in an experiment, she was told exactly what the experiment was about. She then agreed to take part in it. The researchers conducting this experiment acted ethically in that they received _____ from Alicia.
    a. confidentiality
    b. good data
    c. informed consent
    d. deceptive consent

24. Research by Richard Atkinson indicated which of the following about the SATs?
    a. They are a highly valid test.
    b. They do *not* do a good job of predicting college performance.
    c. They are unaffected by SAT preparation classes.
    d. They should *not* be changed in any way.

25. When data are stable and consistent over time they are
    a. reliable.
    b. valid.
    c. central.
    d. accurate.

26. When data are free from error they are
    a. reliable.
    b. valid.
    c. central.
    d. accurate.

27. A statistical measure of how far away each value is on average from the mean is the
    a. mode.
    b. median.
    c. standard deviation.
    d. mean.

28. The average score on a general psychology test was 75%; 75% is, then, the _____.
    a. mode
    b. median
    c. standard deviation
    d. mean

29. If a study found a high positive correlation between the amount of soda people drink and their weight, this means that
    a. people who drink more soda weigh more.
    b. people who drink more soda weigh less.
    c. soda drinking is unrelated to weight.
    d. sometimes soda drinking causes weight gain and sometimes it does not.

30. Your text describes a *New York Times* article that summarized a scientific study on marijuana and heart attacks. What did the authors of your text conclude about the *Times* article?
    a. The *Times* summary was an excellent critical analysis of the scientific study.
    b. The *Times* summary presented all the possible problems with the scientific study.
    c. Critical thinkers would question what the *Times* reported.
    d. The *Times* accurately reported all the variables controlled for in the scientific study.

MATCHING QUESTIONS

Fill in the letter from Column B corresponding to the term that is most associated with the description presented in Column A.

COLUMN A

____ 1. A research method that involves intensive examination of one person.
____ 2. The most frequent score or value in a set of numbers.
____ 3. How widely dispersed the values are in a set of numbers.
____ 4. A measure of speed of a response.
____ 5. A research method for testing causal hypotheses in which variables are both measured and manipulated.
____ 6. A descriptive study in which the researcher is actively involved in the situation.
____ 7. When knowledge that one is being observed alters the behavior being observed.
____ 8. The board that reviews research to ensure it meets ethical standards.
____ 9. A set of procedures used to make judgments about whether differences actually exist between sets of numbers.
____ 10. Objective observations or measurements.

COLUMN B

A. Case study
B. IRB
C. Relative risk
D. Inferential statistics
E. Survey
F. Reactivity
G. Mode
H. fMRI
I. Reaction time
J. Random assignment
K. Central tendency
L. Variability
M. Participant observation
N. Data
O. Experiment

____ 11. The procedure for placing research participants into the conditions of an experiment in which each participant has an equal chance of being assigned to any level of the independent variable.
____ 12. A kind of self-report method.
____ 13. A brain imaging technique.
____ 14. A part of the ethical review process where potential for harm is considered.
____ 15. The measure that represents the typical behavior of a group as a whole.

THOUGHT QUESTIONS

1. What is a "theory"? What makes a theory a "good" theory? Why was Freud's theory *not* a good theory?

2. What ethical issues must be considered before performing research with human participants? What board makes the decision about whether the research is ethical?

3. What is the difference in the kind of information provided by descriptive statistics, correlations, and inferential statistics?

APPLICATIONS

Thinking Critically about Naturalistic Observation and Psychological Research

As the text discusses, naturalistic observation can be an important way in which to collect data. However, the data gathered through this method must be reliable, valid, and accurate to be useful. This exercise will focus specifically on the reliability. Reliability means your data are consistent.

You will need a friend to participate in the exercise with you. Go to a location where a variety of people will be present, such as a mall or a park. Decide on a behavior to observe and how long you want to observe it. For example, you may want to count the number of people wearing red clothing, the number of young couples holding hands, or some other behavior. Conduct your observation for perhaps 15 minutes. Position yourselves where you will be seeing the same people at the same time, but far enough apart from each other that you cannot see what the other is writing. You should each record all the instances of the behavior that you see, starting and ending at exactly the same time.

After you have done this, compare what you found. Did you see exactly the same number of instances of the behavior? If not, why not? Did you operationally define the behavior you were looking for? Did you carefully look at the people for the whole 15 minutes? Were you ever distracted? What might you do to improve the reliability of your data? Think critically about your experiment and this kind of research. Do you think it is easy to do observational research?

Applications of Levels of Analysis: Research on Sexual Behavior

Sexual behavior is influenced by a wide variety of factors. These include the culture one lives in, the views of one's peers, one's personal beliefs, and even one's neurological responses. Research on sexual behavior, therefore, has crossed several levels of analysis with different research questions growing out of the different levels of analysis.

One important area of research involves what influences condom use. Wehrer & Astor-Stetson (2003) investigated how college students think their friends view the use of condoms and whether friends' views predict the students' own attitudes. Questions about how one's friends view condoms and how that view is related to one's own attitude may be at the social and cultural levels of analysis. The way researchers collect data on this is often with self-report methods. Students are given surveys with questions on their friends' attitudes as well as on their own attitudes. Students may be asked questions such as "Do your friends think it is important to use condoms? Do your friends use condoms every time they have sex?" Students would also be asked whether they think condoms are important and whether they use them. As you might guess, for many people their friends' views were related to their own.

Other research on sexuality may look at different issues. For example, sexuality researchers have investigated changes in the brain when an individual is sexually aroused. Beauregard, Levesque, & Bourgouin (2001) compared brain activity of men told to respond naturally to erotic films with the brain activity of men told to inhibit their arousal by erotic films. There were differences between the two groups, providing evidence that people's conscious decisions can influence biological responses. This research is at the brain systems level of analysis. The methods used to do this research include brain imaging methods and electrophysiology.

Clearly, to understand something as complex as sexual behavior, research must be performed at many levels of analysis.

References

Beauregard, M., Levesque, J., & Bourgouin, P. (2001). Neural correlates of conscious self-regulation of emotion. *Journal of Neuroscience, 21(18),* U11–16.

Wehrer, K., & Astor-Stetson, E. (2003). *Factors predicting college students' condom use.* Presented at the Meeting of the Southeastern Psychological Association, New Orleans.

WEB SITES

Research Methods

www.socialpsychology.org/methods.htm
www.spacetransportation.org/Social_Sciences/Psychology/Research_Methods/

ANSWER KEY

Fill-in-the-Blank Questions

1. Scientific method
2. Hypothesis
3. Theory
4. Research
5. Data
6. Serendipity
7. Variables
8. Dependent variable
9. Operational definition
10. Confound
11. Naturalistic observation
12. Participant observation
13. Observational
14. Reactivity
15. Observer bias
16. Self-report
17. Socially desirable responding
18. Case study
19. Reaction time
20. Electrophysiology
21. Brain imaging
22. EEG
23. Institutional Review Board (IRB)
24. Deception
25. Validity
26. Reliability
27. Accuracy
28. Mean
29. Mode
30. Correlation

Multiple-Choice Questions

1. d. The control group is used for comparison to see the effects of the experimental manipulation.

   Incorrect answers:
   a. An experiment must include a control group for comparison.
   b. The experimental group in this example is the group given the alcohol.
   c. The independent variable is the amount of alcohol consumed—not a group.

2. a. Replication means repeating the experiment and finding the same results.

    Incorrect answers:
    b. Although all experiments should be critically evaluated, that is not what replication means.
    c. Both Dr. Smith and Dr. Hernandez collected data.
    d. Both Dr. Smith and Dr. Hernandez used the scientific method.

3. b. A hypothesis is a specific prediction of what should be observed.

    Incorrect answers:
    a. A data set is made up of objective observations or measurements.
    c. A theory is a model of interconnected ideas and concepts.
    d. Variables are things in the world that can be measured and can vary.

4. d. A major problem with Freud's theory is it did not generate testable hypotheses.

    Incorrect answers:
    a. Because Freud's theory is not testable, it is not known whether dreams represent people's wishes.
    b. Freud's beliefs about dreams are based on his theory.
    c. Variables are things in the world that can be measured and can vary.

5. c. The dependent variable is a measure that is affected by manipulating the independent variable. Time to memorize words was being measured.

    Incorrect answers:
    a. The amount of alcohol was the independent variable.
    b. The age of the students was not relevant in the description of the study.
    d. The number of words recalled was not measured in the study.

6. a. Confounds are anything that may unintentionally affect the dependent variable. Because boys may be more aggressive than girls before the study (or vice versa), gender may be a confound.

    Incorrect answers:
    b. Observational techniques are a different way to collect data and are not relevant here.
    c. The independent variable in this description is the type of video game.
    d. The dependent variable in this description is the number of aggressive behaviors performed by the groups.

7. b. An operational definition is a method by which researchers quantify the variables to measure them; number of hits can be counted and so is quantifiable.

    Incorrect answers:
    a. "Being mean" is not quantified: how is "mean" measured? How is it counted?
    c. To be quantified, "unkind" needs to be defined in a way that can be measured.
    d. "Being inconsiderate" is not quantified: how is "inconsiderate" measured? How is it counted?

8. a. This example describes variables that naturally occur in the real world. The research method that examines this is a correlational study. In a correlational study, the researcher cannot directly manipulate an independent variable. Therefore, the researcher cannot be sure whether some other, third variable is really causing changes in the dependent variable. This is the third variable problem. In this example, size of the city was probably related to both the number of dogs and the number of hydrants: Big cities have lots of dogs and lots of hydrants, whereas small cities have fewer dogs and fewer hydrants.

    Incorrect answers:
    b. The example does not describe an experiment. In an experiment the researcher directly manipulates the independent variable.
    c. This example did not describe an experiment. One must do an experiment to make a causal statement.
    d. Researchers can have random assignment only when they do an experiment. This example did not describe an experiment.

9. d. Descriptive studies involve observing and noting behavior.

    Incorrect answers:
    a. Reaction time is a measure of the speed of a response.
    b. Case studies are intensive examinations of one person.
    c. Experiments involve direct manipulation of the independent variable.

10. b. In naturalistic observation observers do not change or alter ongoing behavior.

    Incorrect answers:
    a. In participant observation the researcher becomes actively involved in the situation.
    c. Case studies are intensive examinations of one person.
    d. Response performance is a method whereby perceptual or cognitive processes are measured.

11. a. The Hawthorne effect refers to changes in behavior that occur when people know that other people are watching them.

   Incorrect answers:
   b. The study described is an observational study. The third variable problem is an issue that arises in correlational studies.
   c. The study described is an observational study. The directionality problem is an issue that arises in correlational studies. In correlational studies (as in observational studies) the researcher cannot know whether one variable caused a change in the other, or which variable caused the change. Therefore, the direction of causality is not known. That is the directionality problem.
   d. "Causation problem" is not a real term.

12. c. Observer bias refers to systematic errors due to an observer's expectations.

   Incorrect answers:
   a. "Self-report method bias" is not a real term.
   b. The study described is an observational study. The directionality problem is an issue that arises in correlational studies. In correlational studies (as in observational studies) the researcher cannot know whether one variable caused a change in the other, or which variable caused the change. Therefore, the direction of causality is not known. That is the directionality problem.
   d. When people change their behavior because they are being observed, that is reactivity.

13. c. In self-report methods of data collection, people provide information about themselves.

   Incorrect answers:
   a. Observational techniques involve careful and systematic assessment and coding of behavior.
   b. Response performance is a method where perceptual or cognitive processes are measured.
   d. Psychophysiological methods assess how changes in bodily functions are associated with behavior or mental states.

14. b. Socially desirable responding occurs when a person responds in a way that is socially acceptable.

   Incorrect answers:
   a. When someone keeps selecting the same answer for every question on a survey, that reflects a response set.
   c. Experimenter expectancy effects occur when observer bias leads to changes in people's or animals' behaviors.
   d. "Participant observation effects" is not a real term.

15. a. The tendency to express positive things about oneself is more true in Western cultures than in Eastern cultures.

   Incorrect answers:
   b. The United States is a Western culture.
   c. France is a Western culture.
   d. Germany is a Western culture.

16. c. Case studies are intensive examinations of one person.

   Incorrect answers:
   a. Response performance is a method where perceptual or cognitive processes are measured.
   b. Reaction time is a measure of the speed of a response.
   d. In correlational studies researchers how variables are naturally related to the real world.

17. a. Reaction time is a measure of the speed of a response.

   Incorrect answers:
   b. Response accuracy refers to how well a stimuli was perceived.
   c. Reliability is the degree to which a measure is stable and consistent.
   d. Electrophysiological measures record electrical activity in the brain.

18. c. Because of their age, young killers' frontal lobes have not yet matured.

   Incorrect answers:
   a. Both young killers and older killers were often abused as children.
   b. Dopamine levels in killers were not discussed in chapter.
   d. The intelligence of killers was not discussed in the chapter.

19. d. An EEG is an electrophysiological measure that provides a record of overall brain activity.

   Incorrect answers:
   a. A PET scan is a brain imaging technique that measures changes of blood flow in the brain.
   b. MRI was not discussed in the chapter.
   c. fMRI is a brain imaging technique that measures changes of blood flow in the brain.

20. b. A PET scan is a brain imaging technique that measures changes of blood flow in the brain.

   Incorrect answers:
   a. Electrophysiological measures record electrical activity in the brain.

c. Reaction time is a measure of the speed of a response.

d. An EEG is an electrophysiological measure that provides a record of overall brain activity.

21. b. The Institutional Review Board (IRB) reviews research to ensure it meets ethical standards.

Incorrect answers:

a. The university board that ensures research meets accepted ethical standards is the IRB.

c. The American Psychological Association is a professional organization and was not discussed in this chapter.

d. The American Psychological Society is a professional organization and was not discussed in this chapter.

22. d. The neurochemical level of analysis studies chemicals such as neurotransmitters and hormones.

Incorrect answers:

a. The cognitive level addresses thinking and decision making.

b. The social level studies groups and relationships.

c. The individual level addresses personality traits.

23. c. Informed consent is the process by which people are given full information about an experiment. Based on this they can make a knowledgeable decision about whether to participate.

Incorrect answers:

a. Confidentiality implies that participants' responses will be kept private.

b. Good data are reliable, valid, and accurate.

d. "Deceptive consent" is not a term.

24. b. Richard Atkinson questioned the use of SATs because data indicated that they did not do a good job in predicting college performance.

Incorrect answers:

a. Valid tests do a good job predicting performance,

c. Atkinson proposed that SAT classes did influence performance.

d. Atkinson's criticisms influenced large changes in the SATs.

25. a. Reliability is the degree to which a measure is stable and consistent.

Incorrect answers:

b. Validity refers to the extent to which the data address the research question.

c. "Central" in not a term discussed in this context.

d. Accurate data are free from error.

26. d. Accurate data are free from error.

Incorrect answers:

a. Reliability is the degree to which a measure is stable and consistent.

b. Validity refers to the extent to which the data address the research question.

c. "Central" in not a term discussed in this context.

27. c. The standard deviation is a measure of how far each value is from the mean.

Incorrect answers:

a. The mode is the most common score in a set of numbers.

b. The median is the value that is halfway between the lowest and highest values in a set of numbers.

d. The mean is the arithmetic average of a set of numbers.

28. d. The mean is the arithmetic average of a set of numbers—for example, the scores on a test.

Incorrect answers:

a. The mode is the most common score in a set of numbers.

b. The median is the value that is halfway between the lowest and highest values in a set of numbers.

c. The standard deviation is a measure of how far each value is from the mean.

29. a. A positive correlation between two variables means that the variables increase or decrease together.

Incorrect answers:

b. A negative correlation means that as one variable increases (e.g., soda drinking) the other decreases (e.g., weight).

c. When two variables are unrelated, the correlation is close to zero.

d. Nothing can be said about causality from a correlation.

30. c. The authors' critical analysis of the article indicated the article did not present enough information to support its conclusion.

Incorrect answers:

a. The article was not an excellent critical analysis of the scientific study.

b. The article did not discuss problems with the study.

d. The article oversimplified the study and did not report all the variables controlled for in the study.

Matching Questions

1. A   Case study
2. G   Mode
3. L   Variability
4. I   Reaction time
5. O   Experiment
6. M   Participant observation
7. F   Reactivity
8. B   IRB
9. D   Inferential Statistics
10. N   Data
11. J   Random assignment
12. E   Survey
13. H   fMRI
14. C   Relative risk
15. K   Central tendency

Thought Questions

1. A theory is a model or set of interconnected ideas that explains how something works. The theory is based on observation and makes predictions about future events. A good theory produces testable hypotheses, or specific predictions of what should occur. Freud's theory was not a good theory because it did not generate testable hypotheses. There is no way to test whether his ideas are correct.

2. One ethical concern is privacy. When is it all right to observe someone's behavior without their knowledge? Clearly this depends in part on what behavior is being watched. A second issue to consider is sensitivity. Some topics may be inappropriate or hurtful to some people. Researchers need to be respectful of people's feelings in addressing these topics. A third issue is confidentiality. Access to data should be carefully controlled, especially if the data involve sensitive topics. In addition, researchers need to consider informed consent and relative risk to the participant. Informed consent means that volunteers in research are given information about the experiment. This allows them to make an informed decision about whether to participate. Consideration of relative risk means examining the trade-off between the risks of participation versus the benefits of participation. The benefits must clearly outweigh the risks. Before any human research is conducted in a university, an IRB (Institutional Review Board) must approve the research.

3. Descriptive statistics summarize basic patterns. For example, descriptive statistics indicate what is a typical response. One way to define "typicality" is the arithmetic average, or mean. Another way to define what is typical is by looking at what is most common, or the mode. A third way to define typicality is to determine the middle score, or median. Correlations provide a numerical value that describes the strength of the relationship between two variables. When two variables are strongly related, one can be predicted from the other. Sometimes researchers have two sets of numbers and need to determine whether there are real differences between them. This is done with inferential statistics.

CHAPTER 3 | Genetic and Biological Foundations

GUIDE TO THE READING

This chapter provides the genetic and biological foundations for psychological science and lays the groundwork for presentation of the workings of the brain in the next chapter. With the research publication of the first phase of the *Human Genome Project* in 2001, an explosion of information has furthered our understanding of brain, mind, and behavior. The chapter traces the work of behavioral geneticists from Mendel's time until today. The knowledge of how genes operate and how they are influenced by the environment has furthered our knowledge of psychological science. From here we transition to look at the biological foundations of behavior at the cellular level. Insights into how neurons communicate with each other can help explain both adaptive and maladaptive behavior. A substantial part of this communication system occurs electrochemically through neurotransmitters that are liberated into the synapse between neurons. The excitatory and inhibitory signals these neurotransmitters send greatly influence our experiences of emotion, thought, and behavior. Finally, the chapter looks at how these neural messages are integrated into specialized communication systems. These communication systems help us cope with the tasks and stressors of daily life.

What Is the Genetic Basis of Psychological Science?

The Human Genome Project is a massive undertaking designed to map the entire structure of human genetic material. This is an international project involving hundreds of scientists, and it has the potential to vastly improve our understanding of human behavior and suggest new treatment for many heretofore resistant diseases. Our understanding of the genetic basis of psychological science goes back to the work of Gregor Mendel, a monk who in 1866 studied the reproduction of pea plants. He discovered that the mechanisms for heredity involved passing along genes through reproduction. Mendel's work and that of his successors led to our understanding that human beings have 23 pairs of chromosomes organized into DNA segments called genes. Certain physical characteristics are passed from parents to children through the interaction of dominant and recessive genes; however, much human behavior is determined polygenically. Be sure to understand the difference between an organism's genotype (its genetic material) and its phenotype (its observable physical characteristics). Behavioral geneticists study how genes and the environment interact to influence psychological activity. Some of the methods they use to study this are twin studies, adoption studies, and comparisons of identical twins reared together and reared apart. From these methods they can estimate the heritability of a trait, which is the portion of observed variation in a population that is caused by differences in heredity. It is also important to understand that social and environmental contexts influence genetic expression and vice versa.

How Does the Nervous System Operate?

The nervous system operates via billions of neurons, nerve cells that are specialized for communication. Although there are a wide variety of neurons, they all generally share four structural regions. The dendrites receive information across the synapse from neighboring neurons. This information is sent along to the cell body where it is collected and processed. From the cell body, electrical signals are transmitted along a long narrow outgrowth known as the axon. At the end of the axon are the terminal buttons that receive electrical signals and release chemicals into the synapse, the space between neurons. There are three basic types of neurons. Sensory neurons detect information from the physical world and transmit it to the brain. Motor neurons direct the muscles to contract or relax; thus they are vital for movement. Interneurons communicate within local or short-distance circuits. The resting membrane potential of a neuron is slightly negatively charged. An action potential or neuronal firing causes this balance to change. The action potential is the electrical signal that passes along the axon and causes the release of chemicals that transmit signals to other neurons. These signals can be excitatory, which causes other neurons to be more likely to fire, or inhibitory, which causes other neurons to be less likely to fire. You need to understand the chemical nature of polarization and depolarization, how the myelin sheath over the axon aids in communication, and how neurotransmitters bind to receptors across the synapse. In addition, you need to understand the three processes that terminate the influence of transmitters in the synaptic cleft: reuptake, enzyme deactivation, and autoreception.

How Do Neurotransmitters Influence Emotion, Thought, and Behavior?

Neurotransmitters are chemical substances contained in the terminal buttons that, when they cross the synapse to the next neuron, act to enhance or inhibit action potentials. There are over 60 neurotransmitters in the body that influence emotions, thoughts, and behaviors. Drugs that enhance the actions of neurotransmitters are known as agonists; drugs that inhibit their action are known as antagonists. The chapter focuses on four categories of neurotransmitters: acetylcholine, monoamines, amino acids, and peptides.

Acetylcholine (ACh) is involved with motor control, memory and attention, and dreaming. Botulism inhibits the release of Ach, and botulism injections can reduce wrinkles by paralyzing facial muscles. Acetylcholine is implicated in Alzheimer's disease, which is characterized by severe memory deficits. In addition, people wearing a nicotine patch to stop smoking (which activates acetylcholine neurons) report very vivid dreams.

The monoamines are a group of neurotransmitters whose major functions are to regulate states of arousal and affect (feelings). Epinephrine, also known as adrenaline, is found more in the body than in the brain. Norepinephrine is involved in states of arousal and alertness. Serotonin is especially important for emotional states, impulse control, and dreaming. Drugs that block the reuptake of serotonin are used to treat depression, obsessive-compulsive disorders, eating disorders, and obesity. Dopamine serves many brain functions including motivation and motor control. It has been implicated in many activities that are rewarding and is involved in the effects of cocaine. Dopamine has also been associated with Parkinson's disease and schizophrenia.

Recent research has established important roles for amino acids in general levels of inhibition and activation of the nervous system. GABA (gamma-aminobutyric acid) is the primary inhibitory neurotransmitter in the nervous system. Drugs (such as benzodiazepines) that influence GABA are widely used to treat anxiety disorders. Glutamate is the primary excitatory transmitter in the nervous system.

Peptides are long chains of amino acids that serve as neurotransmitters or neuromodulators. Over 30 known peptides serve this function. Three examples given in the chapter are cholecystokinin (CCK), endorphins, and Substance P.

How Are Neural Messages Integrated into Communication Systems?

Neurons and neurotransmitters are part of a larger communication network known as the nervous system. The nervous system sends messages throughout the body and is necessary for our survival. The nervous system is comprised of the central nervous system, which consists of the brain and the spinal cord, and the peripheral nervous system, which consists of all other nerve cells in the body. The central nervous system is separated from the rest of the body by the blood–brain barrier that prevents certain toxins from passing through.

The peripheral nervous system is comprised of the somatic nervous system and the autonomic nervous system. The somatic nervous system transmits sensory messages to the central nervous system, while the autonomic nervous system regulates the body's internal environment by stimulating glands and by maintaining internal organs. The autonomic nervous system also has two divisions. The sympathetic division of the autonomic nervous system prepares the body for action should there be an immediate need. This is often known as the fight-or-flight reaction. The parasympathetic division of the autonomic nervous system calms you down and returns your body to a resting state after sympathetic activation. Chronic activation of the sympathetic nervous system may result in medical problems such as ulcers, heart disease, and asthma.

Like the nervous system, the endocrine system is a communication system that influences thoughts, behaviors, and actions. However, the endocrine system communicates via hormones, chemical substances that are released into the bloodstream by ductless endocrine glands. The difference in this form of communication (versus the nervous system) is that it takes longer for the messages to reach their intended target. However, once the message is received, it is longer lasting. The master gland of the endocrine system is the pituitary gland, which is controlled by the hypothalamus. The hypothalamus is a small structure located at the base of the brain, and this is where the actions of the endocrine system and the nervous system are coordinated.

FILL-IN-THE-BLANK QUESTIONS

1. The term _____ is typically used to describe how characteristics, such as height, hair color, and weight, are passed along through inheritance.

2. The process by which the gene produces RNA and then protein is known as gene _____ in that the gene is "switched on."

3. Reproductive cells from each parent divide to produce _____, egg and sperm cells, which contain only half of each pair of chromosomes.

4. The two chromosomes in the 23rd pair of chromosomes are known as the _____.

5. _____ is a genetic disorder that mostly affects African Americans and alters how oxygen is processed in the bloodstream.

6. _____ is a dominant gene disorder that typically strikes around age 40, resulting in mental deterioration and abnormal body movements.

7. _____ compare similarities between different types of twins to determine the genetic basis of specific traits.

8. _____ compare the similarities between biological relatives and adoptive relatives.

9. _____ is a statistical estimate of the portion of observed variation in a population that is caused by differences in heredity.

10. The _____ is a communication network that serves as the foundation for all psychological activity and is comprised of billions of specialized nerve cells.

11. The _____ is the basis of the nervous system and facilitates communication from one cell to another.

12. The electrical charge of a neuron when it is not active is known as the _____.

13. The cell membrane is said to be _____; that is, it allows some types of ions to cross more easily than others.

14. The _____ is the small space that exists between neurons and contains the extracellular fluid.

15. _____ are specialized protein molecules on the postsynaptic membrane that neurotransmitters bind to after passing across the synaptic cleft.

16. _____ is the process whereby the neurotransmitter is taken back into the presynaptic terminal buttons, thereby stopping its activity.

17. _____ is the process whereby the neurotransmitter is destroyed by an enzyme, thereby terminating its activity.

18. _____ are the neuron's own neurotransmitter receptors, which regulate the release of the neurotransmitters.

19. _____ is the neurotransmitter responsible for motor control at the junction between nerves and muscles.

20. _____ are the group of neurotransmitters synthesized from a single amino acid that are involved in a variety of psychological activities.

21. _____ is a monoamine, found primarily in the body, which causes a burst of energy after an exciting event.

22. _____ is a monoamine neurotransmitter involved in states of arousal and vigilance.

23. _____ is a monoamine neurotransmitter that is involved in reward, motivation, and motor control.

24. _____ is the primary inhibitory neurotransmitter in the nervous system.

25. _____ is the primary excitatory transmitter in the nervous system.

26. _____ are chains of two or more amino acids that are found in the brain and the body.

27. A _____ is a neutral substance, such as water, that has no pharmacological effect.

28. _____ is a peptide that acts as a neurotransmitter and is involved in pain perception.

29. The _____ nervous system consists of the brain and the spinal cord.

30. The _____ nervous system consists of all nerve cells excluding those in the brain and spinal cord.

31. The _____ nervous system is a major component of the peripheral nervous system and is involved in regulating the body's internal environment.

32. The _____ system is a communication system that uses hormones.

33. _____ are the main endocrine glands involved in sexual behavior—in males, the testes; in females, the ovaries.

34. The _____ is the brain structure that provides much of the central control of the endocrine system.

35. The _____ is located at the base of the hypothalamus and sends hormonal signals that control the release of hormones from endocrine glands.

MULTIPLE-CHOICE QUESTIONS

1. Which of the following events in 2001 marked the beginning of a major biological revolution within the field of psychological science?
   a. Completion of the first phase of the Human Genome Project.
   b. Identification of the structure of DNA.
   c. Discovery of hemisphere differences in split brain patients.
   d. Finding that neurotransmitters communicate information electrochemically in the brain.

2. One of the most striking findings from the Human Genome Project is that there are only about _____ genes in a human being.
   a. 23 pairs of
   b. 30,000
   c. 15–20 million
   d. one billion

3. George has to be careful about drinking sodas or ingesting certain dairy products. He has a genetic disorder in which he is unable to break down an enzyme (phenylalanine) contained in these products. For him, ingesting these substances could lead to severe brain damage. George's disorder is known as
   a. La Vache Folle disorder.
   b. Phenylketonuria (PKU).
   c. Down syndrome.
   d. cultural-familial retardation.

4. The genetic contribution for most human traits and diseases can be considered
   a. monogenic.
   b. retrogenic.
   c. polygenic.
   d. androgenic.

5. Bennell and Burnell are identical twins. They look alike, act alike, and often have a great time fooling their teacher about who they are. Their similarity is the result of one zygote dividing into two, each having the same chromosomes and the genes they contain. Bennell and Burnell are also known as
   a. dizygotic twins.
   b. fraternal twins.
   c. matching twins.
   d. monozygotic twins.

6. Amanda and Renee were adopted into the Wingate household as infant girls. The Wingates took great pains to raise them similarly and expose them to a similar environment growing up. What could we predict about the influence of genes and the environment on Amanda and Renee's personalities as adults?
   a. They will be as similar as monozygotic twins reared apart.
   b. They will be as similar as dizygotic twins reared together.
   c. They will be as similar as siblings reared together.
   d. They will be as similar as two strangers chosen randomly.

7. From Caspi and his colleagues' studies of New Zealanders, which of the following groups would we expect to engage in the most violent activity?
   a. Individuals with low-level MAO gene activity regardless of environment.
   b. Individuals with high-level MAO gene activity regardless of environment.
   c. Individuals with low-level MAO gene activity and a history of child maltreatment.
   d. Individuals with high-level MAO gene activity and a history of child maltreatment.

8. This region of the neuron receives electrical impulses and releases chemical signals into the synapse:
   a. dendrite.
   b. cell body.
   c. axon.
   d. terminal button.

9. Nelly the Neuron is interested in communicating with his neighboring neuron, Naomi. To tell her what he wants, he has to get his chemicals across a tiny space to the receptive membrane of her dendrites. This space is known as the
   a. interstitial space.
   b. synapse.
   c. molecular cleft.
   d. terminal button.

10. Tony was riding his bicycle at the X-Games when he fell on the half-pipe and broke his arm. Which of the following types of neurons sent pain signals from his broken arm to his brain?
    a. Sensory neurons.
    b. Motor neurons.
    c. Interneurons.
    d. Efferent neurons.

11. The period of time, following an action potential, in which it is impossible for the neuron to fire again is known as
    a. propagation.
    b. depolarization.
    c. absolute refractory period.
    d. relative refractory period.

12. The characteristic that the neuron fires with the same potency each time is known as the
    a. all-or-none principle.
    b. absolute refractory period.
    c. relative refractory period.
    d. consistent velocity phenomenon.

13. Richard is experiencing numbness in his limbs and blurry vision. After visiting his physician, he is told that he has a neurological disorder resulting from the decay of the myelin sheath surrounding his axons. Richard is suffering from
    a. muscular dystrophy.
    b. multiple sclerosis.
    c. Down syndrome.
    d. Huntington's disease.

14. Sara and Dopey are chemicals that hang out in the vesicles of the nervous system. When they receive an action potential, they spill out into the synapse to facilitate communication among the other neurons. Sara and Dopey are part of a family of chemicals known as
    a. antagonists.
    b. neurotransmitters.
    c. agonists.
    d. dendrites.

15. Which of the following is *not* one of the three events that terminate the influence of transmitters in the synaptic cleft?
    a. Reuptake.
    b. Depolarization.
    c. Enzyme deactivation.
    d. Autoreception.

16. Prozac is an antidepressant medication that works by preventing the neurotransmitter serotonin from being taken back into the presynaptic terminal button. Thus, it works by inhibiting the process of
    a. reuptake.
    b. depolarization.
    c. enzyme deactivation.
    d. autoreception.

17. Which of the following is *not* a category of neurotransmitters?
    a. Acetylcholine.
    b. Monoamines.
    c. Amino acids.
    d. Lipids.

18. Indiana is searching for treasures in a South American cave. Just as he is about to find the Lost Ark, he is shot with an arrow containing curare on the tip. The curare enters the bloodstream and binds to receptors, thus inhibiting the mechanisms that produce muscle move-

ment. Thus curare competes with the mechanisms of which neurotransmitter?
    a. Acetylcholine.
    b. Serotonin.
    c. Dopamine.
    d. GABA.

19. Eileen is concerned that she is getting older and craggy. To deal with this, she has botulism injected into her eyebrow region, thus getting rid of some of her wrinkles. Her monthly botulism treatment works by interfering with the actions of which neurotransmitter?
    a. Acetylcholine.
    b. Serotonin.
    c. Dopamine.
    d. GABA.

20. Neal is trying to quit smoking. After consulting with his physician, he decided to try a nicotine patch to help him stop. While he is having some success at stopping smoking, he also is having very vivid dreams (which he enjoys). Neal's vivid dreams are likely the result of the nicotine patch exciting which neurotransmitter?
    a. Acetylcholine.
    b. Serotonin.
    c. Dopamine.
    d. GABA.

21. Which of the following is *not* one of the monoamines?
    a. Epinephrine.
    b. GABA.
    c. Serotonin.
    d. Dopamine.

22. What is the major function of the group of neurotransmitters known as the monoamines?
    a. Regulate states of arousal and affect.
    b. Initiate motor movement.
    c. Inhibit the nervous system.
    d. Enhance memory systems.

23. Barbara is a mess. As far as we can tell, she suffers from depression, obsessive-compulsive disorders, eating disorders, and obesity. Fortunately, drugs that block the reuptake of this monoamine neurotransmitter have been used to treat all these disorders:
    a. epinephrine.
    b. norepinephrine.
    c. serotonin.
    d. dopamine.

24. Cassius suffers from Parkinson's disease, a neurological disorder marked by muscular rigidity, tremors, and difficulty initiating voluntary action. This disease is most likely due to a depletion in which of the following neurotransmitters?
    a. Epinephrine.

b. GABA.

c. Serotonin.

d. Dopamine.

25. Shannon suffers from a number of nonspecific anxiety disorders. Her physician prescribes a benzodiazepine medication to deal with this. The medication works because it assists with the binding of which neurotransmitter?

a. Norepinephrine.

b. GABA.

c. Serotonin.

d. Dopamine.

26. Which of the following is *not* a peptide that acts as a neurotransmitter or modulator?

a. Cholecystokinin (CCK).

b. Morphine.

c. Endorphins.

d. Substance P.

27. Lance is involved a monthlong bicycle race. Although he should be in great pain by the end of the race, his body has produced substances that naturally alleviate his pain. What are the names of these helpful peptides?

a. Morphines.

b. Benzodiazepines.

c. Endorphins.

d. Anxiolytics.

28. Reuben is a contestant on the latest edition of *Survivor*. While in a remote jungle, he unknowingly ingests a plant that is potentially toxic. However, the poison does not enter his brain or spinal cord because of the _____, a group of selectively permeable blood vessels.

a. blood–brain barrier

b. brain levee

c. glial cells

d. nodes of Ranvier

29. Which of the following are the components of the peripheral nervous system?

a. Somatic nervous system; autonomic nervous system.

b. Central nervous system; autonomic nervous system.

c. Somatic nervous system; central nervous system.

d. Sympathetic nervous system; parasympathetic nervous system.

30. While in the remote jungle, Reuben nearly steps on a poisonous snake. His body goes into an alarm reaction (blood flows to skeletal muscles, epinephrine is released, the lungs take in more oxygen) preparing it for action. Which part of the nervous system is preparing for action?

a. The sympathetic division of the autonomic nervous system.

b. The parasympathetic division of the peripheral nervous system.

c. The sympathetic division of the central nervous system.

d. The parasympathetic division of the autonomic nervous system.

31. After the poisonous snake disappears into the jungle, Reuben finally calms down. Which part of his nervous system allows this to occur?

a. The sympathetic division of the autonomic nervous system.

b. The parasympathetic division of the central nervous system.

c. The sympathetic division of the central nervous system.

d. The parasympathetic division of the autonomic nervous system.

32. Amarillis is a chronic worrier and cannot deal with the stressors in her life. Her chronic state of arousal has been going on for many years and her friends' attempts to be of help have mostly failed. Because of her worries, Amarillis suffers from ulcers and heart disease. These diseases are likely associated with chronic activation of which nervous system?

a. The sympathetic division of the autonomic nervous system.

b. The parasympathetic division of the peripheral nervous system.

c. The sympathetic division of the central nervous system.

d. The parasympathetic division of the autonomic nervous system.

MATCHING QUESTIONS

Fill in the letter from Column B corresponding to the term that is most associated with the description presented in Column A.

COLUMN A	COLUMN B
____ 1. Structures in the body that are composed of genes.	A. Genotype
	B. Dominant genes
____ 2. Unit of heredity that determines particular characteristics in an organism.	C. Genes
	D. Phenotype
	E. Dendrites
	F. Sensory neurons
____ 3. Expressed in the organism whenever they are present.	G. Action potential
____ 4. Expressed in the organism only when they match a similar gene from the other parent.	H. Antagonist
	I. Myelin sheath
	J. Excitatory signals

____ 5. Genetic constitution of an organism.

____ 6. Observable physical characteristics of an organism; result from genetic and environmental influences.

____ 7. Study of how genes and environment interact to influence psychological activity.

____ 8. Identical twins

____ 9. Fraternal or nonidentical twins.

____ 10. Branchlike extensions of the neuron that detect information from other neurons.

____ 11. Region of the neuron where information from thousands of other neurons is collected and processed.

____ 12. A long narrow outgrowth of a neuron by which information is transmitted to other neurons.

____ 13. Afferent neurons that detect information from the physical world and pass it along to the brain.

____ 14. Neurons that communicate within a local or specific brain region.

____ 15. Efferent neurons that direct muscles to contract tor relax, thus producing movement.

____ 16. Neuronal firing.

____ 17. Stimulate the neuron to fire.

____ 18. Reduce the likelihood of the neuron firing.

____ 19. Fatty material that insulates the axon and allows rapid movement of electrical impulses.

____ 20. Small gaps of exposed axon between sheath.

____ 21. Any drug that enhances the actions of a specific neurotransmitter.

____ 22. Any drug that inhibits the actions of a specific neurotransmitter.

K. Inhibitory signals
L. Cell body
M. Chromosomes
N. Dizygotic twins
O. Axon
P. Agonist
Q. Nodes of Ranvier
R. Interneurons
S. Motor neurons
T. Monozygotic segments of myelin twins
U. Behavioral genetics
V. Recessive genes

THOUGHT QUESTION

Consider that many of today's leading causes of death (such as heart disease and strokes) are contributed to by an overactivation of the sympathetic nervous system. How might this division of the peripheral nervous system have been more adaptive in the past, and what could be done to help it function better today?

APPLICATIONS

A Group Activity to Demonstrate the Speed of Neural Transmission

It is difficult to conceive that it takes time for sensory and motor messages to travel from one neuron to another. It seems that this process is instantaneous. We believe that when we touch something we feel it immediately. Likewise, it seems that when we wish to move, our arm goes out quickly. However, a simple demonstration will indicate that this is not so. Get a group of 8–10 friends and have them hold hands. Have an outside person serve as timekeeper (you will need a watch with a second hand). When the timekeeper says "Go," the first person in line will squeeze the hand of the next person. When that person perceives the squeeze, she or he will squeeze the hand of the next person, and so on. The last person in line will raise his or her hand when squeezed, and the timekeeper will record the time. Do this twice to get an average time.

Next have the group place their left hands on the right shoulders of the people next to them. When the timekeeper says "Go" in this trial, the first person will squeeze the shoulder of the next person in line. When that is perceived, the squeezes of shoulders will proceed down the line. Again, the last person in line should raise his or her hand when finished. Do this twice to get an average time.

If you are lucky, the time for squeezing shoulders should be less than the time for squeezing hands. Have the group hypothesize why. The primary reason for this is that the signals had less distance to travel (across one rather than two arms for each person). This is an excellent model for how neural transmission occurs—that is, the more distance the signal has to travel the more time it takes. Psychologists who work in the area of human factors use this knowledge when designing flight decks for airlines and space shuttles. More important switches and knobs are placed in the center of the pilot's visual field, while less important ones are placed on the periphery.

In keeping with the theme of psychological science, also consider the independent variable, dependent variable, and possible confounds for your experiment.

An Activity for How Your Brain Tricks You with the Speed of Neural Transmission

A nice follow-up activity to the hand and shoulder squeezing is to have your group of friends close their eyes and touch their noses. Assess which feeling reaches your brain first: the perception of your nose being touched or the perception of your nose on your finger. Of course they will look at you like you are crazy—both perceptions occur simultaneously! In actuality, the touch on your finger has to travel about three feet to get to your brain. The touch on your nose travels about three inches, and brain recording devices indicate that this perception gets to your brain first. However, for a coherent view of reality, your brain tricks you into believing that they occur simultaneously. We will find other examples in the next chapter of how your brain distorts the truth to give you a believable sense of reality.

WEB SITES

Biological Psychology and Neuroscience Information

http://psych.athabascau.ca/html/Psych289/Biotutorials
http://faculty.washington.edu/chudler/ehceduc.html

ANSWER KEY

Fill-in-the-Blank Questions

1. Genetics		18. Autoreceptors
2. Gene expression		19. Acetylcholine
3. Gametes		20. Monoamines
4. Sex chromosomes		21. Epinephrine
5. Sickle-cell disease		22. Norepinephrine
6. Huntington's disease		23. Dopamine
7. Twin studies		24. GABA
8. Adoption studies		25. Glutamate
9. Heritability		26. Peptides
10. Nervous system		27. Placebo
11. Neuron		28. Substance P
12. Resting membrane potential		29. Central
13. Selectively permeable		30. Peripheral
14. Synaptic cleft		31. Autonomic
15. Receptors		32. Endocrine
16. Reuptake		33. Gonads
17. Enzyme deactivation		34. Hypothalamus
		35. Pituitary gland

Multiple-Choice Questions

1. a. The completion of the first phase of the Human Genome Project in 2001 marked the beginning of a major biological revolution within the field of psychological science.

    Incorrect answers:
    b. Identification of the structure of DNA did not spark a biological revolution in psychological science.
    c. The discovery of hemisphere differences in split brain patients did not spark a biological revolution in psychological science.
    d. The discovery of neural transmission did not spark a biological revolution in psychological science.

2. b. There are 30, 000 genes in a human being.

    Incorrect answers:
    a. There are 23 pair of chromosomes in a human; there are 30,000 genes.
    c. There are 30,000 genes in a human being.
    d. There are 30,000 genes in a human being

3. b. Phenlyketonuria is the disorder in which infants are unable to break down the enzyme phenylalanine.

    Incorrect answers:
    a. La Vache Folle disorder is a made-up term. It is French for "mad cow disease."
    c. Down syndrome is a form of mental retardation whose genetic cause stems from problems with the 23rd pair of chromosomes.
    d. Cultural-familial retardation is a form of mental retardation whose cause is mostly unknown.

4. c. The genetic contribution for most human traits and diseases is polygenic—that is, influenced by many genes as well as the environment.

    Incorrect answers:
    a. Monogenic means being caused by one gene. Most human traits are influenced by many genes.
    b. Retrogenic is a made-up term. Most human traits are influenced by many genes.
    d. Androgenic is a made-up term. Most human traits are influenced by many genes.

5. d. Identical twins are also known as monozygotic twins.

    Incorrect answers:
    a. Dizygotic twins are the result of two separately fertilized eggs.

b. Fraternal twins are the result of two separately fertilized eggs.

c. Matching twins is a made-up term.

6. d. They will be as similar as two strangers chosen randomly. Research suggests that genes have a strong influence on personality and that growing up in the same household has little influence.

Incorrect answers:

a. Monozygotic twins would be more similar. Research suggests that genes have a strong influence on personality and that growing up in the same household has little influence.

b. Dizygotic twins would be more similar. Research suggests that genes have a strong influence on personality and that growing up in the same household has little influence.

c. Biological siblings would be more similar. Research suggests that genes have a strong influence on personality and that growing up in the same household has little influence.

7. c. Research indicates that individuals with low-level MAO gene activity *and* a history of child maltreatment are more likely to be convicted of violent crimes.

Incorrect answers:

a. Research indicates that individuals with low-level MAO gene activity *and* a history of child maltreatment are more likely to be convicted of violent crimes.

b. Research indicates that individuals with low-level MAO gene activity *and* a history of child maltreatment are more likely to be convicted of violent crimes.

d. Research indicates that individuals with low-level MAO gene activity *and* a history of child maltreatment are more likely to be convicted of violent crimes.

8. d. The terminal button is the region of the neuron that receives electrical impulses and releases chemical signals into the synapse.

Incorrect answers:

a. The dendrites detect chemical signals from neighboring neurons.

b. The cell body is where information from thousands of other neurons is collected and integrated.

c. The axon transmits information from the cell body and ends at the terminal buttons.

9. b. The synapse is the space between neurons. Chemicals leave one neuron, cross the synapse, and pass signals along to the dendrites of other neurons.

Incorrect answers:

a. The synapse is the space between neurons.

c. The molecular cleft is a made-up term. The synapse is the space between neurons.

d. The terminal button is the region of the neuron that receives electrical signals and releases chemical signals into the synapse.

10. a. Sensory neurons, often called afferent neurons, send pain signals from the body to the brain.

Incorrect answers:

b. Motor neurons send signals from the brain to the body.

c. Interneurons communicate with local or short-distance circuits.

d. Efferent or motor neurons send signals from the brain to the body.

11. c. The period following an action potential in which it is impossible for the neuron to fire again is known as the absolute refractory period.

Incorrect answers:

a. Propagation follows the firing of the neuron when the depolarization of the cell membrane moves along the axon like a wave.

b. Depolarization comes from excitatory signals that increase the likelihood that the neuron will fire.

d. The relative refractory period is a brief period when the neuron is somewhat hyperpolarized and requires a stronger signal to become depolarized.

12. a. The characteristic that the neuron fires with the same potency each time is known as the all-or-none principle.

Incorrect answers:

b. The period following an action potential in which it is impossible for the neuron to fire again is known as the absolute refractory period.

c. The relative refractory period is a brief period when the neuron is somewhat hyperpolarized and requires a stronger signal to become depolarized.

d. The consistent velocity phenomenon is a made-up term.

13. b. Multiple sclerosis is the neurological disorder that results from the decay of the myelin sheath.

Incorrect answers:

a. Muscular dystrophy is a disorder that results in the deterioration of muscle movement.

c. Down syndrome is a form of mental retardation whose genetic cause stems from problems with the 23rd pair of chromosomes.

d. Huntington's disease is a late-appearing genetic disorder that results in jerky limb movements and death.

14. b. Neurotransmitters are a family of chemicals that carry signals across the synapse and facilitate communication among the neurons.

   Incorrect answers:
   a. Antagonists are drugs that inhibit the actions of neurotransmitters.
   c. Agonists are drugs that enhance the actions of neurotransmitters.
   d. The dendrites detect chemical signals from neighboring neurons.

15. b. Depolarization comes from excitatory signals that increase the likelihood that the neuron will fire. The three events that terminate the influence of transmitters in the synaptic cleft are reuptake, enzyme deactivation, and autoreception.

   Incorrect answers:
   a. Depolarization comes from excitatory signals that increase the likelihood that the neuron will fire. The three events that terminate the influence of transmitters in the synaptic cleft are reuptake, enzyme deactivation, and autoreception.
   c. Depolarization comes from excitatory signals that increase the likelihood that the neuron will fire. The three events that terminate the influence of transmitters in the synaptic cleft are reuptake, enzyme deactivation, and autoreception.
   d. Depolarization comes from excitatory signals that increase the likelihood that the neuron will fire. The three events that terminate the influence of transmitters in the synaptic cleft are reuptake, enzyme deactivation, and autoreception.

16. a. Prozac works by blocking the process of reuptake when neurotransmitters are taken back into the presynaptic terminal button.

   Incorrect answers:
   b. Depolarization comes from excitatory signals that increase the likelihood that the neuron will fire.
   c. Enzyme deactivation is when an enzyme destroys the neurotransmitter in the synaptic cleft.
   d. Autoreception is the process when excess transmitter substance is detected and the neuron is signaled to stop releasing it.

17. d. Lipids are fat cells. The four categories of neurotransmitters are acetylcholine, monoamines, amino acids, and peptides.

   Incorrect answers:
   a. Lipids are fat cells. The four categories of neurotransmitters are acetylcholine, monoamines, amino acids, and peptides.
   b. Lipids are fat cells. The four categories of neurotransmitters are acetylcholine, monoamines, amino acids, and peptides.
   c. Lipids are fat cells. The four categories of neurotransmitters are acetylcholine, monoamines, amino acids, and peptides.

18. a. Curare interferes with the action of acetylcholine.

   Incorrect answers:
   b. Serotonin is important for emotional states, impulse control, and dreaming.
   c. Dopamine is involved in motivation and motor control.
   d. GABA is the primary inhibitory neurotransmitter.

19. a. Botulism inhibits the release of acetylcholine.

   Incorrect answers:
   b. Serotonin is important for emotional states, impulse control, and dreaming.
   c. Dopamine is involved in motivation and motor control.
   d. GABA is the primary inhibitory neurotransmitter.

20. a. Vivid dreams may result when a nicotine patch excites the neurotransmitter acetylcholine.

   Incorrect answers:
   b. Serotonin is important for emotional states, impulse control, and dreaming.
   c. Dopamine is involved in motivation and motor control.
   d. GABA is the primary inhibitory neurotransmitter.

21. b. GABA is the primary inhibitory neurotransmitter. Epinephrine, norepinephrine, serotonin, and dopamine are the four monoamines.

   Incorrect answers:
   a. GABA is the primary inhibitory neurotransmitter. Epinephrine, norepinephrine, serotonin, and dopamine are the four monoamines.
   c. GABA is the primary inhibitory neurotransmitter. Epinephrine, norepinephrine, serotonin, and dopamine are the four monoamines.
   d. GABA is the primary inhibitory neurotransmitter. Epinephrine, norepinephrine, serotonin, and dopamine are the four monoamines.

22. a. The regulation of states of arousal and affect is the function of the monoamines.

   Incorrect answers:
   b. Acetylcholine is involved in the initiation of motor movement.
   c. GABA is involved in the inhibition of the nervous system.
   d. The regulation of states of arousal and affect is the function of the monoamines.

23. c. Drugs that block the reuptake of serotonin are used to treat depression, OCD, eating disorders, and obesity.

    Incorrect answers:
    a. Drugs that block the reuptake of serotonin are used to treat depression, OCD, eating disorders, and obesity.
    b. Drugs that block the reuptake of serotonin are used to treat depression, OCD, eating disorders, and obesity.
    d. Drugs that block the reuptake of serotonin are used to treat depression, OCD, eating disorders, and obesity.

24. d. Parkinson's disease is most likely due to a depletion of dopamine.

    Incorrect answers:
    a. Parkinson's disease is most likely due to a depletion of dopamine.
    b. GABA is the primary inhibitory neurotransmitter.
    c. A depletion of serotonin is related to depression and OCD.

25. b. Benzodiazepines assist with the binding of GABA.

    Incorrect answers:
    a. Benzodiazepines assist with the binding of GABA.
    c. Serotonin is involved in depression and OCD.
    d. Dopamine is involved with motor control, reward states, and schizophrenia.

26. b. Morphine is a painkiller. CCK, endorphins, and Substance P are peptides that act as a neurotransmitter or modulator.

    Incorrect answers:
    a. Morphine is a painkiller. CCK, endorphins, and Substance P are peptides that act as a neurotransmitter or modulator.
    c. Morphine is a painkiller. CCK, endorphins, and Substance P are peptides that act as a neurotransmitter or modulator.
    d. Morphine is a painkiller. CCK, endorphins, and Substance P are peptides that act as a neurotransmitter or modulator.

27. c. Endorphins are part of the body's natural defense against pain.

    Incorrect answers:
    a. Morphine is a painkiller; morphines is a made-up term.
    b. Benzodiazepines are medications used to treat anxiety.
    d. Anxiolytics is a general term for substances used to treat anxiety.

28. a. The blood–brain barrier is a group of selectively permeable blood vessels throughout the CNS that prevents certain toxins in the blood from entering the brain or spinal cord.

    Incorrect answers:
    b. The brain levee is a made-up term.
    c. Glial cells are support cells in the nervous system.
    d. The nodes of Ranvier are places along the myelin sheath of the neuron that facilitate neuronal communication.

29. a. The two components of the peripheral nervous system are the somatic nervous system and the autonomic nervous system.

    Incorrect answers:
    b. The two components of the peripheral nervous system are the somatic nervous system and the autonomic nervous system.
    c. The two components of the peripheral nervous system are the somatic nervous system and the autonomic nervous system.
    d. The two components of the peripheral nervous system are the somatic nervous system and the autonomic nervous system.

30. a. The sympathetic division of the autonomic nervous system goes into an alarm reaction and prepares the body for action.

    Incorrect answers:
    b. The parasympathetic division returns the body to a resting state after sympathetic activation.
    c. The sympathetic division is not part of the central nervous system.
    d. The parasympathetic division returns the body to a resting state after sympathetic activation.

31. d. The parasympathetic division of the autonomic nervous system returns the body to a resting state after sympathetic activation.

    Incorrect answers:
    a. The sympathetic division goes into an alarm reaction and prepares the body for action.
    b. The parasympathetic division is not part of the central nervous system.
    c. The sympathetic division goes into an alarm reaction and prepares the body for action. Also, it is not part of the central nervous system.

32. a. Chronic activation of the sympathetic division of the autonomic nervous system is associated with ulcers, heart disease, and asthma.

    Incorrect answers:
    b. The parasympathetic division returns the body to a resting state after sympathetic activation.

c. The sympathetic division is not part of the central nervous system.

d. The parasympathetic division returns the body to a resting state after sympathetic activation.

Matching Questions

1. M   Chromosomes
2. C   Genes
3. B   Dominant genes
4. V   Recessive genes
5. A   Genotype
6. D   Phenotype
7. U   Behavioral genetics
8. T   Monozygotic twins
9. N   Dizygotic twins
10. E   Dendrites
11. L   Cell body
12. O   Axon
13. F   Sensory neurons
14. R   Interneurons
15. S   Motor neurons
16. G   Action potential
17. J   Excitatory signals
18. K   Inhibitory signals
19. I   Myelin sheath
20. Q   Nodes of Ranvier
21. P   Agonist
22. H   Antagonist

Thought Question

Answers will vary. Students should consider that the sympathetic nervous system was designed so that we could react quickly to an emergency, the so-called "fight-or-flight" reaction. This would have been more adaptive in hunter–gatherer societies in which individuals faced more immediate physical dangers. In today's society stressors are more of a psychological nature. However, the body still reacts with sympathetic activation. But because neither "flight" nor "fight" are required, potentially damaging chemicals (e.g., cortisol) remain in the bloodstream, leading to long-term health problems.

One way to deal with this is to reduce the stressors in one's life. This can come from activating appropriate coping mechanisms (e.g., meditation, exercise, assertiveness) or preventing/avoiding the stressors (e.g., simplifying one's life, reducing workload, avoiding stressful situations). It has been theorized that the sympathetic nervous system may eventually have to evolve to meet the changes of modern society.

CHAPTER 4 | The Brain and Consciousness

GUIDE TO THE READING

In the previous chapters the authors focused on the biological underpinnings of the nervous system. This chapter builds on that foundation and explores how the brain, part of the central nervous system, gives rise to mental events and behavior. They articulate how environmental events as well as genetics work together to shape the wiring of our three-pound universe. It is apparent that each hemisphere of the brain is specialized for particular functions and that the mind is a subjective interpreter of these stimuli. The authors go further and explore what consciousness is and how it is related to neural events. Finally, they look more in depth at one fascinating, everyday altered state of consciousness—sleep and dreaming.

What Are the Basic Brain Structures and Their Functions?

After a discussion of the history of discovering that localized brain areas have particular functions, the textbook goes about identifying some of the areas. The spinal cord, a rope of neural tissue inside the vertebrae, responds to sensory inputs and directs muscle responses. The brainstem houses the basic programs of survival including breathing, swallowing, vomiting, urination, and orgasm. Two brain structures in this area are the reticular formation (implicated in attention and arousal) and the cerebellum (involved with the initiation of motor movement).

The limbic system is a subcortical region involved with basic drives and emotion. The limbic system includes the hypothalamus (eating, drinking, body temperature), the thalamus (relays sensory information), hippocampus (formation of new/emotional memories), and the amygdala (processing strong emotional information). The basal ganglia are another system of subcortical structures crucial for planning and producing movement.

The cerebral cortex underlies most complex mental activity. The cortex is divided into four regions known as lobes. The occipital lobe is almost exclusively devoted to vision and is the home of the primary visual cortex. The parietal lobe is devoted to the sense of touch and the spatial layout of the environment. The temporal lobe is taken up with the primary auditory cortex as well as some of the auditory aspects of memory. Finally, the frontal lobe is the one that makes us seem most human because it is involved with planning, empathy, and making choices. The fact that the frontal lobe was severed from the rest of the brain in the infamous frontal lobotomy helped explain the zombie-like quality of some of these individuals. For others, their emotional life had just been disinhibited.

How Does the Brain Change?

The brain changes throughout development via the complex interplay of genes and the environment. Should environmental events cause injury to certain locations in the brain, another brain area will attempt to reorganize and take over those functions. This phenomenon, known as plasticity, decreases with age. In general, this plasticity has critical periods—times in which certain experiences must occur for development to proceed normally. Changes in neuronal connections occur as a result of experience. Neurons that fire together strengthen their connections with one another, increasing the likelihood that they will fire together in the future, a process known as Hebbian learning.

How Is the Brain Divided?

Research on individuals with split brains has provided a great deal of insight for the specialized functions of the two hemispheres. Split brain surgery is accomplished by severing most or all of the corpus callosum, a bundle of nerve fibers that connects the two hemispheres and allows communication. When people undergo split brain surgery, often as a means of controlling intractable epilepsy, they can be tested for the functions of each hemisphere. It appears that the left hemisphere is highly involved in the functions of speech and language. The left hemisphere also has a propensity to try and make sense out of the world (i.e., subjective interpreter) even when the data do not make sense. The right brain seems to be more involved with spatial relationships and emotional recognition.

Can We Study Consciousness?

These neural events give rise to our subjective experience of being conscious, self-aware individuals. However, consciousness has long been a difficult area to study because of its internal properties. We tend to focus on more definable parts such as the subjective experience of consciousness, our access to conscious information, and the experience of it as a unitary phenomenon. Processes outside our mental awareness are labeled unconscious; however, this can be quite adaptive as we are better off putting our knowledge of processes such as heartbeat and breathing on automatic. Unconscious or subliminal processing can influence our awareness and behavior, although these findings have been much overhyped in the media. It also seems that different parts of the brain are responsible for awareness of different types of information.

What Is Sleep?

The final section of the chapter looks in more detail at the complex topic of sleep. When we consider the amount of time we engage in this activity, it is truly surprising that most of the scientific information on sleep is fairly recent. Sleep is an altered state of consciousness that is initiated by biological processes. Our brain waves become slower and more rhythmic as we progress from stage 1 to stage 4 sleep. After about 90 minutes of sleep, we venture into the cycle of REM sleep, also known as paradoxical sleep because of the discrepancy between a sleeping body and an activated brain. Although many view it as a nuisance, sleep appears to be an important survival behavior. Restorative theory suggests that sleep allows the body to rest and repair itself. Circadian rhythm theory proposes that sleep keeps animals quiet and inactive during times of the day when they are in greatest danger. Substantial research also indicates that sleep is important for the facilitation of learning. For students, this points to the limits of cramming all night for an exam.

Finally, the chapter investigates the perplexing topic of dreaming, which, like all of sleeping, is highly regulated by biological factors. The brain actually sends signals to paralyze the body during REM sleep that aid in preventing us from acting out our dreams. Three dream theories are presented along with their supporting evidence (Sigmund Freud, activation–synthesis hypothesis, evolved threat rehearsal). It is interesting that the Freudian theory of dream analysis, which is well known among the general public, has virtually no scientific support.

FILL-IN-THE-BLANK QUESTIONS

1. The _____ is a rope of neural tissue that runs inside the vertebrae from just above the pelvis up into the base of the skull.

2. The _____ is a section of the bottom of the brain that houses the most basic programs of survival such as breathing, swallowing, vomiting, urination, and orgasm.

3. The _____ is a large network of neural tissue within the brainstem involved in behavioral arousal and sleep–wake cycles.

4. The pituitary gland is controlled by the _____, a vital subcortical structure in the brain.

5. Almost all sensory information must go through the _____ in the limbic system before reaching the cortex.

6. The _____ are a system of subcortical structures crucial for planning and producing movement.

7. The _____ is the thin outer layer of brain tissue that forms the convoluted surface of the brain.

8. The _____ is a region of the frontal lobes that is important for attention, working memory, decision making, appropriate social behavior, and personality.

9. _____ is a property of the brain that allows it to change as a result of experience, drugs, or injury.

10. The time in which certain experiences must occur for normal brain development is known as a _____.

11. Amputees are often afflicted with _____, the intense sensation that the amputated body part still exists.

12. _____ are "master" cells that not only are able to regenerate themselves, but also have the capacity to develop into any type of tissue, such as muscles or nerve cells.

13. The fiber of axons that transmits information between the two cerebral hemispheres of the brain is known as the _____.

14. The condition in which the corpus callosum is surgically cut and the two hemispheres do not receive information from each other is known as _____.

15. The left hemispheric propensity to construct a world that makes sense is called the _____.

16. The properties of our subjective, phenomenological awareness are known as _____.

17. The processes that we are not conscious of we label _____, or outside our mental awareness.

18. _____ refers to stimuli that our sensory systems respond to, but that because of their short duration or subtle form, never reach the threshold of entering into consciousness.

19. The _____ is when unconscious thoughts are suddenly expressed at inappropriate times, often to inappropriate people.

20. A condition in which people suffer blindness due to damage in the visual cortex but continue to have some visual capacities in the absence of any visual awareness is known as _____.

21. An influential model of consciousness known as the _____ model posits that consciousness arises as a function of which brain regions are active.

22. Sleep is often considered an _____, one sharing many properties with drug/alcohol intoxication, meditation, and hypnotic states.

23. _____ is a sleep disorder characterized by an inability to sleep.

24. _____ is the stage of sleep marked by rapid eye movements, dreaming, and paralysis of motor systems.

25. Brief, unintended sleep episodes caused by chronic sleep deprivation are known as _____.

26. The regulation of biological cycles into regular patterns are known as _____.

27. _____ are the product of an altered state of consciousness in which images and fantasies are confused with reality.

28. The plot of a dream or the way that it is remembered is known as the _____.

29. What a dream symbolizes or the material that is disguised is known as the _____.

30. The theory that dreams are the result of the sleeping mind trying to make sense of random neuronal firing is known as the _____.

MULTIPLE-CHOICE QUESTIONS

1. Franz was visiting the county fair. A carnie on the midway told him that he could determine his personality by feeling the bumps on his head. Franz was skeptical but paid a dollar to check this claim. The carnie duped Franz by practicing the pseudoscience of
   a. geneology.
   b. phrenology.
   c. neuropsychology.
   d. psychiatry.

2. Franz decided to go on some of the rides at the fair. Unfortunately, a piece of the carousel broke and punctured his skull in Broca's area. We know that when he recovers, he is going to have difficulty with the
   a. production of language.
   b. understanding of language.
   c. hearing of language.
   d. control of his emotions.

3. Little Jorge has contracted a serious infection. He suddenly has difficulty riding his bicycle and coordinating his motor movements. We suspect that Jorge's infection has impaired his
   a. reticular formation.
   b. cerebellum.
   c. limbic system.
   d. hypothalamus.

4. James is a patient in the water intoxication ward. He suffers from polydipsia or an incessant thirst. His motivation to drink is so strong that he has to be monitored when he is walking on the hospital grounds. From our knowledge of neuroscience, we might suspect difficulties in this subcortical structure:
   a. cerebellum.
   b. hypothalamus.
   c. thalamus.
   d. hippocampus.

5. Robert's life is a mess. He cannot remember whether he has eaten his meals or taken a bath. His inability to form new memories is likely due to damage to the
   a. hypothalamus.
   b. thalamus.
   c. hippocampus.
   d. amygdala.

6. Alexis was attacked by a man who hit her and eventually stole her purse. Eventually she was asked to identify him in a police lineup. We would suspect that which part of the brain would be highly activated in response to this fearful face?
   a. Hypothalamus.
   b. Thalamus.
   c. Basal ganglia.
   d. Amygdala.

7. Roger is suffering from severe epilepsy. To control it, he opts to have this brain area severed, thus separating the two hemispheres of the brain:
   a. corpus callosum.
   b. frontal lobe.
   c. hypothalamus.
   d. amygdala.

8. Stevie has been blind since birth. He has an operation to try and regain his sight. Psychological scientists put a small camera on his glasses that runs to a laptop computer on his hip. From here, surgeons run connections into his primary visual cortex in the _____ lobe of the brain.
   a. frontal
   b. parietal
   c. temporal
   d. occipital

9. Kramer suffers hemineglect as a result of a tumor in his right hemisphere. Which of the following behaviors is he most likely to exhibit?
   a. He forgets personal information such as the name of his wife and children.
   b. He is unable to form new memories.
   c. He only sees the left and right outer halves of his visual field.
   d. He only shaves the right side of his face.

10. Desi talked about his family during his first therapy session. At the beginning of the second session he asked his therapist, "Have I ever met you before, sir?" Desi's inability to remember his therapist is likely due to damage to which lobe of the brain?
    a. Frontal.
    b. Parietal.
    c. Temporal.
    d. Occipital.

11. The case of this railroad foreman who had an iron bar go through his head demonstrated that the brain is important for personality and self-control. Who was this important individual in the history of neuroscience?
    a. Tan Tan.
    b. Phineas Gage.
    c. Victor the Wild Boy of Aveyron.
    d. Karl Wernicke.

12. Recent research suggests that if you do not learn a foreign language before the age of 5, you will never speak it without an accent. This window of time that allows the brain to learn the proper neural connections is an example of
    a. a critical period.
    b. plasticity.
    c. discontinuity.
    d. qualia.

13. Mike, a split brain patient, is shown a key in his left visual field and a ring in his right visual field. He is asked what he sees. Which of the following is most likely his answer?
    a. Nothing.
    b. A key.
    c. A ring.
    d. A key ring.

14. Bill visits his father in the hospital following a stroke. His father is paralyzed on the right side, indicating damage in the left hemisphere. Bill knows his father is likely to have problems with which of the following functions?
    a. Spatial relationships.
    b. Emotional intelligence.
    c. Language.
    d. Facial recognition.

15. Hugh is a split brain patient. He is shown a dollar sign in his right visual field and a nude pinup photo in his left visual field. When asked what he sees, his left hemisphere answers, "A dollar sign." However, he is flustered and embarrassed. When asked why, he says, "This is some wild machine you have!" This left hemispheric propensity to construct a world that makes sense is called the
    a. combiner.
    b. reality language device.
    c. split conscious phenomenon.
    d. interpreter.

16. As Eric goes through the day, he normally does not pay attention to how his heartbeat goes up and down to respond to environmental situations. In terms of information processing, we would describe the workings of Eric's heartbeat as
    a. qualia.
    b. unconscious.
    c. preconscious.
    d. subliminal.

17. Larry has lost his vision following a couple of strokes. However, when he takes his kids to the mall he amazes them by guessing fairly accurately the expressions of people without actually seeing them. This phenomenon of visual processing without visual awareness is known as
    a. qualia.
    b. subliminal perception.
    c. blindsight.
    d. unconscious awareness.

18. Brooke and Tom are trying to decide a name for their baby. They get a Ouija board to see if they can get some help. When Brooke is using the board, she spells the name C-H-L-O-E, which is amazing because this was the name she was considering. This phenomenon represents
    a. the power of blindsight.
    b. the supernatural powers of the Ouija board.
    c. the periodic demonstration of extrasensory perception.
    d. the ability of Brooke's mind to direct a behavior that appears to be outside her conscious will.

19. As you enter stage 2 sleep, there are occasional bursts of activity known as sleep spindles and large waves called
    a. alpha waves.
    b. beta waves.
    c. k-complexes.
    d. REM.

20. William often has difficulty getting to sleep. He tosses and turns and thinks about all his problems from the day. William's inability to sleep is known as
    a. hypersomnia.
    b. insomnia.
    c. REM behavior disorder.
    d. paradoxical sleep.

21. For revenge, Joe wants to put shaving cream on his roommate's face and write "STUPID" on his forehead. Which sleep stage should he pick for his roommate to be least likely to detect this?
    a. Stage 1.
    b. Stage 2.
    c. REM.
    d. Stage 4.

22. Which of the following is *not* characteristic of REM sleep?
    a. Dreaming.
    b. Slow-wave sleep.
    c. Muscle paralysis.
    d. Genital arousal.

23. Flipper the Dolphin is playing around his tank at Sea World. Because some new interns like to jump in the tank and ride with Flipper, he keeps an eye on them by watching them with one eye while the other half of his brain sleeps. The peculiar way of sleeping is known as
    a. split brain sleep.
    b. Unihemispherical sleep.
    c. Paradoxical sleep.
    d. Circadian sleep.

24. Which of the following is *not* an explanation for the adaptiveness of sleep?
    a. Restoration.
    b. Wish fulfillment.
    c. Circadian cycles.
    d. Facilitation of learning.

25. Ryan has been up late for several days watching sports on television. At the end of a boring business meeting, he realizes that he missed various parts of the discussion. Which of the following is the most likely explanation for this?
    a. Multiple personality.
    b. Microsleeps.
    c. REM rebound.
    d. REM behavior disorder.

26. Nancy has been depressed throughout the winter. She tries something new and cuts her sleep in half for a week. Amazingly, this helps lift her spirits. This effect likely works because sleep deprivation leads to increased activation of _____ receptors.
    a. acetylcholine
    b. dopamine
    c. serotonin
    d. GABA

27. The finding that many small animals sleep a great deal while vulnerable large animals such as cows and deer sleep little provides support for which sleep theory?
    a. Restorative.
    b. Freudian.
    c. Circadian rhythm.
    d. Facilitation of learning.

28. The finding that college students have more REM sleep during final exams, and infants spend more time sleeping and in REM sleep, provides support for which sleep theory?
    a. Restorative.
    b. Freudian.
    c. Circadian rhythm.
    d. Facilitation of learning.

29. Debbie acts out the activities in her dreams. She beats on her husband while dreaming of playing the drums and jumps around the bedroom while dreaming of dancing. This acting out of dreams that comes from the lack of the normal muscle paralysis is known as
    a. cataplexy.
    b. narcolepsy.
    c. REM behavior disorder.
    d. sleep apnea.

30. Kendall describes a dream during her first year of college in which her teeth fell out. Jaime tells her that this dream symbolizes the anxiety that is associated with the transition to college. According to Freud, Jaime is describing the _____ content of Kendall's dream.
    a. manifest
    b. latent
    c. activation–synthesis
    d. epiphenomenal

31. Barry describes a dream in which he is climbing a ladder. Alan tells him that his dream reflects the fact that his eyes were going up and down during REM sleep and that dreams are epiphenomenal. Alan obviously supports which theory of dreaming?
    a. Freudian.
    b. Restorative.
    c. Circadian rhythm.
    d. Activation–synthesis hypothesis.

MATCHING QUESTIONS

Fill in the letter from Column B corresponding to the term that is most associated with the description presented in Column A.

COLUMN A

____ 1. Central nervous system tissue dominated by the cell bodies of neurons.

____ 2. Central nervous system tissue dominated by axons and surrounding fatty sheaths.

____ 3. Clumsiness and loss of motor coordination.

____ 4. Consists of the two cerebral hemispheres.

____ 5. Subcortical region involved with eating, drinking, and emotions.

COLUMN B

A. Ataxia
B. Gray matter
C. Lobotomy
D. Parietal
E. Materialism
F. Hebbian learning
G. White matter
H. Neurogenesis
I. Freudian slip
J. Altered states of consciousness
K. Circadian rhythm

____ 6. Lobe of the brain involved with vision.

____ 7. Lobe of the brain involved with touch and spatial layout of the environment.

____ 8. Lobe of the brain involved with memory and processing auditory information.

____ 9. Lobe of the brain involved with thought, planning, and movement.

____ 10. Early 20th-century procedure that involves damaging the frontal lobes.

____ 11. "Fire together, wire together."

____ 12. New neurons produced in adult brains.

____ 13. Two hemispheres are surgically separated.

____ 14. Belief that the brain and mind are inseparable.

____ 15. Unconscious thoughts are expressed at inappropriate times.

____ 16. Sleep, meditation, hypnosis.

____ 17. Short, frequent, desynchronized brain signals when people are awake.

____ 18. Brain signals characteristic of deep sleep.

____ 19. Paradoxical sleep.

____ 20. Sleep theory that the body needs to rest and repair itself.

____ 21. Sleep theory that it keeps animals inactive when it is dark.

____ 22. Sleep theory that it strengthens neuronal connections.

L. Restorative theory
M. Temporal
N. Beta waves
O. Frontal
P. Delta waves
Q. Facilitation of learning
R. REM sleep
S. Limbic system
T. Occipital
U. Split brain
V. Forebrain

THOUGHT QUESTIONS

1. The debate in neuroscience over the last 100 years has been that parts of the brain have specialized functions (i.e., localization) versus that all parts of the cortex contribute equally to mental abilities (i.e., equipotentiality).

With the improvements in imaging techniques, localization of function won out. What if this idea is fundamentally wrong? What if the brain has the tendency to wire in certain ways but adapts based on need, injury, infection, and the like? What impact would this have on our ideas of neuroscience?

2. It has been estimated that individuals slept an average of 10 hours per day at the beginning of the 20th century. Today people average a little over 7 hours per night. Speculate about the various causes for this change. Also, considering the seemingly adaptive nature of sleep and dreaming, consider how this change has influenced our society. What do you think will happen if this reduction in sleep continues?

APPLICATIONS

An Activity to Demonstrate the Specialized Functions of the Left and Right Hemispheres

Here is a fun, if not totally scientific, way to explore the specialized functions of the left and right hemispheres of the brain. You will recall that the left hemisphere of the brain is specialized for the functions of speech and language. The right hemisphere seems to be more involved with the functions of spatial localization, recognition of faces (particularly fear-producing), and emotional recognition.

At one time there was a theory that people moved their eyes in a direction that would activate the preferred hemisphere of the brain. For example, if you asked someone the words in the Preamble to the Constitution, she would look to the right to activate the left hemisphere for this verbal question. Likewise, if you asked someone which way Lincoln's head faced on the penny, he would look to the left to activate the right hemisphere for this question requiring spatial localization.

Although this correlation between eye movement and hemisphere activation has never been satisfactorily demonstrated, it is an educational activity nonetheless. Get a group of friends to act as scorers, main participant, and questioner. The main participant (who is blind to the hypothesis of the activity) will sit in a chair facing the group. The questioner sits behind the main participant and instructs him or her to imagine (not verbally answer) the answers to 10 questions. The group should construct a list of 5 right hemisphere questions and 5 left hemisphere questions. It can be quite challenging to come up with questions that the group will agree tap the main functions of that hemisphere. Finally, the group will score whether the main participant looks left for right hemisphere activation or looks right for left hemisphere activation. See whether the main participant responds in the hypothesized direction at a rate better than chance. Assessing the difficulties of this activity can be the best part of it. Talk about how you are dealing with an intact brain that shares information across the hemispheres. Also, identify the independent variable, dependent variable, and potential confounds. Getting the main participant not to focus on the group scoring eye movement can also be challenging.

An Activity to Demonstrate Common Types of Dream Content

As mentioned in the chapter, it is amazing how little we know about dreams given their provocative nature and the amount of time we spend engaged in them throughout our lives. The text presents three theories of dream interpretation: Freudian, activation–synthesis hypothesis, and evolved threat rehearsal. However, this does not get at the uniqueness and commonality of dream content. *Psychology Today* questioned its readers about the content of their dreams. While far from scientific, it is enlightening. Gather a group of friends and compare their responses to salient ones from the survey:

1. Do you typically remember your dreams? (95% yes)

2. Have you ever been able to control either what you dream about or how your dream unfolds? (39% yes).

3. Have you ever died in a dream? (28% yes)

4. Do you have a recurring dream? (68% yes)

5. Do you ever dream about celebrities? (45% yes)

You can also query them about whether they incorporate outside noises into their dream. This is an indication that the body (particularly the reticular formation) never stops processing external information. Also ask your group whether they have dreamed about a sexual experience, being naked in public, killing someone, finding money, being attacked or pursued, arriving late for something important, being locked up, or war. Consider how each of these dreams would fit the three theories of interpretation.

WEB SITES

Brain Imaging

www.med.harvard.edu/AANLIB/home.html
www.hlm.nih.gov/research/visible/visible_human.html
www.bic.mni.mcgill.ca/demos

ANSWER KEY

Fill-in-the-Blank Questions

1. Spinal cord
2. Brainstem
3. Reticular formation
4. Hypothalamus
5. Thalamus
6. Basal ganglia
7. Cerebral cortex
8. Prefrontal cortex
9. Plasticity
10. Critical period
11. Phantom limbs
12. Stem cells
13. Corpus callosum
14. Split brain
15. Interpreter
16. Qualia
17. Unconscious
18. Subliminal perception
19. Freudian slip
20. Blindsight
21. Neuronal workspace
22. Altered state of consciousness
23. Insomnia
24. REM sleep
25. Microsleeps
26. Circadian rhythms
27. Dreams
28. Manifest content
29. Latent content
30. Activation–synthesis hypothesis

Multiple-Choice Questions

1. b   Phrenology is the pseudoscience of determining personality by feeling the bumps on one's head.

   Incorrect answers:
   a. Geneology is the study of one's ancestry.
   c. Neuropsychology is a branch of psychology (a science) that studies the interaction between behavior and neural events.
   d. Psychiatry is a branch of medicine that treats abnormal behavior.

2. a. Broca's area is involved with the production of language.

   Incorrect answers:
   b. Wernicke's area is involved with the understanding of language.
   c. Wernicke's area is involved with the hearing of language.
   d. The emotional area of the brain is more in the limbic system.

3. b. The cerebellum coordinates motor movements.

   Incorrect answers:
   a. The reticular formation is involved with attention and arousal.
   c. The limbic system is involved with emotional expression.
   d. The hypothalamus is involved with a number of functions including eating, thirst, temperature regulation, and hormone control.

4. b. The hypothalamus is involved with the regulation of thirst.

   Incorrect answers:
   a. The cerebellum coordinates motor movements.
   c. The thalamus relays sensory information.
   d. The hippocampus is involved with emotional memory.

5. c. The hippocampus is involved with the formation of new memories.

   Incorrect answers:
   a. The hypothalamus is involved with a number of functions including eating, thirst, temperature regulation, and hormone control.
   b. The thalamus relays sensory information.
   d. The amygdala is involved with processing emotional information.

6. d. The amygdala is involved with processing strong (particularly fearful) information.

   Incorrect answers:
   a. The hypothalamus is involved with a number of functions including eating, thirst, temperature regulation, and hormone control.
   b. The thalamus relays sensory information.
   c. The basal ganglia are important for the initiation of planned movement.

7. a. The corpus callosum connects the two hemispheres of the brain.

   Incorrect answers:
   b. The frontal lobe is involved with planning and movement.
   c. The hypothalamus is involved with a number of functions including eating, thirst, temperature regulation, and hormone control.
   d. The amygdala is involved with processing emotional information.

8. d. The occipital lobe contains the primary visual cortex.

   Incorrect answers:
   a. The frontal lobe is involved with planning and movement.
   b. The parietal lobe is involved with touch and spatial information.
   c. The temporal lobe is involved with audition and memory.

9. d. Hemineglect involves a failure to attend to the left side of space.

   Incorrect answers:
   a. Hemineglect involves a failure to attend to the left side of space.

b. Hemineglect involves a failure to attend to the left side of space.

c. Hemineglect involves a failure to attend to the left side of space.

10. c. The temporal lobe is involved with audition and memory.

Incorrect answers:

a. The frontal lobe is involved with planning and movement.

b. The parietal lobe is involved with touch and spatial information.

d. The occipital lobe contains the primary visual cortex.

11. b. Phineas Gage was the famous railroad foreman.

Incorrect answers:

a. Tan Tan was the aphasic patient of Paul Broca.

c. Victor the Wild Boy of Aveyron was a feral child who was seen by Jean Itard.

d. Karl Wernicke studied the brain areas involved with the comprehension of language.

12. a. Critical periods are the term for these optimal periods of time.

Incorrect answers:

b. Plasticity is the term for when one brain area takes over the functions for another.

c. Discontinuity is a characteristic of development when growth takes place in qualitatively different stages.

d. Qualia are the properties of our subjective, phenomenological awareness.

13. c. Mike will reply "a ring" as information in the right visual field goes to the left hemisphere—the one that talks.

Incorrect answers:

a. Mike will reply "a ring" as information in the right visual field goes to the left hemisphere—the one that talks.

b. The stimulus of the key goes to the right hemisphere—the one that does not talk.

d. Mike will reply "a ring" as information in the right visual field goes to the left hemisphere— the one that talks.

14. c. Damage in the left hemisphere would create problems with language.

Incorrect answers:

a. Spatial relationships are functions of the right hemisphere.

b. Emotional intelligence is more a function of the right hemisphere.

d. Facial recognition is more a function of the right hemisphere.

15. d. The left hemispheric propensity to construct a world that makes sense is called the interpreter.

Incorrect answers:

a. The combiner is a made-up term.

b. The reality language device is a made-up term.

c. The split conscious phenomenon is a made-up term.

16. b. The processes of which we are not conscious we label unconscious.

Incorrect answers:

a. Qualia are the properties of our subjective, phenomenological awareness.

c. Preconscious is the term given stimuli of which we are not conscious, but are brought easily into conscious awareness.

d. Subliminal refers to stimuli that our sensory systems respond to but never enter consciousness.

17. c. Blindsight is the phenomenon of visual processing without visual awareness.

Incorrect answers:

a. Qualia are the properties of our subjective, phenomenological awareness.

b. Subliminal refers to stimuli that our sensory systems respond to but never enter consciousness.

d. The processes of which we are not conscious we label unconscious.

18. d. This phenomenon represents the ability of Brooke's mind to direct a behavior that appears to be outside her conscious will.

Incorrect answers:

a. Blindsight is the phenomenon of visual processing without visual awareness.

b. This phenomenon represents the ability of Brooke's mind to direct a behavior that appears to be outside her conscious will.

c. This phenomenon represents the ability of Brooke's mind to direct a behavior that appears to be outside her conscious will.

19. c. The large waves in stage 2 are called k-complexes.

Incorrect answers:

a. Alpha waves occur just before sleep when people close their eyes and relax.

b. Beta waves are characteristic of alert wakefulness.

d. REM sleep is characterized by dreams and brain activation.

20. b. The inability to sleep is known as insomnia.

   Incorrect answers:
   a. Hypersomnia is excessive sleep.
   c. REM behavior disorder is when you act out your dreams.
   d. Paradoxical sleep is the term given to REM sleep in that your body is asleep but your brain is quite active.

21. d. It is difficult to awaken individuals in Stage 4 sleep.

   Incorrect answers:
   a. Stage 1 is a relatively light stage of sleep.
   b. Stage 2 is a relatively light stage of sleep.
   c. REM sleep is a relatively light stage of sleep characterized by dreaming.

22. b. Slow-wave sleep is not a characteristic of REM sleep. The brain is quite active during REM sleep.

   Incorrect answers:
   a. Dreaming, muscle paralysis, and genital arousal are characteristics of REM sleep.
   c. Dreaming, muscle paralysis, and genital arousal are characteristics of REM sleep.
   d. Dreaming, muscle paralysis, and genital arousal are characteristics of REM sleep.

23. b. The ability to keep one eye open while half the brain sleeps is known as unihemispherical sleep.

   Incorrect answers:
   a. Split brain sleep is a made-up term.
   c. Paradoxical sleep is the term given to REM sleep in that your body is asleep but your brain is quite active.
   d. Circadian sleep is a made-up term.

24. b. Wish fulfillment is a Freudian term about dreams. It is not an explanation for the adaptiveness of sleep.

   Incorrect answers:
   a. Restoration, circadian cycles, and facilitation of learning are explanations for the adaptiveness of sleep.
   c. Restoration, circadian cycles, and facilitation of learning are explanations for the adaptiveness of sleep.
   d. Restoration, circadian cycles, and facilitation of learning are explanations for the adaptiveness of sleep.

25. b. Microsleeps are brief, unintended sleep episodes causes by sleep deprivation.

   Incorrect answers:
   a. Multiple personality is a term for individuals exhibiting two or more personalities.
   c. REM rebound is when you go into REM sleep quicker and spend a greater percentage of time in REM sleep because of REM deprivation.
   d. REM behavior disorder is when you act out your dreams.

26. c. This effect likely works because sleep deprivation leads to increased activation of serotonin receptors, as do drugs used to treat depression.

   Incorrect answers:
   a. This effect likely works because sleep deprivation leads to increased activation of serotonin receptors.
   b. This effect likely works because sleep deprivation leads to increased activation of serotonin receptors.
   d. This effect likely works because sleep deprivation leads to increased activation of serotonin receptors.

27. c. Circadian rhythm theory indicates that the amount an animal sleeps depends on how much time it needs to obtain food, how easily it can hide, and how vulnerable it is to attack.

   Incorrect answers:
   a. Restorative theory indicates that sleep is for rest and restoration of the body.
   b. Freudian theory has more to do with dreams, which serve the function of wish fulfillment.
   d. This theory suggests that sleep aids in the facilitation of learning.

28. d. This theory suggests that sleep aids in the facilitation of learning.

   Incorrect answers:
   a. Restorative theory indicates that sleep is for rest and restoration of the body.
   b. Freudian theory has more to do with dreams, which serve the function of wish fulfillment.
   c. Circadian rhythm theory indicates that the amount an animal sleeps depends on how much time it needs to obtain food, how easily it can hide, and how vulnerable it is to attack.

29. c. REM behavior disorder is the acting out of dreams because of the lack of normal muscle paralysis.

   Incorrect answers:
   a. People with cataplexy experience REM muscle paralysis while awake.
   b. Narcolepsy is the disorder in which people collapse into sleep when awake.

d. Sleep apnea is a disorder characterized by lack of breathing for extended periods while asleep.

30. b. The latent content of the dream is what the dream symbolizes.

Incorrect answers:
a. The manifest content is the plot of the dream, what is remembered.
c. The activation–synthesis hypothesis says that the sleeping mind tries to make sense of random neural firing.
d. Epiphenomenal is the term from the activation–synthesis hypothesis that dreams are the side effects of random neural firing.

31. d. The activation–synthesis hypothesis says that the sleeping mind tries to make sense of random neural firing.

Incorrect answers:
a. The Freudian model of dreaming says that dreams are wish fulfillment.
b. Restorative theory indicates that sleep is for rest and restoration of the body.
c. Circadian rhythm theory indicates that the amount an animal sleeps depends on how much time it needs to obtain food, how easily it can hide, and how vulnerable it is to attack.

Matching Questions

1. B Gray matter
2. G White matter
3. A Ataxia
4. V Forebrain
5. S Limbic system
6. T Occipital
7. D Parietal
8. M Temporal
9. O Frontal
10. C Lobotomy
11. F Hebbian learning
12. H Neurogenesis
13. U Split brain
14. E Materialism
15. I Freudian slip
16. J Altered states of consciousness
17. N Beta waves
18. P Delta waves
19. R REM sleep
20. L Restorative theory
21. K Circadian rhythm
22. Q Facilitation of learning

Thought Questions

1. Answers will vary, but this is exactly the hypothesis being explored by a new generation of neuroscientists. These scientists trace the history of the localization versus equipotentiality debate and argue that we are on the wrong track by focusing on localization. The impact of this is that we would be restricted in our ability to understand the function, usage, and rehabilitation of the brain. It is a provocative theory.

2. Answers will vary. Idea for reasons why we sleep less may include the invention of the electric lightbulb and that there are more activities available at night, including television and the Internet. The effect of less sleep on society is unclear, but one might address how this undermines the adaptive function of sleeping (restoration, facilitation of learning) that took thousands of years to evolve. Other possible influences may be increased stress, loss of coping mechanisms (e.g., road rage), sleep-related errors (e.g., work and vehicle accidents), and bodily breakdown (e.g., immune problems, cancer, coronary heart disease). Either we will need to concede the need for more sleep or other bodily systems will have to pick up these functions.

CHAPTER 5 | Sensation, Perception, and Attention

GUIDE TO THE READING

We have knowledge of the physical world and all the objects and people in it through information picked up by our sensory systems. This chapter focuses on two phases of how we gain this information: sensation and perception. The study of sensation involves understanding both how sense organs respond to physical stimuli in the environment, and also how the sense organs convert these stimuli to neural impulses the brain can interpret. The study of perception concerns how the brain makes sense of the incoming signals, organizing them into useful information. The authors discuss the sensory processes of gustation, olfaction (smell), touch, hearing, and vision. The basic perceptual processes are demonstrated primarily through a discussion of visual abilities including object perception, depth perception, size perception, and motion perception. The chapter ends with a discussion of attention, or how the brain selects information for further processing.

How Do We Sense Our Worlds?

Our sense organs respond to physical stimuli in the world by changing these stimuli into neural impulses. This process is called transduction. Psychological scientists have used the methods of psychophysics to understand the relationship between the physical stimulus and sensation of it. Research included both sensory thresholds, or how much physical energy a stimulus must have before it is detected, and difference thresholds, or how much change is required before a difference between stimuli can be sensed. More recent investigators dropped the idea of a threshold, above which one can sense a stimulus and below which one cannot sense it, to focus instead on signal detection theory. Signal detection theory includes not only the strength of the stimulus but also other factors that may influence people's judgments about whether they sense a stimulus.

What Are the Basic Sensory Processes?

This section describes how sensation occurs for each of the basic sensory systems. First, receptors in the sense organs respond to the physical world; they send signals to neurons; neurons transmit the signals to the brain. The text briefly covers gustation, olfaction, and touch. In gustation, the sensory receptors are on the taste buds. The receptors respond to chemical substances in food. In the upper back portion of the nasal cavity is the olfactory epithelium, which contains the olfactory receptors that convey signals related to smell. Like the gustatory receptors, the olfactory receptors respond to chemical stimuli. Touch, or the haptic sense, conveys signals related to pain, pressure, and temperature. Receptors are located on the skin. The text covers hearing and vision in more detail. For hearing, the text presents the relationship between physical components of sound waves, such as amplitude, to sensory responses, such as loudness. The parts of the ear follow. How temporal coding and place coding account for sensation of pitch is discussed. Vision, the sense humans generally rely on most, is presented in the most detail. Coverage includes sensory information going from the receptor cells, the rods and cones, through the visual system to the brain, followed by a discussion of color perception.

What Are the Basic Perceptual Processes?

How does the brain create the conscious experience of perception from nerve impulses stimulated by the sensory receptors? The authors present brief discussions of the role of the primary auditory cortex (called A1) for hearing and the primary somatosensory cortex (called S1) for touch. The remainder of the section considers vision. Some scientists believe that up to half of the cerebral cortex may be in some way related to vision. Modern researchers focus on how neurons in different parts of the brain process different kinds of information. These neurological processes allow complex perceptual experiences, such as object perception, depth perception, size perception, and motion perception. For example, one of the most important jobs of the visual system is locating objects in space. To accomplish this we must be capable of depth perception. The authors discuss the roles of binocular depth cues, which are based on both eyes working together, and monocular depth cues, which can be used with one eye alone. Frequently much can be learned about the nature of perception when what people experience and the actual stimulus do not match. Perception of illusory contours (or seeing lines when none are actually there) and visual illusions demonstrate this. For example, you may have noticed the moon illusion—the moon looks bigger when it is low on the horizon than when it is higher in the sky. Understanding why this occurs will give psychological scientists increased insight into the nature of vision.

How Does Attention Help the Brain Manage Perceptions?

Have you ever tried to read a difficult chapter while a friend is trying to have a conversation with you? If so, you already know that people cannot process all the stimuli they are exposed to. Rather, the brain has to select some stimuli for further processing. Attention is the study of how the brain does this. Anne Treisman developed one theory of attention. She proposed two stages of visual processing: preattentive processing of simple targets and serial processing, which requires attention, of complex targets. Cherry described the cocktail party phenomenon. You may have experienced this if you have ever been engrossed in a conversation at a loud party, yet you still heard your name when someone in another part of the room said it. Donald Broadbent proposed a filter theory of attention based on early selection of information for further processing, even before basic characteristics of the stimulus are processed. Although data like the cocktail party phenomena show he was wrong, Broadbent had an enormous influence on the study of attention.

FILL-IN–THE-BLANK QUESTIONS

1. _____ is the brain's processing of sensory signals that leads to an internal representation.

2. The way sense organs translate the physical properties of a stimulus into neural impulses is _____.

3. In an experiment Janelle thought she heard a stimulus when in fact none was presented. This is an example of a _____.

4. Decreasing sensory responsiveness to repeated presentations of a stimulus is _____.

5. The four primary taste sensations are _____ .

6. _____ is the only sense that does not go to the thalamus.

7. _____ are chemicals released by animals that cause behavior reactions in other animals.

8. When he cut himself shaving, Urich could feel the pain because he has a functioning _____ sense.

9. The ossicles transfer vibrations to the _____, a membrane of the cochlea.

10. The light-sensitive chemicals inside the eye are _____.

11. The region of the retina densely packed with cones is the _____.

12. The exit of the optic nerve at the back of each eye leaves a _____.

13. _____ occurs when a stimulated cell sends information to the brain while also inhibiting the activity of neighboring neurons.

14. Perception of color is influenced by hue, saturation, and _____.

15. Red, yellow, and blue are the _____ primary colors.

16. If you stare at a green square and then look at a white wall you will see a _____ afterimage.

17. Ryan believes that he can move things with his mind. He believes that he has a kind of _____.

18. In A1, the neurons at the rear respond best to low frequencies while those at the front respond best to high frequencies. This demonstrates a _____ organization.

19. After a stroke Joyce could no longer recognize objects. Her condition is known as _____.

20. Although there is a gap in your vision where the optic nerve leaves the eye, you do not notice it because of the process of _____.

21. Jamal is in an experiment where he has to locate the letter "h" in an array of a hundred other letters as quickly as possible. He is performing a _____ task.

22. Primitive parts that can be put together to form complex objects are called_____.

23. Sarah can recognize many objects, like cars, gloves, and cups, but she cannot recognize any faces. She has a condition called _____.

24. Julie lost the vision in her right eye, but she can still see depth through use of _____ cues.

25. Using the knowledge that distant objects project smaller retinal images than near objects do reflects which monocular cue for depth? _____

26. In a painting, a house depicted low on the horizon should be seen as _____ than a tree depicted higher in the picture.

27. _____ are rooms constructed with distorted linear perspective such that small people, like children, seem much larger than bigger people, like their parents.

28. The inability to perceive motion is _____.

29. Leo has a little booklet that contains line drawings of a man. If Leo flips the pages of the book quickly, it looks like the man moves his arms. Leo's impression of the man moving is an example of _____.

30. Helmholtz's idea that the brain unconsciously connects information is called _____.

MULTIPLE-CHOICE QUESTIONS

1. When Mary hears her alarm ring, the sensory receptors in her ears respond to the sound waves producing neural impulses. This process is called
   a. sound localization.
   b. pheromone production.
   c. transduction.
   d. place coding.

2. When Pete sees a bright light, his neurons fire more rapidly than when he sees a dim light. This is an example of
   a. quantitative sensory coding.
   b. qualitative sensory coding.
   c. psychophysics.
   d. JNDs.

3. When they went into the mall, Mickey complained that she could hear a high-pitched whine. Her friend Donna could not hear it. When they asked a mall employee about it, he told them that it was the security system and most people could not hear it. Mickey and Donna have different _____ for sound.
   a. signal detectors
   b. absolute thresholds
   c. false alarms
   d. transduction mechanisms

4. When Kumar sat down to study his biology, he noticed that his lamp made a buzzing noise. After a while, he no longer heard it. This demonstrates
   a. sensory adaptation.
   b. response bias.
   c. a correct rejection.
   d. threshold detection.

5. Mehdi was in an experiment where he had to say whether a very faint light was shown. Sometimes the lights were presented and sometimes they were not. He often had to guess. Which perspective takes into account the factors that influence his judgments about the lights?
   a. Threshold theory.
   b. Signal detection theory.
   c. Pheromone theory.
   d. Gustation theory.

6. When Lili eats very spicy food her mouth hurts; she hates bitter foods, and she has many more taste buds than most people do. Lili may be a(n)
   a. supertaster.
   b. somnambulist.
   c. olfactory respondent.
   d. JND.

7. Which sense has the most direct route to the brain?
   a. Gustation.
   b. Olfaction.
   c. Hearing.
   d. Vision.

8. Company X developed a perfume that contains a hormone the company believes will sexually excite men. This company believes their perfume contains a(n)
   a. epithelium.
   b. receptor.
   c. cone.
   d. pheromone.

9. Children born with a rare disease that leaves them insensitive to pain have a problem with their
   a. olfactory sense.
   b. gustatory sense.

c. auditory sense.

d. haptic sense.

10. Endorphins are believed to influence a part of the midbrain that when stimulated results in the reduction of pain. This supports the _____ theory of pain.
    a. amplitude
    b. haptic screening
    c. cochleal
    d. gate control

11. Kambon was in an experiment where he was presented with sounds varying in amplitude. He will hear these sounds as varying in
    a. brightness.
    b. pitch.
    c. loudness.
    d. frequency.

12. Judy had an accident that damaged her hammer, anvil, and stirrup. She damaged her
    a. cochleas.
    b. ossicles.
    c. basilars.
    d. ovals.

13. _____ coding is used to encode low frequencies of sound, and the number of times the hair cells fire matches the frequency of the tone.
    a. Temporal
    b. Place
    c. Thalamic
    d. Location

14. Someone who has hearing in only one ear will most probably have difficulties with
    a. place coding in their good ear.
    b. temporal coding in their good ear.
    c. basalar processing.
    d. auditory localization.

15. As he got older, Brett had increased difficulties visually focusing on objects close to his eyes. He was having problems with
    a. place vision.
    b. photopigments.
    c. accommodation.
    d. his optic nerve.

16. When walking through town on a moonless night, Harry noticed that everything looked gray. He was relying on which receptors for vision that night?
    a. Cones.
    b. Rods.
    c. Pupils.
    d. Iris.

17. Axons from _____ cells are gathered into a bundle to form the optic nerve.
    a. ganglion
    b. horizontal
    c. amacrine
    d. bipolar

18. Cheryl and Tomas are both wearing blue shirts, but all their friends can see that the shirt are not the same color even though both are blue. The shirts are seen as different colors because
    a. perception of color is influenced by many factors.
    b. the shirts differ in saturation, the only important variable for seeing color.
    c. the shirts differ in hue, the most important variable for seeing color.
    d. perception of color is tremendously unpredictable.

19. Meagan mixes yellow and blue paint to get green paint. This demonstrates
    a. additive color mixing.
    b. subtractive color mixing.
    c. primary color mixing.
    d. place color mixing.

20. If you stare at a yellow square and then look at a white wall, you will see a blue afterimage. This is explained by the functioning of the
    a. cones in the retina.
    b. retinal ganglion cells.
    c. rods in the retina.
    d. bipolar cells.

21. According to the text, most of the research on ESP indicates that
    a. it is stronger in some people than in others.
    b. it is stronger in some animals than in others.
    c. some countries have proven it exists.
    d. it probably does not exist.

22. For most senses, information goes to the thalamus and then to the
    a. hypothalamus.
    b. olfactory regions.
    c. primary sensory regions.
    d. retinotopic regions.

23. Janice was hit on her occipital lobe, which resulted in stimulation of which sensory region?
    a. The somatosensory cortex.
    b. The retinotopic cortex.
    c. The primary visual cortex.
    d. The tonotopic cortex.

24. What perspective describes why we see "21 21 21" as the number twenty-one repeated three times rather than

the number two followed by the number one followed by the number two, and so on?

a. The Gestalt principles.
b. The geon descriptors.
c. The fusiform gyrus.
d. The binocular cue.

25. After Maria photocopied an article she noticed that one letter was chopped off the end of each line. She was happy to find she had no trouble reading the article even though the letters were missing. Her ability to read the article reflects

a. Thatcher processing.
b. deep processing.
c. bottom-up processing.
d. top-down processing.

26. Research indicates that a person will be best at recognizing a face if

a. the face is upside down.
b. the person has prosopagnosia.
c. the person has damage to the fusiform gyrus.
d. the face is from the same ethnic group as the person.

27. When bored in class, Denise stares at her index finger first with only her left eye, then with only her right eye, to watch her finger seem to dance back and forth. Denise's dancing finger demonstrates

a. the effects of relative size.
b. monocular cues for depth.
c. motion parallax.
d. binocular disparity.

28. When staring out the passenger window in his dad's car while riding down the highway, Steve noticed that the fence close to the road seemed to flash past him while trees at the far end of a field seemed to move by more slowly. This demonstrates

a. the effects of relative size.
b. a pictorial cue for depth.
c. motion parallax.
d. binocular disparity.

29. When Dave and Chuck walk past Anne, Anne knows that Dave is closer to her because he blocks part of Chuck from view. Anne is using _____ to make her judgment about who is closer.

a. occlusion
b. relative size
c. binocular vision
d. linear perspective

30. Sally was sitting in her car staring out the window when suddenly she thought she was moving! She stomped her brake, and then realized she had not

moved at all. Rather, the car next to her had moved. Sally's confusion is an example of

a. stroboscopic movement.
b. the waterfall effect.
c. the induced movement illusion.
d. the sensitivity effect.

31. You know that a car driving away from you into the distance is not shrinking because you have

a. size constancy.
b. stroboscopic constancy.
c. good continuation.
d. lightness constancy.

32. At a party, Frank was listening to his friend Eddy. Suddenly Frank told Eddy to be quiet: He heard a pretty girl across the room mention his name, and he wanted to listen in on her conversation. Frank's hearing his name from across the room reflects

a. binding.
b. visual search.
c. unconscious inference.
d. the cocktail party phenomenon.

MATCHING QUESTIONS

Fill in the letter from Column B corresponding to the term that is most associated with the description presented in Column A.

COLUMN A	COLUMN B
____ 1. The study of how sense organs detects external stimuli.	A. Monocular
	B. Somatotopic organization
____ 2. The process of changing physical or chemical stimulation to neural stimulation.	C. Optic chiasm
	D. "What" pathways
____ 3. The minimum change between two stimuli needed to sense a difference.	E. Direct perception
	F. Shape constancy
____ 4. Failing to detect a stimulus.	G. JND
____ 5. A tendency to report, or not report, a stimulus on ambiguous trials.	H. Simple cells
	I. Attention
	J. Response bias
____ 6. Short, hairlike structures at the tips of the taste buds.	K. Receptive field
	L. Sensation
____ 7. The brain center for smell.	M. Additive color mixing
____ 8. Location of the receptor cells for hearing.	N. Olfactory bulb
	O. A miss
	P. Transduction

___ 9. Where the two parts of the optic nerve cross.

___ 10. The receptors that influence activity in a sensory neuron.

___ 11. Producing colors by mixing lights of different wavelengths.

___ 12. What A1 represents.

___ 13. The mapping of the body in the brain such that body areas close to each other are next to each other in the cortex.

___ 14. Neurons in the brain that respond to lines of a particular orientation (e.g., vertical).

___ 15. Visual pathway specialized for recognizing objects.

___ 16. Brain area specialized for perceiving faces.

___ 17. Depth cues that can be used by one eye alone.

___ 18. Correctly perceiving an object's shape despite misleading sensory data.

___ 19. Selecting some stimuli while not processing others.

___ 20. Gibson's theory that the brain does not need unconscious inference to have perception.

Q. Microvilli
R. Fusiform gyrus
S. Cochlea
T. Primary auditory cortex

THOUGHT QUESTIONS

1. Imagine humans evolved without the sense of vision. Could we have adapted to our environment without it? Would we have needed another sense to replace it such as the sonar that bats or dolphins use?

2. Design a study to determine which interferes more with paying attention to the road when driving, talking on a cell phone or listening to the radio. What would you expect based on Treisman's ideas about parallel and serial processing?

APPLICATIONS

Thinking Critically about Two-Point Discrimination

As described in the textbook, the skin contains receptors that respond to pressure. Different areas of the skin have different degrees of sensitivity. Areas with relatively large amounts of S1 dedicated to them are more sensitive; body areas with lesser amounts of S1 dedicated to them are less sensitive. Two-point discrimination is a method to test sensitivity to pressure.

Enlist the help of a willing friend. You must explain what you will be doing to your friend, and have his or her consent, before you start. Find two implements with small *dull* points, such as the tops of pen caps or dull pencil points. (You do not want to stab your friend!) Tell your friend that you will be gently pressing the points on his or her arm; sometimes you will press with just one point, and other times you will press with both points. Ask your friend to indicate whether he or she feels one point or two points. While your friend's eyes are shut, put the two points on your friend's forearm at the same time. Ask whether your friend feels one or two. You might want to start with the points about three inches apart. Your friend will probably say he or she feels two. Repeat this for several trials, sometimes pressing with only one point, sometimes with two. Gradually move the points closer to each other. Note when your friend feels only one even though both are being pressed down. Now try the same procedure on your friend's fingertip.

Why can your friend feel two points when they are much closer on the fingertip than on the forearm? Do you think the distance needed to tell there are two points will be the same for all of your friends? (You may want to have your friend try this on you.) What are some confounding variables that may have interfered with this demonstration?

Applications of Levels of Analysis: The Debate about Cochlear Implants

Cochlear implants transmit sound to deaf individuals. Unlike hearing aids, which just make sounds louder, cochlear implants transmit electrical impulses directly to the auditory nerve. People who cannot respond to hearing aids may be able to process sounds with a cochlear implant. So far this may sound all good, but there are limitations to cochlear implants' effectiveness. First, the auditory nerve must be intact or the device will not work. The auditory nerve stops working properly after hearing loss. Cochlear implants are most effective, then, when implanted as soon as possible. What the cochlear implant transmits is not exactly the same as normal hearing. People who have experience with sound and who already developed language skills before they lose their hearing generally benefit most from cochlear implants. People who are prelingually deaf—who lost their hearing very young and so did not have experience with sound or speech—need more therapy to use cochlear implants.

Different levels of analysis explain why cochlear implants work. At the brain systems level, they work by stimulating the auditory nerve. The greater effectiveness of cochlear implants for people who already acquired speech may reflect top-down processing, a cognitive and perceptual process. People who already acquired language may use their knowledge to recognize and organize the signals provided by the implant.

Use of cochlear implants has generated a controversy at another level: Some deaf people argue that cochlear implants threaten deaf culture. Deaf culture is based on commonalities shared by deaf people, including their heritage and their visual language. Some deaf people fear that cochlear implants will eliminate the need for visual language and undermine deaf culture. Other deaf individuals disagree. They believe that cochlear implants do not turn deaf people into hearing people, and individuals may both use implants and visual language. For a more detailed discussion, you may want to visit the National Association of the Deaf Web site: www.nad.org.

WEB SITES

Sensory Systems

http://faculty.washington.edu/chudler/introb.html
www.ncbi.nlm.nih.gov/books/bv.fcgi?rid=stryer.
    chapter.4573

Visual Illusions

http://dragon.uml.edu/psych/illusion.html

ANSWER KEY

Fill–in-the-Blank Questions

1. Perception
2. Sensory coding
3. False alarm
4. Sensory adaptation
5. Sweet, sour, salty, and bitter
6. Olfaction
7. Pheromones
8. Haptic
9. Oval window
10. Photopigments
11. Fovea
12. Blind spot
13. Lateral inhibition
14. Brightness
15. Subtractive
16. Red
17. ESP
18. Tonotopic
19. Object agnosia
20. Filling-in
21. Visual search
22. Geons
23. Prosopagnosia
24. Monocular
25. Relative size
26. Closer
27. Ames boxes
28. Akinetopsia
29. Stroboscopic motion
30. Unconscious inference

Multiple-Choice Questions

1. c. Transduction occurs when sensory receptors change physical or chemical stimulation to nerve impulses.

Incorrect answers:
a. Sound localization is determining where a sound is.
b. Pheromones are chemicals released by animals that cause behavioral responses in members of the same species.
d. Place coding involves the frequency of a sound being encoded by the location of hair cells on the basilar membrane.

2. a. In quantitative sensory coding, the brighter or louder the stimulus, the faster the neural firing.

Incorrect answers:
b. Qualitative sensory coding involves different receptors for different qualities of a stimulus.
c. Psychophysics is the study of the relationship between physical properties of a stimulus and perception.
d. JNDs are just noticeable differences, related to difference thresholds.

3. b. Absolute thresholds are the minimum intensity a stimulus must have for it to be perceived.

Incorrect answers:
a. Sensory receptors would be signal detectors.
c. A false alarm occurs when a stimulus is not presented in an experiment but the participant reports it is present.
d. "Transduction mechanisms" is not used in this context.

4. a. Sensory adaptation occurs when responding to a stimulus decreases over time.

Incorrect answers:
b. Response bias is a tendency to report, or not report, perceiving a stimulus when it is ambiguous.
c. In an experiment, when an stimulus has not been presented and the participant correctly says so, that is a correct rejection.
d. Threshold detection is not used in this context.

5. b. Signal detection theory says that detecting a stimulus involves making judgments.

Incorrect answers:
a. Threshold theory is not used in this context
c. Pheromones are chemicals released by animals that cause behavioral responses in members of the same species.
d. Gustation is related to taste.

6. a. Supertasters have many more taste buds than other people and are very sensitive to qualities of food.

Incorrect answers:
b. A somnambulist is a sleepwalker.

c. Olfactory respondent is not a term.

d. JNDs are just noticeable differences, related to difference thresholds.

7. b. Olfaction has the most direct route to the brain.

Incorrect answers:

a. The route to the brain for gustation is not as direct.

c. The route to the brain for hearing is not as direct.

d. The route to the brain for vision is not as direct.

8. d. Pheromones are chemicals released by animals that cause behavioral responses in other animals.

Incorrect answers:

a. The olfactory epithelium is the tissue that contains the olfactory receptors.

b. Receptors receive information.

c. Cones are photosensitive cells in the retina that code color.

9. d. The haptic sense includes pain, temperature, and pressure.

Incorrect answers:

a. The olfactory sense is about smell.

b. The gustatory sense is related to taste.

c. The auditory sense is about hearing.

10. d. Parts of the midbrain appear to influence whether the gate is open or shut.

Incorrect answers:

a. There was no amplitude theory of pain presented.

b. There was no haptic screening theory presented.

c. The cochlea is a part of the inner ear and is not involved in pain.

11. c. Amplitude of sound waves is related to loudness.

Incorrect answers:

a. Brightness is a characteristic of visual stimuli.

b. Pitch is related to the frequency of a sound wave.

d. The frequency of a sound wave is related to pitch.

12. b. The small bones in the ear are collectively labeled the ossicles.

Incorrect answers:

a. The cochlea is the inner ear.

c. The basilar membrane divides the cochlea into three parts.

d. The oval window is a membrane of the cochlea.

13. a. The question defines temporal coding.

Incorrect answers:

b. Place coding involves the frequency of a sound

being encoded by the location of hair cells on the basilar membrane.

c. Thalamic coding is not used in this context.

d. Location coding is not a term.

14. d. Auditory localization is the ability to locate sounds, a process that requires coordination of information from both ears.

Incorrect answers:

a. Place coding in the good ear would not be influenced.

b. Temporal coding in the good ear would not be influenced.

c. Basalar processing is not a term.

15. c. Accommodation is changing the shape of the lens depending on whether the focus is on a near object or a distant object.

Incorrect answers:

a. Place vision is not a term.

b. Photopigments are light-sensitive chemicals in the rods and cones.

d. The optic nerve carries information to the brain.

16. b. The receptors used for night vision are the rods.

Incorrect answers:

a. The cones are used in the light and code information on color.

c. The pupil is the opening in front of the lens that allows light into the eye.

d. The iris is the muscle that controls the pupil.

17. a. Ganglion cells are gathered into a bundle to form the optic nerve.

Incorrect answers:

b. Horizontal cells relay information to the ganglion cells.

c. Amacrine cells relay information to the ganglion cells.

d. Bipolar cells relay information to the ganglion cells.

18. a. Perception of color is influenced by many factors including hue, brightness, and saturation.

Incorrect answers:

b. Saturation is just one factor that influences color perception.

c. Hue is just one factor that influences color perception.

d. The perception of color is often predictable.

19. b. Mixing paints is an example of subtractive color mixing. The pigments absorb wavelengths, so they are not reflected to the eye.

Incorrect answers:
- a. Mixing different wavelengths of lights is additive color mixing.
- c. Red, yellow, and blue are the primary colors for subtractive color mixing. Red, green, and blue are the primary colors for additive color mixing.
- d. Place color mixing is not a term.

20. b. Afterimages are caused by the workings of the ganglion cells.

Incorrect answers:
- a. The three types of cones are most sensitive to blue light, green light, or red light. They are not related to afterimages.
- c. Rods do not code color.
- d. Bipolar cells relay information to ganglion cells.

21. d. According to the research presented in the text, little evidence exists to support the existence of ESP.

Incorrect answers:
- a. The evidence does not show that some people have ESP.
- b. The evidence does not show that some animals have ESP.
- c. No countries have proven the existence of ESP.

22. c. For all senses except olfaction, sensory information goes to the thalamus and then to each sense's corresponding primary sensory region.

Incorrect answers:
- a. The hypothalamus regulates vital functions and is related to motivation.
- b. Olfaction involves smell.
- d. Retinotopic regions is not a term.

23. c. The primary visual cortex is in the occipital lobe.

Incorrect answers:
- a. The somatosensory cortex is in the parietal lobe.
- b. There is no retinotopic cortex.
- d. There is no tonotopic cortex.

24. a. The Gestalt principles describe how we organize perceptual information.

Incorrect answers:
- b. There are no geon descriptors. Geons are simple shapes that can be combined to form more complex objects.
- c. The fusiform gyrus is an area of the brain that may be related to face perception.
- d. A binocular cue is a cue for depth that involves both eyes.

25. d. In top-down processing what is perceived is influenced by expectations and context.

Incorrect answers:
- a. Thatcher processing is not a term.
- b. Deep processing is related to memory.
- c. Bottom-up processing is based on responses to lower-level stimuli.

26. d. People are most accurate when recognizing others of their own ethnic group.

Incorrect answers:
- a. People have difficulty recognizing upside-down faces.
- b. People with prosopagnosia cannot recognize faces.
- c. Damage to the fusiform gyrus may result in problems recognizing faces.

27. d. Binocular disparity occurs because each eye has a slightly different view of the world.

Incorrect answers:
- a. Relative size, a monocular depth cue, is based on distant objects projecting smaller retinal images than near objects.
- b. Monocular cues for depth are seen with one eye.
- c. Motion parallax is based on the relative movement of objects at different distances. Near objects move across our vision faster than distant objects.

28. c. Motion parallax is based on the relative movement of objects at different distances. Near objects move across our vision faster than distant objects.

Incorrect answers:
- a. Relative size, a monocular depth cue, is based on distant objects projecting smaller retinal images than near objects.
- b. Pictorial cues for depth are presented in pictures.
- d. Binocular disparity occurs because each eye has a slightly different view of the world.

29. a. Occlusion, a monocular depth cue, is when a near object blocks a more distant object.

Incorrect answers:
- b. Relative size, a monocular depth cue, is based on distant objects projecting smaller retinal images than near objects.
- c. Binocular vision results from the coordination of information from both eyes.
- d. Linear perspective, a monocular depth cue, means that parallel lines converge in the distance.

30. c. The induced movement illusion occurs when your frame of reference is wrong and you mistake which object is moving.

Incorrect answers:

a. Stroboscopic movement occurs when two images presented in rapid succession give the impression of movement.

b. The waterfall effect is an example of motion aftereffects. If you stare at a waterfall falling downward, and then look at something stationary, the stationary object seems to move upward.

d. There is no sensitivity effect.

31. a. Seeing familiar objects as the same size regardless of their distance from you is size constancy.

Incorrect answers:

b. Stroboscopic constancy is not a term.

c. Good continuation is one of the Gestalt principles.

d. Lightness constancy is realizing an object's lightness does not change as its background changes.

32. d. The cocktail party phenomenon is the ability to focus on one conversation and yet hear particularly significant information from a previously unattended conversation.

Incorrect answers:

a. Binding is determining which features go with which objects.

b. A visual search involves using vision to locate information.

c. Unconscious inference occurs when the brain automatically and unconsciously connects information.

Matching Questions

1. L Sensation
2. P Transduction
3. G JND
4. O A miss
5. J Response bias
6. Q Microvilli
7. N Olfactory bulb
8. S Cochlea
9. C Optic chiasm
10. K Receptive field
11. M Additive color mixing
12. T Primary auditory cortex
13. B Somatotopic organization
14. H Simple cells
15. D "What" pathways
16. R Fusiform gyrus
17. A Monocular
18. F Shape constancy
19. I Attention
20. E Direct perception

Thought Questions

1. To approach the question, you must consider the kinds of information vision gives you—for example, perception of objects, movement, distance, and size. Are these kinds of information necessary for survival? If so, what could compensate for vision?

2. In designing any experiment, first define your independent and dependent variables. What will you play on the radio? Will you write scripts for the phone conversation? Will some topics be more distracting than others? How will you control for this? What will be your measure of attention to the road (the dependent variable)? In considering Treisman's theory, what kinds of stimuli would allow parallel processing and what kinds would require attention?

CHAPTER 6 | Learning and Reward

GUIDE TO THE READING

The study of learning dramatically influenced our understanding of both human and animal behavior, and so helped form a foundation for all other major areas of psychology. The authors define *learning* as an enduring change in behavior resulting from experience. In their coverage of learning, Gazzaniga and Heatherton present how the behavioral study of learning developed. They then describe classical and operant conditioning, followed by discussions of how learning may occur through observation, the biological basis of learning, and learning at the neuronal level.

How Did the Behavioral Study of Learning Develop?

American psychologist John Watson championed the behavioral study of learning in the early twentieth century. He believed that psychology should focus only on that which could be directly observed and measured; things such as thoughts and feelings may exist but could not be studied scientifically. Strongly influenced by the work of Russian physiologist Ivan Pavlov, Watson founded the school of behaviorism.

Pavlov won the Nobel Prize for his work on digestion in animals. He studied the salivary reflex in dogs. He would put food in the dogs' mouths and measure their salivary responses. In his work he noticed that dogs started salivating when they saw the bowls containing the food—well before they tasted the food. His investigation of why this occurred led to the development of the principles of classical conditioning.

In classical conditioning a neutral stimulus is paired with a stimulus that causes a reflexive response. In Pavlov's work, the stimulus causing the reflexive response was food. The response was salivation. The food is called the unconditioned stimulus (US). Salivating to the food is called the unconditioned response (UR). This relationship is automatic and unlearned. Pavlov then introduced a neutral stimulus, one that had no influence on salivation, such as a bell. Following repeated presentations with the food, the bell by itself caused the dog to salivate. The bell was now the conditioned stimulus (CS). Salivating to the bell was the conditioned response (CR). The dog learned to salivate to the bell.

A number of additional terms were introduced in this section: acquisition, the initial learning of a behavior; extinction, the process of undoing conditioning; stimulus generalization, when stimuli similar to the CS also produce a CR; and stimulus discrimination, the animal's ability to differentiate between stimuli. The authors also discussed the role of classical conditioning in the development of phobias and drug addiction.

When Pavlov developed his theory he focused on contiguity: Presenting two events together in time results in a learned association. He believed that all stimuli are equally capable of producing conditioning, a concept called equipotentiality. More recent researchers have demonstrated the limitations of equipotentiality. For example, current models may focus on how biological adaptation or cognitive processes influence conditioning.

How Is Operant Conditioning Different from Classical Conditioning?

The animal is fairly passive during classical conditioning: The dogs did not look for food; it was given to them. However, many of our actions are actively performed for a purpose: They are instrumental. Animals learn to behave in ways to get rewards and to avoid other behaviors that result in punishment. B. F. Skinner used the term *operant* to describe animals' operating on the environment to achieve a particular outcome. Edward Thorndike performed the first studies on operant conditioning. He placed cats in a puzzle box and timed how long it took them to escape. Based on this research, Thorndike developed the Law of Effect, which states that behaviors that are followed by a positive outcome are more likely to occur, whereas behaviors followed by a negative outcome are less likely to occur. Skinner labeled the stimuli that increase the likelihood of the response *reinforcers*.

Skinner developed a device for studying operant conditioning called a Skinner box or operant chamber. In it an animal, such as a rat, may press a lever that dispenses some reinforcer, like food. Skinner also described the process of shaping, or reinforcing behaviors increasingly similar to the desired response.

In addition to reinforcement, which increases the likelihood of behavior, there is punishment, which decreases the likelihood of behavior. Both reinforcement and punishment may be positive or negative. Reinforcement may be presented on varying schedules. In a continuous reinforcement schedule, the reinforcement follows every targeted response. Partial reinforcement schedules may be based on either the number of responses necessary before the reinforcement is given (ratio schedule) or the amount of time that elapses between reinforced responses (interval schedules). As was the case for classical conditioning, the roles of biology and cognition in operant conditioning are studied.

How Does Watching Others Affect Learning?

The cultural transmission of knowledge is referred to as a *meme*. Memes are found for both animals and humans. They may be acquired through conditioning or by watching others. Observational learning occurs when we acquire new behaviors or modify previous behaviors by observing others. Albert Bandura conducted classic studies of children's acquisition of aggressive behaviors through observing films. Recent research indicates special neurons in the brain, mirror neurons, become activated when one animal observes another.

What Is the Biological Basis of Reward?

Milner and Olds performed some of the earliest research on the biological basis of reward. They found rats would give themselves shocks to stimulate pleasure centers in the brain, a process called intracranial self-stimulation (ICSS). More recent research revealed the importance of the neurotransmitter dopamine for the experience of reward. For example, dopamine is released during ICSS. It is activated in the nucleus accumbens, a part of the limbic system, during pleasurable activities. The drugs people use for pleasure, such as alcohol, heroin, and cannabis, appear to increase dopamine activation.

How Does Learning Occur at the Neuronal Level?

Learning was earlier defined as relatively permanent changes resulting from experience. Scientists believe these changes include alterations in the brain, specifically in synaptic connections. Donald Hebb, an early researcher in the area, proposed that when one neuron excites another the synapse between the two is strengthened: In his words, "Cells that fire together wire together." Two simple kinds of learning, habituation and sensitization, demonstrate the roles of neurotransmitters. In habituation the animal decreases its response to repeated presentations of a non-threatening stimulus. A reduction of neurotransmitter release is related to habituation. In sensitization there is an increase in responding with exposure to threatening stimuli. An increase in release of neurotransmitters results in sensitization. Understanding simple learning provides a basis for understanding complex processes, such as long-term potentiation (LPT). LPT involves strengthening synaptic connections so that postsynaptic neurons are more easily activated. LPT may be influential in several different parts of the brain.

The authors' presentation of behaviorism and learning clearly demonstrated how psychological research is based on cumulative principles and how different levels of analysis may be used to understand key concepts.

FILL-IN-THE-BLANK QUESTIONS

1. _____ is a relatively enduring change in behavior that results from experience.

2. _____ founded behaviorism.

3. _____ is the Latin term meaning "blank slate."

4. _____ was the Russian physiologist who developed classical conditioning.

5. The response elicited by the conditioned stimulus is the _____.

6. The response to the unconditioned stimulus that does not have to be learned is the _____.

7. _____ is unlearning previous associations between the CS and US.

8. If after classical conditioning an animal responds to a low-pitched tone but not a high-pitched tone, the animal demonstrates_____.

9. If after being scratched by a bird, an individual is terrified of all birds, that individual is suffering from a _____.

10. _____ is the process by which addicts need more and more of a drug to experience the same effects.

11. When Watson conditioned Albert the US was a _____ and the CS was a _____.

12. The finding that some associations are more likely to produce conditioning than others shows that Pavlov's idea of _____ is wrong.

13. The _____ model states that the strength of the CS–US association is determined by the extent to which the US is unexpected.

14. _____ is the learning process in which the consequences of an action determine the likelihood that it will be performed in the future.

15. After eating her supper, a child gets candy, making the child more likely to eat her supper in the future. This demonstrates Thorndike's _____.

16. _____ involves reinforcing behaviors that are increasingly similar to the desired response.

17. Children who do their homework to earn stickers are working for _____ reinforcers.

18. When Joey makes his bed his mother gives him a dollar. He is then likely to continue to make his bed in the future. Joey's mother is using _____ to increase his bed making.

19. When Janet's room is messy, her mother doesn't let her watch TV. Janet's mother is trying to decrease Janet's messiness through _____.

20. According to the research on punishment, which mother in the previous two questions should be more successful in modifying her child's behavior? _____

21. A teacher who gives her students stickers every third time they hand in their homework is using a _____ schedule of reinforcement.

22. _____ refers to using operant conditioning techniques to eliminate unwanted behaviors and replace them with desirable behaviors.

23. _____ are demonstrated when an innate adaptive behavior interferes with conditioning an incompatible behavior.

24. A _____ is a spatial representation of the environment.

25. When someone suddenly realizes the solution to a problem after not thinking about it for a while, this person is demonstrating _____.

26. _____ did the most thorough work on observational learning.

27. The term for cultural transmission of knowledge is _____.

28. _____ neurons are activated when one monkey observes another monkey.

29. Feelings of pleasure result from the release of dopamine in the part of the limbic system called the _____.

30. _____ is the strengthening of synaptic connections so that postsynaptic neurons are more easily activated.

MULTIPLE-CHOICE QUESTIONS

1. Watson believed that any baby could be made into any kind of person based on the environment in which the baby was brought up. This idea indicates he thought of the baby as a(n)
   a. tabula rasa.
   b. unconditionable participant.
   c. spontaneous participant.
   d. positive reinforcer.

2. Every time Jon feeds his dog he first opens the can with an electric can opener. He then gives the dog its food. Initially the dog would salivate while eating. Now the dog salivates when it hears the can opener. What is the unconditioned stimulus in this example?
   a. The dog.
   b. The food.
   c. The sound of the can opener.
   d. Salivation.

3. Denise was recently in a car accident, which made her very afraid. Following the accident, she was also afraid of cars. What is the conditioned stimulus in this example?
   a. The accident.
   b. The car.
   c. The fear.
   d. An increase in her heart rate.

4. Even though she was afraid of cars following her accident, Denise forced herself to get back in the car and keep driving. After a while, she noticed that she was no longer afraid of the car. This elimination of fear of the car represents
   a. extinction.
   b. stimulus generalization.
   c. stimulus discrimination.
   d. operant conditioning.

5. A few days after Denise drove around in the car, she went back to the car and noticed that she was slightly afraid again. Just a little bit of driving, however, eliminated her fear. The return of the fear is known as
   a. second-order conditioning.
   b. mirror conditioning.
   c. spontaneous recovery.
   d. incomplete generalization.

6. When Chris went to the dentist he had to have his teeth drilled. Following the visit, Chris was very afraid of the dentist. Soon after, Chris had to go to the doctor. Which of the following would indicate Chris generalized from the situation with the dentist to the situation with the doctor?
   a. He would be comfortable with the doctor.
   b. He would have no feelings about the doctor.
   c. He would also be afraid of the doctor.
   d. He would choose going to the doctor over going to the dentist.

7. After a bad fall from her bicycle, Jenny was afraid to ride any bicycle. She was not afraid to ride on a motorcycle. The difference in her reaction to bicycles and motorcycles reflects
   a. extinction.
   b. spontaneous recovery.
   c. stimulus generalization.
   d. stimulus discrimination.

8. Pavlov trained dogs to salivate by presenting a tone followed by food. After this, he repeatedly presented the dogs with a black square concurrent with the tone. He did not present the food. After many trials he found the dogs salivated when presented with the black square alone. This is a demonstration of
   a. stimulus discrimination.
   b. spontaneous recovery.
   c. equipotentiality.
   d. second-order conditioning.

9. People are more likely to have irrational fears of snakes or dogs than of flowers or butterflies. This reflects
   a. biological preparedness.
   b. equipotentiality.
   c. operant conditioning.
   d. the contiguity principle.

10. Teresa wants to classically condition her dog to salivate. According to the Rescorla-Wagner model, which of the following would be the most effective conditioned stimulus to pair with food?
    a. The smell of dog biscuits.
    b. The sight of the can of dog food.
    c. The smell of the dog food.
    d. The smell of almonds.

11. In his study of learning, Thorndike put cats in a _____ and timed how long it took them to escape.
    a. puzzle box
    b. operant chamber
    c. Skinner box
    d. harness

12. When a hungry rat presses a lever and gets food, he is more likely to press the lever again. According to Thorndike, this demonstrates
    a. classical conditioning.
    b. the Law of Effect.
    c. use of an unconditioned stimulus.
    d. secondary reinforcement.

13. Which of the following is most likely to be a primary reinforcer?
    a. Food.
    b. Money.
    c. Stickers.
    d. Gold stars.

14. Which of the following is most likely to be a secondary reinforcer?
    a. Food.
    b. Water.
    c. Sex.
    d. Gold stars.

15. When Luis wanted to teach his puppy to roll over, he first rewarded the puppy for lying down, then he rewarded the puppy for moving to its side, then for moving to its back, and finally for totally rolling over. The process through which Luis trained his puppy is called
    a. classical conditioning.
    b. shaping.
    c. observational learning.
    d. mirror learning.

16. After trying a number of different products, Meagan finds that her headaches will go away if she takes ibuprofen. Now she takes ibuprofen every time she has a headache. Her taking of ibuprofen has increased because of
    a. positive reinforcement.
    b. negative reinforcement.

c. positive punishment.

d. negative punishment.

17. Selma's mother saw Selma speeding on the highway. Following this, to try to make Selma less likely to speed, Selma's mother took the car keys away for a week. Selma's mother is using _____ to decrease Selma's speeding.

a. negative reinforcement

b. positive punishment

c. negative punishment

d. extinction

18. Dr. King wants to use a fixed ratio schedule when training her rats to lever press. To do this, Dr. King may

a. reward the rats every time they lever press.

b. reward the rats 30 seconds after each lever press.

c. reward the rats on a random schedule.

d. reward the rats after every fourth lever press.

19. Mr. Smith rewards his son every time he gets an A on an exam. This is an example of

a. continuous reinforcement.

b. noncontingent reinforcement.

c. a fixed ratio schedule.

d. partial reinforcement.

20. What is a benefit of partial reinforcement?

a. It is the fastest way to get acquisition of a behavior.

b. It is the only way to modify a behavior.

c. It is the most effective way of combining classical and operant conditioning.

d. It makes the behavior resistant to extinction.

21. Rebecca has a mental representation of the locations of the dorms, the library, and the commons on her campus. This is called

a. observational learning.

b. latent learning.

c. operant finding.

d. a cognitive map.

22. After watching his older sister make herself breakfast by pouring her cereal and adding milk, 4-year-old Joey tried to make his own breakfast—and he did a pretty good job. Joey learned how to make breakfast through

a. observational learning.

b. stimulus discrimination.

c. operant finding.

d. a cognitive map.

23. Judy saw her brother sneak some cookies before dinner and then get punished by their dad for doing it. Judy could describe what her brother did—but she would not do the behavior herself. Her reaction reflects

a. the effects of a partial reinforcement schedule.

b. latent learning.

c. vicarious learning.

d. modeling.

24. Which neurotransmitter has been associated with reward?

a. GABA.

b. Epinephrine.

c. Dopamine.

d. ICSS.

25. Tim was teasing his friend Rita by tapping her on the back. At first Rita jumped when Tim tapped her, but after a while she stopped responding to the taps entirely. Her decrease in responding reflects

a. an orienting response.

b. habituation.

c. sensitization.

d. potentiation.

26. Sensitization is associated with

a. a reduction of neurotransmitters.

b. a complete cessation in the production of neurotransmitters.

c. an increase in the release of neurotransmitters.

d. extinction of neurotransmitter production.

27. The strengthening of synaptic connections so that postsynaptic neurons are more easily activated is called

a. an orienting response.

b. long-term potentiation.

c. intracranial self stimulation.

d. latent learning.

28. Tsien altered which receptors in what he called "Doogie mice" resulting in more rapid learning?

a. NMDA receptors.

b. LTP receptors.

c. ICSS receptors.

d. JND receptors.

MATCHING QUESTIONS

Fill in the letter from Column B corresponding to the term that is most associated with the description presented in Column A.

Column A	Column B
____ 1. The book in which Skinner dismissed mental states and questioned free will.	A. Acquisition
	B. *Walden Two*
____ 2. The stimulus initially unrelated to the unconditioned response.	C. Optimal foraging theory
	D. Modeling
____ 3. In classical conditioning, a stimulus that causes an automatic response.	E. Reinforcement
	F. Systematic desensitization
	G. Neutral stimulus

____ 4. In classical conditioning, an acquired response that is learned.

____ 5. Initial learning of behavior.

____ 6. When stimuli that are similar but not identical to the CS produce the CR.

____ 7. An acquired fear that is out of proportion to the real threat.

____ 8. A treatment for phobias.

____ 9. The idea that animals are genetically programmed to fear certain objects.

____ 10. A stimulus that occurs following a response that increases the likelihood of the response.

____ 11. Rewarding successive approximations to a desired response.

____ 12. Reinforcers that do not satisfy biological needs.

____ 13. A consequence that decreases the probability of a response.

____ 14. Reinforcement schedule based on a specific unit of time.

____ 15. Learning that takes place in the absence of reinforcement.

____ 16. Theory that describes how animals in the wild choose to provide their own schedules of reinforcement.

____ 17. Term for transmission of cultural knowledge.

____ 18. Imitation of an observed behavior.

____ 19. Areas stimulated during ICSS.

____ 20. Neurotransmitter involved in reward.

____ 21. Increase in behavioral response following exposure to a threatening stimulus.

H. Punishment
I. Conditioned response
J. Latent learning
K. Unconditioned stimulus
L. Meme
M. Secondary reinforcers
N. Phobia
O. Interval schedule
P. Pleasure centers
Q. Generalization
R. Sensitization
S. Shaping
T. Dopamine
U. Biological preparedness

THOUGHT QUESTIONS

1. What were the assumptions made by the original behaviorists about the roles of cognition, the brain, and the nervous system on behavior? What are some examples of how the roles of these are addressed now?

2. Parents, teachers, and others often use some form of punishment with children. What should be the goal of punishment? Under what conditions is punishment effective? Under what conditions is it ineffective? What are the best ways to change a child's behavior?

3. Which neurotransmitter is currently believed to be crucial for positive reinforcement? Describe the varying roles this neurotransmitter may play.

APPLICATIONS

Thinking Critically about Shaping

Shaping involves rewarding behaviors that are increasingly similar to a target behavior. You can try this playing a game similar to "hotter/colder." First you need to find a friend willing to try this out with you. Then agree with your friend on what will be the reward: Presentation of this stimulus will increase the behavior. It can be a primary reinforcer like candy or a secondary reinforcer like clapping hands. Send your friend out of the room where you will do the shaping and think of a simple behavior you would like the friend to perform. (Be sure to *not* tell your friend what it is!) Do not make the behavior too complex because it will be difficult to shape. Shaping your friend to sit backward in a specified chair may work well. For example, when your friend reenters the room, you may first reward him or her for walking toward the chair, then for facing the chair, then for sitting in the chair.

As you do this, note what difficulties you face. Did your friend stay motionless so you could not reward any behavior? Did you inadvertently reward incorrect behaviors so your friend repeated responses irrelevant to your goal? Did you forget to reward appropriate behaviors?

After you shape your friend, you may want to reverse roles and have your friend shape you. The original behaviorists excluded the role of cognition (thinking, decision making) in learning. Do you believe that cognition affected your behavior? Did you generate hypotheses about what was being shaped?

Applications of Levels of Analysis: Autistic Disorder

The *DSM-IV* (the main diagnostic manual used by mental health professionals) classifies autistic disorder as one of the pervasive developmental disorders. These disorders generally start in childhood and affect many types of functioning. For example, children with pervasive developmental disorders may have difficulty with language, social skills, and behaviors. The character portrayed by Dustin Hoffman in the film *Rainman* was an autistic savant. Like other people with autism, he had difficulties with social interaction. For example, he did not look other people in the eyes, nor did he use normal facial expressions. His use of language was not normal: He did not inflect his voice, and he tended to repeat words and phrases. His behaviors were also abnormal: His movements were awkward, and he tended to rock. In addition the character was a savant, meaning he had exceptional skills, in this case in math. It is worth noting that the character in *Rainman* was very unusual: Many people with autism are even more emotionally and linguistically limited than he was, and few people with autism are savants.

What causes autism is not entirely known. Researchers propose that genes, brain structures, and neurotransmitters may all be implicated (see Treffert 1999 for a review). Children with autism are frequently treated, at least in part, with behavior modification. Behavior modification is based on the principles of operant and classical conditioning. For example, children with autism may not look other people in the eyes. To increase this, the children may be shaped with positive reinforcement. First the child may be given a treat just for glancing at another person's face, then for looking the other person in the eyes, then for maintaining eye contact. After the child acquires the behavior, the therapist may shift to a partial schedule to make the behavior more resistant to extinction.

Autistic disorder exemplifies how a syndrome evidenced by social, cognitive, and behavioral problems is caused by biological abnormalities and may be treated with behavior techniques. To fully understand the disorder many levels of analysis must be employed.

Reference

Treffert, D. A. (1999). Pervasive developmental disorders. In S. D. Netherton, D. Holmes, & C. E. Walker (Eds.), *Child and adolescent psychological disorders: A comprehensive textbook* (pp. 76–97). New York: Oxford University Press.

WEB SITES

http://psychclassics.yorku.ca/Watson/emotion.htm
http://psychclassics.yorku.ca/Skinner/Twotypes/twotypes.htm
http://psychclassics.yorku.ca/Skinner/Theories/
http://psychclassics.yorku.ca/Bandura/bobo.htm

ANSWER KEY

Fill-in-the-Blank Questions

1. Learning	16. Shaping
2. Watson	17. Secondary
3. Tabula rasa	18. Positive reinforcement
4. Pavlov	19. Negative punishment
5. Conditioned response	20. Joey's mother
6. Unconditioned response	21. Partial (ratio) schedule
7. Extinction	22. Behavior modification
8. Stimulus discrimination	23. Biological constraints
9. Phobia	24. Cognitive map
10. Tolerance	25. Insight learning
11. Noise, rat	26. Bandura
12. Equipotentiality	27. Meme
13. Rescorla-Wagner	28. Mirror
14. Operant conditioning	29. Nucleus accumbens
15. Law of Effect	30. Long-term potentiation

Multiple-Choice Questions

1. a. Watson adopted philosopher John Locke's idea that the baby is born a tabula rasa or clean slate.

   Incorrect answers:
   b. Unconditionable participant is not a psychological concept.
   c. Spontaneous participant is not a psychological concept.
   d. A positive reinforcer is a stimulus that increases the likelihood of a response.

2. b. The food causes a reflexive response, salivating, and so is the unconditioned stimulus.

   Incorrect answers:
   a. The dog is the participant in the experiment.
   c. The sound of the can opener is the conditioned stimulus.
   d. Salivation to the food is the unconditioned response; salivation to the can opener is the conditioned response.

3. b. Denise learned to be afraid of the car through its association with the accident.

   Incorrect answers:
   a. The accident is the unconditioned stimulus.
   c. Fear is the response.
   d. Increase in heart rate is a response associated with fear.

4. a. The process through which a conditioned response disappears is extinction.

   Incorrect answers:
   b. Generalization occurs when stimuli similar to the conditioned stimulus also produce the response.
   c. Discrimination occurs when the organism can differentiate betweenstimuli.
   d. Operant conditioning is when consequences of an action determine whether it will be performed again.

5. c. The return of a conditioned response after extinction is called spontaneous recovery.

   Incorrect answers:
   a. Second-order conditioning involves pairing a neutral stimulus with the conditioned stimulus.
   b. The is no such thing as mirror conditioning. Mirror neurons are activated when one animal observes another.
   d. Incomplete generalization was not a concept in the chapter.

6. c. Generalization occurs when the conditioned response also occurs to stimuli similar to the conditioned stimulus.

   Incorrect answers:
   a. Comfort with the doctor indicates Chris can discriminate between the doctor and dentist.
   b. No feeling would also indicate discrimination.
   d. Choosing the doctor might indicate discrimination.

7. d. Jenny differentiates between the bicycle and the motorcycle.

   Incorrect answers:
   a. Extinction occurs when the conditioned stimulus no longer results in the conditioned response.
   b. Spontaneous recovery is indicated when a conditioned response reoccursafter extinction.
   c. Generalization occurs when the conditioned response also occurs to stimuli similar to the conditioned stimulus.

8. d. Second-order conditioning occurs when a stimulus associated with the conditioned stimulus also produces the conditioned response.

   Incorrect answers:
   a. Stimulus discrimination occurs when a participant can differentiate between stimuli.
   b. Spontaneous recovery is indicated when a conditioned response reoccurs after extinction.
   c. Equipotentiality is an incorrect assumption that all stimuli are equally capable of producing conditioning.

9. a. Biological preparedness means animals are genetically prewired to fear specific objects.

   Incorrect answers:
   b. Equipotentiality is an incorrect assumption that all stimuli are equally capable of producing conditioning.
   c. Operant conditioning is when consequences of an action determine whether it will be performed again.
   d. The contiguity principle is Pavlov's idea that any two stimuli presented at the same time will form a learned association.

10. d. According to the Rescorla-Wagner model, novel stimuli will be more easily associated with an unconditioned stimulus than will familiar stimuli.

    Incorrect answers:
    a. The smell of dog biscuits is likely to be familiar to the dog.
    b. The sight of the can of dog food is likely to be familiar to the dog.
    c. The smell of the dog food is likely to be familiar to the dog.

11. a. Thorndike studied cats in a puzzle box.

    Incorrect answers:
    b. Skinner developed the operant chamber to study learning.
    c. Another name for an operant chamber is a Skinner box.
    d. Neither Skinner nor Thorndike harnessed their animals.

12. b. The Law of Effect states that behaviors that are followed by a positive outcome are more likely to occur, whereas behaviors followed by a negative outcome are less likely to occur.

    Incorrect answers:
    a. Classical conditioning is based on forming associations between a neutral stimulus and a stimulus that causes a response.
    c. An unconditioned stimulus results in a reflexive response.
    d. Secondary reinforcers are learned through classical conditioning. They serve as reinforcers but do not satisfy a biological need.

13. a. Primary reinforcers satisfy a biological need.

    Incorrect answers:
    b. Money can be a secondary reinforcer; it does not satisfy a biological need.
    c. Stickers can be secondary reinforcers.
    d. Gold stars can be secondary reinforcers.

14. d. Secondary reinforcers such as gold stars are learned through classical conditioning. They serve as reinforcers but do not satisfy a biological need.

    Incorrect answers:
    a. Food satisfies a biological need.
    b. Water satisfies a biological need.
    c. Sex satisfies a biological need.

15. b. Shaping involves reinforcing behaviors that are increasingly similar to the desired response.

    Incorrect answers:
    a. Classical conditioning is based on forming associations between a neutral stimulus and a stimulus that causes a response.
    c. Observational learning occurs when behaviors are acquired or changed after watching the behaviors of others.
    d. The is no such thing as mirror learning. Mirror neurons are activated when one animal observes another.

16. b. Negative reinforcement increases behavior (in this case, taking ibuprofen) through the removal of an aversive stimulus (in this case, the headache).

    Incorrect answers:
    a. Positive reinforcement increases behavior by following the behavior with a pleasurable stimulus.
    c. Positive punishment decreases behavior by following the behavior with an aversive stimulus.
    d. Negative punishment decreases behavior by following the behavior with the removal of a pleasurable stimulus.

17. c. Negative punishment decreases behavior by following the behavior with the removal of a pleasurable stimulus. The pleasurable stimuli removed in this example are the car keys. The behavior to be reduced is speeding.

    Incorrect answers:
    a. Negative reinforcement increases behavior through the removal of an aversive stimulus.
    b. Positive punishment decreases behavior by following the behavior with an aversive stimulus.
    d. Extinction occurs when the participant stops responding after the reinforcement has been withdrawn.

18. d. In a fixed ratio schedule, reinforcement is given consistently after a specific number of responses (in this case, four).

    Incorrect answers:
    a. Rewarding the rats every time they lever press reflects a continuous reinforcement schedule.

    b. Reinforcement schedules based on time between reinforcement are interval schedules.
    c. Random rewards are not following a schedule.

19. a. A continuous reinforcement schedule involves rewarding participants every time they perform the target response.

    Incorrect answers:
    b. In noncontingent reinforcement the reward is not based on a response.
    c. In a fixed ratio schedule, reinforcement is given consistently after a specific number of responses.
    d. In partial reinforcement schedules, rewards are given intermittently.

20. d. The partial reinforcement extinction effect means behaviors have greater persistence when acquired through partial schedules of reinforcement.

    Incorrect answers:
    a. The fastest way to get acquisition of a behavior is generally with a continuous schedule of reinforcement.
    b. Behaviors may be modified in a variety of ways: Classical conditioning, continuous schedules, and observational learning all modify behavior.
    c. Partial reinforcement makes the absence of reinforcement more difficult to detect.

21. d. A cognitive map is a spatial representation of the environment.

    Incorrect answers:
    a. Observational learning occurs when behaviors are acquired or changed after watching the behaviors of others.
    b. Latent learning occurs in the absence of reinforcement.
    c. Operant finding is not a term.

22. a. Observational learning occurs when behaviors are acquired or changed after watching the behaviors of others.

    Incorrect answers:
    b. Discrimination occurs when the organism can differentiate between stimuli.
    c. Operant finding is not a term.
    d. A cognitive map is a spatial representation of the environment.

23. c. Vicarious learning occurs when people learn a behavior by watching others being rewarded or punished for performing it.

    Incorrect answers:
    a. A partial schedule was not described in the question.

b. Latent learning occurs in the absence of reinforcement.

d. Modeling involves imitating an observed behavior.

24. c. The authors discussed the role of dopamine in reward.

Incorrect answers:

a. The neurotransmitter epinephrine was not discussed in this context.

b. The neurotransmitter GABA was not discussed in this context.

d. ICSS stands for intracranial self-stimulation and is not a neurotransmitter.

25. b. Habituation refers to a decrease in responding to repeated presentations of a nonthreatening stimulus.

Incorrect answers:

a. An orienting response is attention paid to a novel stimulus when it is first encountered.

c. Sensitization is an increase in responding to repeated presentations of a threatening stimulus.

d. "Potentiate" means to strengthen.

26. c. An increase in neurotransmitter release leads to sensitization.

Incorrect answers:

a. A reduction in neurotransmitter release leads to habituation.

b. Sensitization is associated with increases in neurotransmitter release.

d. Extinction was not used in this context.

27. b. The description defines long-term potentiation.

Incorrect answers:

a. An orienting response is attention paid to a novel stimulus when it is first encountered.

c. Intracranial self-stimulation involves self-administration of shocks to pleasure centers of the brain.

d. Latent learning occurs in the absence of reward.

28. a. Joseph Tsien studied long-term potentiation (LTP) and NMDA receptors.

Incorrect answers:

b. LTP stands for long-term potentiation.

c. ICSS stands for intracranial self-stimulation.

d. "JND receptors" is not a term.

Matching Questions

1. B   *Walden Two*
2. G   Neutral stimulus
3. K   Unconditioned stimulus
4. I   Conditioned response
5. A   Acquisition
6. Q   Generalization
7. N   Phobia
8. F   Systematic desensitization
9. U   Biological preparedness
10. E   Reinforcement
11. S   Shaping
12. M   Secondary reinforcers
13. H   Punishment
14. O   Interval schedule
15. J   Latent learning
16. C   Optimal foraging theory
17. L   Meme
18. D   Modeling
19. P   Pleasure centers
20. T   Dopamine
21. R   Sensitization

Thought Questions

1. The original behaviorists focused only on what could be directly observed and measured. They did not include study of cognition or the brain. Today both cognitive science and neuroscience influence the study of learning and reward. For example, the Rescorala-Wagner model takes a cognitive approach to classical conditioning. Research on its biological basis is one example of the way neuroscience is influencing the study of learning.

2. The goal of punishment is to decrease behavior. It is most effective if it is applied immediately, it is unpleasant, and it is reasonable. When applied to children, it may not be effective if it makes the child unreasonably afraid of the person administering the punishment. The child will then learn to fear the punisher rather than to stop performing the undesired behavior. In addition, punishment alone may not make clear what appropriate behavior is: Punishment may indicate to children what they should not do but not clarify what they should do. Many psychological scientists believe that reinforcing appropriate behavior is more effective than punishing inappropriate behavior.

3. The role the neurotransmitter dopamine plays in reward is currently the focus of study. It appears to be activated in the nucleus accumbens, a part of the limbic system, during pleasurable activities. Secondary reinforcers also release dopamine. Drugs associated with pleasure are also associated with dopamine production.

CHAPTER 7 | Memory

GUIDE TO THE READING

The study of memory concerns how new information is acquired and retained. The authors begin with Atkinson and Shiffrin's modal memory model, so called because it is most widely used. In this model information goes through three kinds of storage: sensory memory, short-term memory, and long-term memory. Following explanations of these, the authors describe the different systems that make up long-term memory, including two types of processes, explicit memory and implicit memory. How long-term memory is organized and the brain processes involved in memory are presented. After this discussion of processes involved in remembering, the authors describe the influences on why people forget and what may cause distortions in memory.

What Are the Basic Stages of Memory?

In Atkinson and Shiffrin's information processing model of memory, information goes through a three-stage system: sensory memory, short-term memory (STM), and long-term memory (LTM). Sensory memory is brief but accurate. Some of the information in sensory memory is attended and passed on to STM. Information lasts only around 20 seconds in STM unless it is rehearsed. According to George Miller, STM has a limited span of about seven meaningful units, called *chunks*. More recently Baddeley developed a model of working memory to replace traditional views of STM. In Baddeley's model working memory includes three components: the central executive, which coordinates information; the phonological loop, which processes auditory information; and the visuospatial sketchpad, which is independent of the phonological loop and processes visual information.

The authors introduce their discussion of LTM by presenting the data supporting it as a distinct system from STM. The most convincing data are from the biological level of analysis, showing that some kinds of brain damage disrupt STM while other kinds of damage interfere with LTM. The authors propose that information that is important from an evolutionary perspective, in that it facilitates adaptation to the environment, is most likely to be transferred into LTM.

What Are the Different Memory Systems?

Many researchers believe that LTM includes a variety of systems. The authors draw a distinction between the processes involved in recalling information and the content of the information recalled. Explicit memory refers to the processes underlying conscious recall. What is recalled is declarative memory. For example, if asked what you ate for breakfast this morning, you use explicit memory to recall you had cereal. Tulving divided declarative memory into two types. Episodic memory involves recall of events involving the individual. Semantic memory is general knowledge. In contrast to explicit memory, implicit memory does not involve conscious recall. It involves neither effort nor awareness. One kind of implicit memory is procedural memory, which includes motor memories of how to do things, such as tying your shoes.

How Is Information Organized in Long-Term Memory?

The authors divide memory into three stages: encoding, or changing sensations into some kind of representation; storage, or retaining information; and retrieval, or remembering information. Meaning forms the basis for storage in LTM. Craik and Lockhart developed a levels of processing model proposing that as information is more deeply encoded, it is given more meaning, resulting in easier recall. According to their model, maintenance rehearsal, or just saying the information over and over, results in shallow encoding and poor recall. In contrast, elaborative rehearsal, which encodes meaning, results in deep processing and better recall. In LTM, information is organized based on schemas, which influence perception and organization of information. Network models, made of nodes and links, show the associations between information in LTM. Retrieval cues facilitate access of information in LTM.

What Brain Processes Are Involved in Memory?

Memory is not stored in just a single area of the brain. Rather, memories are stored in many areas linked together, with different areas storing different kinds of information. The medial temporal lobes appear to be important for consolidation, or moving information into LTM. The memories then seem to be stored in the part of the brain important for perceiving and using that specific information. The frontal lobes also appear to have a significant role in memory. Damage here results in inability to recall the order of events or from where information was acquired. Neurotransmitters also impact memory. Neurotransmitters that influence the strength of memory are called memory modulators. The part of the brain important for controlling these is the amygdala. During arousing events the neurotransmitter epinephrine, which is not formed in the brain, influences norepinephrine, a neurotransmitter in the brain. Norepinephrine influences receptors in the amygdala. The increase in activity in the amygdala then results in stronger memories.

When Do People Forget?

Gazzaniga and Heatherton discuss three typical causes of forgetting: transience, blocking, and absentmindedness. Transience involves the loss of information over time, probably resulting from one set of information interfering with another set of information. Blocking refers to a short-term inability to recall information. The tip-of-the-tongue phenomenon, where you just cannot think of some information that you know you know, demonstrates this. Absentmindedness occurs when people cannot recall an event because they did not pay enough attention to it while it was occurring. The authors end this section with a discussion of amnesia, which involves long-term loss of a significant amount of memory.

How Are Memories Distorted?

Memory is not a permanent and accurate record of past events. Even when people say they have vivid, detailed recall of a startling emotional event, a flashbulb memory, they are often not totally correct. One distortion of memory involves source misattributions—incorrect recall of from whom or where one acquired information. Because of memory distortion, people often make poor eyewitnesses. False memories of events that never occurred can also be created in some people. These distortions in recall help form the basis of a major controversy facing psychological scientists today: Can repressed memories, especially of childhood sexual abuse, be recalled, or are people who report this recall actually suffering from memory distortions?

FILL-IN-THE-BLANK QUESTIONS

1. The most widely used model of memory is referred to as the _____ memory model.

2. Sensory memory for auditory information is _____ memory.

3. _____ is a memory system that can hold about seven items.

4. A meaningful unit in STM is called a _____.

5. _____ memory replaces the concept of STM and is made of three components.

6. The _____ encodes auditory information in working memory.

7. Better recall of the beginning and end of a list as compared to the middle demonstrates the _____ effect.

8. _____ is continuing to rehearse material you already know.

9. One's general knowledge of facts reflects _____ memory.

10. Remembering how to ride a bicycle reflects _____ memory.

11. Improvement in identifying a previously presented stimulus reflects _____.

12. Agatha studied her psychology by putting all the definitions in her own words and making up her own examples. She used _____ rehearsal.

13. Jim studied his psychology by reading the definitions over and over. He used _____ rehearsal.

14. _____ is the act of recalling or remembering information.

15. _____ models of LTM are made of nodes and links.

16. A stimulus that helps you get information from LTM is a _____.

17. The idea that memory is distributed throughout the brain is _____.

18. A character in a film who cannot put new memories into LTM is suffering from _____.

19. Putting memories back in storage after they have been activated is called _____.

20. The areas of the medial temporal lobes believed to be most essential for declarative memory are the _____ and the _____.

21. Chuck did a study in which he put a rat in a small pool of water and the rat had to learn to swim to a platform. This procedure is the _____.

22. _____ is the neurotransmitter in the brain associated with memory of emotionally arousing events.

23. _____ is a mental health disorder that results from having suffered a traumatic experience.

24. Alicia knows she knows the name of the disorder where people suddenly fall asleep. In fact, she's sure it starts with an "n" but she just cannot think of the word (narcolepsy). Alicia is experiencing _____.

25. Rod studied Spanish at 10 A.M. and French at 11 A.M. When he went back to study Spanish again after lunch, he could only recall French words. This may be an example of _____ interference.

26. _____ are vivid memories for surprising or emotional events.

27. _____ occurs when people believe they have come up with an original idea but have actually recalled information from memory.

28. _____ occurs when people modify their memory based on misleading information.

29. _____ occurs when people falsely recall or recognize events that did not really occur.

30. _____ occurs when someone has false episodic memories but has no intent to lie.

MULTIPLE-CHOICE QUESTIONS

1. Joe looked up his friend Jack's phone number. He was repeating the number to himself as he looked for the phone. He repeated the number to keep it in which memory system?
   a. Sensory memory.
   b. Short-term memory.
   c. Echoic memory.
   d. Long-term memory.

2. Which of the following lists would probably be most difficult to keep in STM?
   a. WXZCRNQP.
   b. CATDOGMOUSE.
   c. PSYCHOLOGY.
   d. 20052004.

3. Sara is with a group of her friends when they are introduced to a guy she would really like to meet. According to the research on primacy effects, when among her friends should she be introduced if she wants the guy to remember her?
   a. First.
   b. Last.
   c. In the middle.
   d. Either first or last.

4. Avi wrote a grocery list of 12 items. Unfortunately he forgot the list at home and could only remember the first few items on the list and the last few. His recall demonstrates
   a. anterograde amnesia.
   b. the encoding specificity principle.
   c. the serial position effect.
   d. equipotentiality effects.

5. Which of the following is *not* recommended as a strategy to improve memory?
   a. Try to restate key ideas in your own words.
   b. Go over material even after you think you know it.
   c. Stay up as late as is necessary to review material right before the exam.
   d. Study in advance of a test instead of cramming.

6. When Cybil asked Marcia what the word *mnemonics* means, Marcia had no difficulty providing the definition. Marcia's knowledge of the word exemplifies her
   a. procedural memory.
   b. episodic memory.
   c. implicit memory.
   d. semantic memory.

7. Which of the following is an example of procedural memory?
   a. Remembering you first learned about Freud in high school.
   b. Knowing the definition of the word *implicit*.
   c. Knowing how to ride a bicycle.
   d. Recalling you had a really terrible meal at a specific restaurant.

8. When studying for a biology test John just repeated the definitions of the words over and over to himself. Which of the following is true of this method of study?
   a. It is maintenance rehearsal.
   b. It results in deep processing.
   c. It is the most effective way to study for an exam.
   d. It makes use of networks.

9. Terri studied for her psychology test in the room where the test was given. Jenn studied for the exam in her dorm. If everything else about Jenn and Terri was the same, but Terri did better on the exam, what could account for this?
   a. Procedural memory.
   b. Iconic memory storage.
   c. Encoding specificity.
   d. Equipotentiality of memory.

10. According to the research on state-dependent memory, if you drink a lot of coffee when studying, what should you do when taking the exam?
    a. You should drink coffee.
    b. You should avoid coffee to highlight the differences between studying and testing.
    c. You should drink alcohol.
    d. You should avoid all fluids.

11. The idea that memory is distributed throughout the brain is known as
    a. the engram.
    b. state-dependent learning.
    c. equipotentiality.
    d. anterograde amnesia.

12. When he recovered from his accident, Bruce discovered he could remember things like his name, his elementary school, and his mother's birthday. However, he could not put any new information into LTM. Bruce is probably suffering from
    a. problems with short-term memory.
    b. disruption of the occipital lobe.
    c. reconsolidation.
    d. damage to the medial temporal lobe.

13. Which of the following demonstrates spatial memory?
    a. The ability to recall what you had for breakfast.
    b. The ability to define STM.
    c. The ability to tie your shoes.
    d. The ability to point in the direction of the library.

14. Which part of the brain was found to be most active during encoding of verbal information?
    a. The left frontal lobe.
    b. The right frontal lobe.
    c. The left occipital lobe.
    d. The right occipital lobe.

15. Which brain structure seems to be most important for influencing the effects of neurotransmitters on memory?
    a. The corpus callosum.
    b. The amygdala.
    c. The cerebellum.
    d. The basal ganglia.

16. When people forget information with the passage of time, this is termed
    a. transience.
    b. blocking.
    c. repression.
    d. proactivation.

17. Susie just got a new combination lock. She is upset because she keeps trying to open it with her old combination. Her problem demonstrates
    a. blocking.
    b. proactive interference.
    c. retroactive interference.
    d. transience.

18. Ginny knows that she knows the name of the guy who sat next to her in Biology, but she just can't think of it! Her memory lapse exemplifies
    a. blocking.
    b. transience.
    c. nepotism.
    d. retrograde amnesia.

19. When Brett was introduced to a friend's cousin, he was not paying attention. Later, when asked the cousin's name, Brett had no idea. Brett's memory problem exemplifies
    a. transience.
    b. amnesia.
    c. absentmindedness.
    d. concussion.

20. Suki watched a TV show in which following an accident the main character could not remember her name, her husband, or her profession. This character is suffering from
    a. retrograde amnesia.
    b. anterograde amnesia.
    c. blocking.
    d. the von Restorff effect.

21. Mary has a very vivid memory of where she was when she first heard the *Challenger* exploded. This demonstrates
    a. retroactive interference.
    b. proactive interference.
    c. flashbulb memory.
    d. shallow encoding.

22. The von Restorff effect refers to the finding that
    a. distinctive information is recalled more easily than less distinctive information.
    b. flashbulb memories are less accurate than other kinds of episodic recall.
    c. semantic memory is not encoded in LTM.
    d. alcohol abuse can cause anterograde amnesia.

23. Jose believes he first learned about the facts of life from his older brother. In reality, his parents were the first to discuss this subject with him. Jose's mistaken recall reflects
    a. cryptomnesia.
    b. absentmindedness.
    c. Korsakoff's syndrome.
    d. source misattribution.

24. When writing a paper, Jenn thought she defined a term in a new way; in fact she directly quoted one of the articles she read. This exemplifies
    a. cryptomnesia.
    b. absentmindedness.
    c. Korsakoff's syndrome.
    d. source misattribution.

25. Liz, a Caucasian American, was an eyewitness to a crime. She will be most likely to correctly identify the perpetrator if the perpetrator
    a. is a college student.
    b. is Caucasian American.
    c. is African American.
    d. carried a gun.

26. Donna's older sisters kept telling her that she had been lost as a little kid and they could not find her for two hours. In fact, this never happened. But Donna believes that she can remember it. Donna is demonstrating
    a. cryptomnesia.
    b. suggestibility.
    c. source misattribution.
    d. absentmindedness.

27. Jodi surprised all her friends when she could supply the definition of *narcolepsy* in class. When asked where she had learned it, Jodi had no idea. She just knew it. Jodi is demonstrating
    a. false recognition.
    b. childhood amnesia.
    c. suggestibility.
    d. source amnesia.

28. After his stroke, Mr. Smith had problems with his memory. When asked about his family he will report what he knows and then will seem to just make things up—even though he has no intent to deceive anyone. Mr. Smith demonstrates
    a. false recognition.
    b. suggestibility.
    c. confabulation.
    d. source amnesia.

29. A person who believes that their family has been replaced by imposters is probably suffering from
    a. Capgras syndrome.
    b. damage to the parietal lobes.
    c. confabulation.
    d. amnesia.

30. At present, what may be concluded about repressed memories?
    a. Almost all repressed memories have been found to be true events.
    b. Some therapeutic techniques may contribute to formation of false memories.
    c. There is no evidence that people may recall instances of early abuse.
    d. Suggestibility does *not* influence recall of repressed memories.

MATCHING QUESTIONS

Fill in the letter from Column B corresponding to the term that is most associated with the description presented in Column A.

COLUMN A	COLUMN B
____ 1. Retention of encoded representations over time.	A. Maintenance rehearsal
____ 2. Better memory for items at the end of a list.	B. Declarative memory
____ 3. Component of working memory that coordinates information from other sources.	C. Hippocampus D. Mnemonics E. Chunking
____ 4. The information retrieved in explicit memory.	F. Distributed practice G. Recency effect
____ 5. The process where information is transferred from STM to LTM.	H. Node I. Schemas J. Elaborative rehearsal
____ 6. Deficits in LTM resulting from trauma.	K. Amnesia L. Engram

___ 7. A brain region important for spatial memory.

___ 8. Memory of one's personal past experiences.

___ 9. Rehearsing an item by focusing on meaning.

___ 10. Neurotransmitters that influence memory.

___ 11. A unit of information in a network.

___ 12. Memory without awareness or effort.

___ 13. Studying information over a spread-out period.

___ 14. The process of organizing information into meaningful units.

___ 15. Hypothetical cognitive structures that help us perceive and organize information.

___ 16. Repeating an item over and over.

___ 17. Strategies to improve memory.

___ 18. The component of working memory involved in processing visual information.

___ 19. Sensory memory for visual information.

___ 20. The physical site of a memory.

M. Episodic
N. Central executive
O. Iconic
P. Consolidation
Q. Implicit
R. Visuospatial sketchpad
S. Memory modulators
T. Storage

THOUGHT QUESTIONS

1. Invent a character with short-term memory problems. Invent a second character who has problems putting new information into long-term memory. Specifically describe how each of these characters would demonstrate the problem.

2. Draw an association network representing your knowledge of fast-food restaurants and the items they serve.

APPLICATIONS

Thinking Critically about Working Memory

Baddeley's model of working memory is described in your textbook as comprised of three components: the central executive, the phonological loop, and the visuospatial sketchpad (VSSP). The phonological loop and the VSSP work independently of each other. The phonological loop is involved in processing auditory and verbal information, while the VSSP processes visual and spatial information. The following demonstration is a test of their independence.

You will need at least two willing friends to participate with you, two copies of a simple maze (which you may find in a children's magazine or the children's sections of newspapers), two lists of about 15 words each, paper, and pencils. First you will inform your friends that you will be asking them to recall words. You will inform one friend that he or she will be working on a maze at the same time as the words are presented. You will inform the other friend that he or she will just listen. You will then read them the first word list. About 30 seconds after the words have been read, ask your friends to write down all the words they can recall. Next reverse the roles of your friends, so the friend who just listened now completes a maze and the friend who had the maze just listens. Follow the same procedure with the second word list. When finished, find the number of words recalled for each friend when they just listened, the number they recalled when they did the maze, and the total number recalled for both lists.

If solving the maze required processing from only the VSSP, it should have no impact on the number of words recalled. Is this what you found? Or did your friends recall more words when just listening than when doing the maze? If they recalled more when just listening, what may account for this? Do people talk to themselves while solving mazes? If so, does this involve the phonological loop? How many tasks involve only the phonological loop or only the VSSP? What are some confounds that may have influenced your finding?

Applications of Levels of Analysis: Further Ideas on Treatment of Posttraumatic Stress Disorder

In their discussion of posttraumatic stress disorder (PTSD) Gazzaniga and Heatherton explain that some people develop extreme emotional reactions following a traumatic event. For example, they may have thoughts about the event that they cannot control, or recurrent dreams, or feelings that the event keeps happening. Given the seriousness of the problem, how may it be treated?

Three of the treatment types that have been studied are psychological debriefing, cognitive behavioral therapy (CBT), and use of beta blockers, a drug treatment for high blood pressure. Psychological debriefing and CBT both reflect the individual category of analysis. Psychological debriefing is usually run soon after the traumatic event. The affected individual is generally asked to ventilate emotionally, going over thoughts and feelings related to the event. The data are mixed on whether this works. Some researchers feel that the venting and reviewing of the traumatic event just makes it more memorable. It allows the person to encode the event into long-term memory even more effectively than would have been possible without the debriefing. CBT is not conducted until weeks or months after the event. In this way, the people affected by the event can determine whether therapy is needed. Because people vary widely in their reactions to traumatic events, some people develop PTSD while others do not. People treated with CBT are often taught how to change their thinking about the event, a cognitive therapy technique, while also learning relaxation exercises like deep breathing, a behavioral technique. Some researchers believe that CBT is a more effective treatment than psychological debriefing. Use of beta blockers to treat PTSD reflects the biological category of analysis. Scientists hypothesize that the beta blockers interfere with the way memories are encoded by hindering the actions of the neurotransmitter epinephrine. At this time it is not clear which therapeutic technique, or which combination of techniques, is most effective.

In the Thinking Critically section on use of drugs to increase or decrease memory, Gazzaniga and Heatherton discuss the ethics of using a drug to forget an event. Can this argument also be applied to psychological therapies?

References

Doskoch, P. (2002). Can beta blockers prevent PTSD? A first look. *NeuroPsychiatry.* http://www.neuro psychiatriyreviews.com/march02/ptsd.html. Downloaded 8/17/05.

McNally, R., Bryant, R., & Ehlers, A. (2003). Does early psychological intervention promote recovery from posttraumatic stress? *Psychological Science in the Public Interest, 4,* 45–79.

WEB SITES

Neurochemical Basis of Memory

www.apa.org/monitor/apr04/vagus.html

Recovered Memory of Child Abuse

www.apa.org/pubinfo/mem.html

ANSWER KEY

Fill-in-the-Blank Questions

1. Modal
2. Echoic
3. Short-term memory
4. Chunk
5. Working
6. Phonological loop
7. Serial position
8. Overlearning
9. Semantic
10. Procedural
11. Repetition priming
12. Elaborative
13. Maintenance
14. Retrieval
15. Network
16. Retrieval cue
17. Equipotentiality
18. Anterograde amnesia
19. Reconsolidation
20. Hippocampus and rhinal cortex
21. Morris water maze test
22. Norepinephrine
23. Posttraumatic stress disorder (PTSD)
24. Blocking (or the tip-of-the-tongue phenomena)
25. Retroactive
26. Flashbulb memories
27. Cryptomnesia
28. Suggestibility
29. False recognition
30. Confabulation

Multiple-Choice Questions

1. b. Short-term memory lasts only about 20 seconds unless the information is rehearsed.

   Incorrect answers:
   a. Sensory memory is a brief buffer that stores information in its original sensory form.
   c. Echoic memory is sensory memory for auditory information.
   d. Long-term memory is relatively permanent and does not require rehearsal.

2. a. Short-term memory can hold about seven chunks, or meaningful units. "WXZCRNQP" is a string of eight unrelated letters and so is made of eight chunks.

   Incorrect answers:
   b. Although "catdogmouse" is made of 11 letters, it is three words and so only three chunks.
   c. The word *psychology* is one chunk made of 10 letters.
   d. "20052004" can be two dates, 2005 and 2004, and so is only two chunks.

3. a. Research on primacy effects indicates people have better recall for the first items presented in a list than for middle items.

   Incorrect answers:
   b. Better recall of the last items in a list is a recency effect.
   c. Middle items are not recalled as well as the first or last items.
   d. Primacy refers specifically to the beginning of the list.

4. c. Better recall of the first and last items in a list as compared to the middle items is known as the serial position effect.

    Incorrect answers:
    a. Anterograde amnesia is the inability to store new information in long-term memory.
    b. According to the encoding specificity principle, any stimulus that is encoded with an experience can facilitate recall of the experience.
    d. Equipotentiality is Lashley's mostly incorrect idea that memory is distributed throughout the brain.

5. c. Data indicate that getting enough sleep helps memory while disrupting sleep hinders memory.

    Incorrect answers:
    a. Restating ideas in your own words is a form of elaborative rehearsal, which results in deep processing and facilitates memory.
    b. Reviewing the material you know is a form of overlearning and helps recall.
    d. Studying in advance is more effective than is cramming.

6. d. Semantic memory includes one's knowledge of facts.

    Incorrect answers:
    a. Procedural memory is motor memory of skills and habits.
    b. Episodic memory is memory of personal events and past experiences.
    c. Implicit memory occurs without effort or awareness.

7. c. Procedural memory is motor memory of skills and habits.

    Incorrect answers:
    a. Remembering when you first learned some information is episodic memory.
    b. Knowing the definition of a word demonstrates semantic memory.
    d. Recalling an event involves episodic memory.

8. a. Maintenance rehearsal is just repeating information over and over.

    Incorrect answers:
    b. Maintenance rehearsal results in shallow processing.
    c. When studying for an exam, it is more effective to use elaborative rehearsal, which then results in deep processing and better recall.
    d. Networks are ways to represent information in LTM.

9. c. Studying in the room where you take the test makes use of encoding specificity: According to the encoding specificity principle, any stimulus that is encoded with an experience can facilitate recall of the experience.

    Incorrect answers:
    a. Procedural memory is motor memory of skills and habits.
    b. Iconic memory is sensory memory for visual information.
    d. Equipotentiality is Lashley's mostly incorrect idea that memory is distributed throughout the brain.

10. a. According to the research on state-dependent memory, memory is best when internal, physical cues at learning are similar to those at recall. Drinking coffee both at learning and recall provides similar cues.

    Incorrect answers:
    b. Avoiding coffee for the exam will result in different internal cues.
    c. Drinking alcohol before the exam will interfere with recall.
    d. Avoiding all fluids will not help recall.

11. c. Equipotentiality is Lashley's mostly incorrect idea that memory is distributed throughout the brain.

    Incorrect answers:
    a. The engram is the place where memory is physically located.
    b. According to the research on state-dependent memory, memory is best when internal, physical cues at learning are similar to those at recall.
    d. Anterograde amnesia is the inability to store new information in long-term memory.

12. d. The medial temporal lobes are important for putting information into LTM.

    Incorrect answers:
    a. Problems with STM are not described in the question.
    b. The occipital lobe is important for vision.
    c. Reconsolidation is the process of putting a memory back into LTM after it has been activated.

13. d. Spatial memory involves recall of the physical environment, such as the location of buildings.

    Incorrect answers:
    a. Recalling what you had for breakfast is episodic memory.
    b. Defining STM involves semantic memory.
    c. Tying your shoes involves procedural memory.

14. a. The left frontal lobes are more active during encoding of verbal information.

    Incorrect answers:
    b. The right frontal lobes may be more active during retrieval of information or when the information is visual rather than verbal.
    c. The occipital lobes are important for vision.
    d. The occipital lobes are important for vision.

15. b. Recent research points to the amygdala as the brain structure most important for influencing the effects of neurotransmitters on memory.

    Incorrect answers:
    a. The corpus callosum connects the left and right hemispheres.
    c. The cerebellum plays a significant role in motor memory.
    d. The basal ganglia plays a significant role in motor memory.

16. a. Forgetting over time is called transience.

    Incorrect answers:
    b. Blocking refers to a temporary inability to recall information.
    c. Repression is a psychoanalytic term referring to motivated forgetting of an anxiety-producing event.
    d. Proactivation is not a term.

17. b. Proactive interference occurs when earlier learning interferes with later learning.

    Incorrect answers:
    a. Blocking refers to a temporary inability to recall information.
    c. Retroactive interference occurs when recent learning interferes with recall of material learned earlier.
    d. Transience is forgetting that occurs over time.

18. a. Blocking, including the tip-of-the-tongue phenomenon, is a temporary inability to recall information.

    Incorrect answers:
    b. Transience is forgetting that occurs over time.
    c. *Nepotism* means preferred hiring of one's relatives.
    d. Retrograde amnesia is loss of memory for past events.

19. c. Absentmindedness refers to not recalling information due to inattentiveness.

    Incorrect answers:
    a. Transience is forgetting that occurs over time.

    b. Amnesia refers to problems in long-term memory as a result of physical or psychological trauma.
    d. A concussion is a result of a head injury.

20. a. Retrograde amnesia is loss of memory for past events.

    Incorrect answers:
    b. Anterograde amnesia is the inability to store new information in long-term memory.
    c. Blocking is a temporary inability to recall information.
    d. The von Restorff effect describes the finding that distinctive information is recalled more easily than ordinary information.

21. c. A flashbulb memory is a vivid memory of a surprising emotional event.

    Incorrect answers:
    a. Retroactive interference occurs when recent learning interferes with recall of material learned earlier.
    b. Proactive interference occurs when earlier learning interferes with later learning.
    d. Shallow encoding involves processing little meaning.

22. a. The von Restorff effect describes the finding that distinctive information is recalled more easily than ordinary information.

    Incorrect answers:
    b. Flashbulb memories are not less accurate than other kinds of episodic recall.
    c. Semantic memory is a kind of LTM.
    d. Although alcohol abuse can cause anterograde amnesia, this is not the von Restorff effect.

23. d. Source misattribution is incorrect recall of where or from whom one learned information.

    Incorrect answers:
    a. Cryptomnesia occurs when people believe they have come up with a novel idea without realizing they are really recalling it from another source.
    b. Absentmindedness refers to not recalling information due to inattentiveness.
    c. Korsakoff's syndrome is a form of brain damage caused by alcohol abuse, one symptom of which is anterograde amnesia.

24. a. Cryptomnesia occurs when people believe they have come up with a novel idea without realizing they are really recalling it from another source.

Incorrect answers:

b. Absentmindedness refers to not recalling information due to inattentiveness.

c. Korsakoff's syndrome is a form of brain damage caused by alcohol abuse, one symptom of which is anterograde amnesia.

d. Source misattribution is incorrect recall of where or from whom one learned information.

25. b. People are more accurate when identifying others of their own race.

Incorrect answers:

a. Given the description in the question, there is no reason for a college student to be more easily identified.

c. Liz, a Caucasian, would have more difficulty identifying an African American.

d. Eyewitness accuracy tends to decrease if the perpetrator carries a gun because people tend to focus on the gun.

26. b. Suggestibility is demonstrated when people's recall of events is modified by misleading information.

Incorrect answers:

a. Cryptomnesia occurs when people believe they have come up with a novel idea without realizing they are really recalling it from another source.

c. Source misattribution is incorrect recall of where or from whom one learned information.

d. Absentmindedness refers to not recalling information due to inattentiveness.

27. d. Source amnesia is the inability to recall from where you learned information.

Incorrect answers:

a. False recognition occurs when people believe an event occurred previously when it did not.

b. Childhood amnesia is the inability to recall events that occurred before about age 3.

c. Suggestibility is demonstrated when people's recall of events is modified by misleading information.

28. c. Confabulation involves false recall of events with no intent to lie.

Incorrect answers:

a. False recognition occurs when people believe an event occurred previously when it did not.

b. Suggestibility is demonstrated when people's recall of events is modified by misleading information.

d. Source amnesia is the inability to recall from where you learned information.

29. a. Capgras syndrome apparently results from brain damage and is the belief that family members have been replaced by imposters.

Incorrect answers:

b. The frontal lobes and limbic brain regions seem to be damaged in people with Capgras syndrome.

c. Confabulation involves false recall of events with no intent to lie.

d. Amnesia refers to problems in LTM resulting from physical or psychological trauma.

30. b. Recent research indicates some therapies may increase false memories.

Incorrect answers:

a. Many recovered repressed memories have not been found to be true.

c. The is evidence that people may recall incidents of early abuse later in their lives.

d. Suggestibility does influence recall of repressed memories.

Matching Questions

1. T   Storage
2. G   Recency effect
3. N   Central executive
4. B   Declarative memory
5. P   Consolidation
6. K   Amnesia
7. C   Hippocampus
8. M   Episodic
9. J   Elaborative rehearsal
10. S   Memory modulators
11. H   Node
12. Q   Implicit
13. F   Distributed practice
14. E   Chunking
15. I   Schemas
16. A   Maintenance rehearsal
17. D   Mnemonics
18. R   Visuospatial sketchpad
19. O   Iconic
20. L   Engram

Thought Questions

1. When describing characters with short-term memory problems, you need to include problems they would

have in attending to relevant information while being able to recall the gist of events after they are over. In contrast, characters with problems putting new information into long-term memory could focus on immediate events. They could not recall the event when it was over.

2. In the network, highly associated information would be directly linked while the links between weakly associated information would be long and indirect. For example, two restaurants that serve similar food, like French fries and burgers, would be directly linked both to each other and to the burgers and fries. These restaurants would be indirectly linked to foods they do not serve, like tacos.

CHAPTER 8 | Thinking and Intelligence

GUIDE TO THE READING

How is information represented in our minds? How do we use this information to solve problems and make decisions? Are more intelligent people better at this than less intelligent people? Why? This chapter addresses these basic issues. The authors first discuss how information may be represented and organized. Ways to use information to solve problems, including deductive reasoning and inductive reasoning, follow. Gazzaniga and Heatherton then describe the research on people's use of heuristics, or rules of thumb, to make decisions. The last part of the chapter addresses intelligence, including what intelligence is and what approaches are used to study intelligence. The chapter concludes with discussion of a major controversy in the field: To what extent are racial differences in performance on intelligence tests caused by genes or the environment?

How Does the Mind Represent Information?

Cognitive psychology focuses on how the brain represents information. Two basic types of representation include analogical representation and symbolic representation. Analogical representations share some physical traits with the information. For example, if you imagine an apple in your mind, that representation includes visual similarities to the apple, though it is not identical to the apple. In contrast, symbolic representations are not similar to the information. Rather, symbolic representations are abstract and often verbal: The word *apple* does not look at all like the fruit.

Concepts include categories (such as animals) and relations (such as size) and are symbolically represented. The authors describe a number of models of how concepts may be organized in our minds. Defining attribute models hierarchically organize concepts, so that sparrow is attached to

bird, which in turn is attached to animal. Characteristics specific to each level of the hierarchy are connected to that level (for example, "feathers" would connect to "bird"). This does not work well because the model is too inflexible. Prototype models are based on the idea that some members of a category are more representative than other members. However, this model does not make clear what *representative* means: Is it what is most common, or most similar to others, or most average? Exemplar models define a category with all its examples; prototypical members of a category are those most often encountered.

Information broader than specific categories may be represented with schemas. For example, you may have a schema for how a kitchen is organized: pots and pans in cabinets, spoons and forks in a drawer. Schemas influence what we see, what we expect, and how we act. Schemas that follow a clear temporal sequence are called *scripts*. Using the drive-through window at a fast-food restaurant is a highly scripted event.

How Do We Make Decisions and Solve Problems?

Given that we have information organized in our mind, how do we use it? The authors first describe inductive and deductive reasoning. In deductive reasoning you start with a general premise and decide if a particular outcome is possible based on it. Deductive reasoning may be represented by a syllogism, a kind of logical argument. Problems can arise when the premises are questionable. Inductive reasoning starts with a specific outcome. A general principle is developed from that. Problems here may occur when the specific instances are too limited to justify the general conclusion.

Often decision making in everyday situations relies on heuristics, or rules of thumb. Gazzaniga and Heatherton describe Tversky and Kahneman's research on heuristics and the pitfalls associated with these. Some of the heuristics in the chapter include the availability heuristic, the representativeness heuristic, and confirmation bias. Using the availability heuristic, decisions are based on information that is easily recalled. When using the representativeness heuristic, we make decisions based on the degree to which a specific instance is typical of a category. Confirmation bias involves using only information that supports one's expectations while ignoring information that does not.

This section concludes with a discussion of problem solving. Gazzaniga and Heatherton propose that one has a problem when one has a goal and no clear way to attain it. The authors present several strategies for solving problems. Use of subgoals involves breaking a complex problem into smaller, more manageable problems. Sudden insight occurs when a problem solver abruptly sees the answer to a problem. Restructuring, or changing the way you look at a problem, may make the solution to a problem more obvious. If the strategies used for solving a problem do not work, problem solvers may consciously alter their approach. At other times, unconscious problem solving may actually be most effective. For example, in complex situations when there is no clear way to evaluate the pros and cons of a situation, quick unconscious choices may be best.

How Do We Understand Intelligence?

The nature of intelligence may have generated more debate in psychology than any other topic. What is intelligence? How can it be assessed? To what degree is it the result of nature or of nurture? What underlies group, and especially racial, differences in intelligence test scores? The section begins by describing three approaches to intelligence: the psychometric approach, the cognitive approach, and the biological approach.

The psychometric approach is based on testing. It began when Alfred Binet developed the first important assessment to identify children who needed extra attention in school. In doing this, Binet invented the concept of mental age: how well a child performs intellectually compared to other children. Later Wilhelm Stern developed the Intelligence Quotient (IQ) by dividing mental age by chronological age and multiplying by 100. Today IQs are calculated by comparing an individual's performance on an IQ test to the average performance on the test.

An obvious question about IQ tests is whether they do what they are supposed to. In other words, are they valid? Research indicates that people with higher IQs tend to do better in school and have higher-paying careers than people with lower IQs. However, many other variables also seem to be important for school and job success. In addition, IQ tests may be culturally biased: They may be based on the experiences of a particular culture or subculture and so would not be fair to other groups.

Binet viewed intelligence as a general ability. Today researchers believe that intelligence may be made up of specific abilities. Cattell proposed a distinction between fluid intelligence, which involves reasoning and flexible thinking, and crystallized intelligence, which includes knowledge of information. Gardner's theory of multiple intelligences includes a variety of skills, such as verbal, spatial, and interpersonal, all of which he assumed to be independent.

Both cognitive skills and brain structures are related to intelligence. More intelligent people respond more quickly on visual tasks and on tests of working memory than do less intelligent people. Recent research indicates people with larger brains, perhaps particularly in the frontal lobes, tend to be more intelligent.

Clearly people differ in intelligence. What causes this difference? This leads to one of the most basic, and often controversial, topics in psychology: the nature–nurture debate. To what degree is intelligence the result of environmental factors, and to what degree is it genetically determined? Current data indicate the significance of both. However, this debate becomes even more heated when applied to differences in IQ scores found between racial groups. On average, Caucasian Americans score higher on IQ tests than do African Americans. What does this mean? Before discussing racial differences it should first be established that race is a valid biological category. There is actually a lot of debate about this. Assuming race is a category, can environmental differences account for the differences in performance? At this time there is no clear answer, but it is certain that many environmental differences exist.

FILL-IN–THE-BLANK QUESTIONS

1. _____ is the act of thinking and representing information.

2. _____ representations have some characteristics of actual objects.

3. The word *dog* is a _____ representation of the animal we call dog.

4. A class or category that includes some number of individuals or subtypes is referred to as a _____.

5. The model proposing that the traits "long nose, gray, and tusks" are stored with "elephant" is the _____.

6. Within each category, the fact that some members are more representative of the category than other members is the premise for the _____ model.

7. According to the _____ model is there no single best representation of a concept, so all examples form the concept.

8. When going through a drive-through at a fast-food restaurant, first you pull to the menu where you order, next you go to a window where you pay, then you go to a window where you pick up your food, and finally you drive out of the restaurant's lot. This sequence indicates this event follows a strong _____.

9. Evaluating information, arguments, and beliefs to draw conclusions refers to _____.

10. A logical argument containing two premises and a conclusion that can be determined to be either valid or invalid is a _____.

11. In _____ reasoning general conclusions are reached from specific instances.

12. _____ models of decision making view people as optimal decision makers.

13. Mental shortcuts or rules of thumb that people typically use during inductive reasoning and decision making are called _____.

14. When asked whether people are more likely to die in an airplane crash or during a stay at the hospital, Georgie replies "airplane crash" because she just read about one in the newspaper. Her incorrect decision is most probably influenced by the _____ heuristic.

15. The chances that the next car you see will be blue must be greater than the chances that the next car you see will be blue and have four doors because being blue and having four doors is a _____.

16. The tendency to focus selectively on some information and not use other information is the basis of _____.

17. _____ means that the way information is presented can alter how people perceive it.

18. Jerome overestimated how long it would take him to get over his sadness when his dog ran away. This demonstrates he has problems with _____, an instance of the affective heuristic.

19. The sudden realization of the solution to a problem is _____.

20. Not realizing you can use your stapler as a paperweight because you do not usually use it that way reflects _____.

21. _____ is the human ability to use knowledge to solve problems, understand complex ideas, learn quickly, and adapt to environmental changes.

22. A test to determine whether someone has the skills needed to become a good manager in a company is a/n _____ test.

23. _____ developed the first important intelligence tests.

24. According to Stern, a child with a mental age of 12 and a chronological age of 10 has an IQ of _____.

25. A test that measures what it is supposed to measure is _____.

26. According to Cattell, knowledge that we acquire through experience is _____ intelligence.

27. According to Gardner, a person with excellent social understanding is demonstrating which kind of intelligence? _____

28. _____ are people with minimal intellectual capacity in most areas but who at a very early age show an exceptional ability in some sort of intelligent process.

29. According to Sternberg, understanding how people deal with everyday tasks is _____ intelligence.

30. _____ is a measure of how quickly people solve visual problems.

31. The rise in IQ scores over the last century of intelligence testing is referred to as the _____.

32. Right before a math test, Anita's teacher told the class that he did not expect the girls to do well because girls are not good in math. Sure enough Anita, an excellent math student, did worse on the test than she should have. Anita's performance reflects _____.

MULTIPLE–CHOICE QUESTIONS

1. Your mental image of a bicycle shares some physical characteristics with an actual bicycle and so is a(n) _____ representation.
   a. symbolic
   b. deficient
   c. analogical
   d. physical

2. The word *bicycle* is not physically similar to the actual object and so is a(n)
   a. symbolic representation.
   b. deficient representation.
   c. analogical representation.
   d. image representation.

3. In an experiment, Janice was given a rose, a toy car, a toy truck, a tulip, a daisy, and a toy ambulance. When told to put these in groups, she put the rose, tulip, and daisy together because they had petals, leaves, and stems. This kind of grouping is called
   a. categorization.
   b. shared knowledge.
   c. defining representation.
   d. mental mapping.

4. Which model would represent a concept as part of a hierarchical network?
   a. Prototype model.
   b. Representativeness model.
   c. Defining attribute model.
   d. Availability model.

5. According to which model is an apple more representative of the category of fruits than a kiwi is?
   a. Conceptual model.
   b. Defining attribute model.
   c. Representativeness model.
   d. Prototype model.

6. John believes that classrooms contain seats, desks, blackboards, students, and professors, so this is what he expects to see. This may be a description of John's _____ for classrooms.
   a. script
   b. validity
   c. schema
   d. analog

7. Mary is a philosophy professor. Sue believes that all philosophy professors are fascinating. She is therefore sure that Mary will be fascinating. Sue is using which kind of reasoning to make this judgment?
   a. Inductive reasoning.
   b. Deductive reasoning.
   c. Analysis reasoning.
   d. Meta-reasoning.

8. After meeting four intelligent people on the swim team, Albert concludes that swimmers must be a bright group. Albert drew this conclusion based on what kind of reasoning?
   a. Inductive reasoning.
   b. Deductive reasoning.
   c. Analysis reasoning.
   d. Meta-reasoning.

9. When asked whether more words begin with the letter "k" or whether more have "k" in the third position, Meagan said that more started with "k" because she could think of them more easily. She is using which heuristic?
   a. Confirmation bias.
   b. Availability heuristic.
   c. Representativeness heuristic.
   d. Framing heuristic.

10. When Marion first met Stan she figured he must be an engineer because he liked math puzzles, woodworking, and computers. Her guess about his profession can be explained by the
    a. affective heuristic.
    b. availability heuristic.
    c. representativeness heuristic.
    d. framing heuristic.

11. The tendency to focus selectively on information that fits our preexisting views is
    a. confirmation bias.
    b. representative heuristic.
    c. availability heuristic.
    d. framing heuristic.

12. After her car was wrecked on Wednesday, Tanika thought she would be depressed for weeks. To her surprise, by the weekend she was in a good mood and had already figured out a plan to use the insurance money to get a new car. Tanika's overestimate of how bad she thought she would feel reflects which heuristic?
    a. Affective.
    b. Simulation.
    c. Availability.
    d. Framing.

13. Little Tony's room is a mess: Books are on the floor, clothing is all over, the bed is unmade, and so on. His mother helps him out by telling him to first put the books back on the shelf. When that is done she tells him to hang up the clothing. Finally she tells him to make his bed. Tony's mom has helped him solve his problem by using
    a. framing.
    b. subgoals.
    c. functional fixedness.
    d. a mental set.

14. Sheryl was trying to solve a statistics problem and getting nowhere until she suddenly saw how to get to the answer. Once she saw this, the problem was easy. Sheryl's experience demonstrates
    a. functional fixedness.
    b. affective problem solving.
    c. counterfactual reasoning.
    d. sudden insight.

15. When she got to class, Marie noticed that the seam of her shirt was opened. She was embarrassed by this and wanted some way to close the seam until she could get home and mend it. Although she knew she had tape with her, it did not occur to her that she could tape the seam closed. Marie is suffering from
    a. counterfactual thinking.
    b. the availability heuristic.
    c. the framing effect.
    d. functional fixedness.

16. When trying to solve a maze, Jay started at the end-point and worked toward the beginning instead of the reverse. This strategy is called
    a. working by analogy.
    b. working backward.
    c. unconscious processing.
    d. deductive reasoning.

17. Ryan had only minutes to finish scheduling his classes before the scheduling period ended. He had to pick one class from two possible choices. One of the courses seemed interesting and had a good professor but was not at a great time. The other class seemed less interesting, had a good professor, and was at a somewhat better time. Ryan had no time to think about this and chose the first class—which turned out to be an excellent decision. His choice was probably based on
    a. working backward.
    b. unconscious processing.
    c. mental sets.
    d. restructuring.

18. The human ability to use knowledge to solve problems, understand complex ideas, learn quickly, and adapt to environmental changes is known as
    a. framing.
    b. intelligence.
    c. heuristic.
    d. insight.

19. Gary took a test in his math class that assessed his knowledge of the material in the first three chapters of the textbook. This test was an
    a. achievement test.
    b. aptitude test.
    c. invalid test.
    d. intelligence test.

20. The SATs are used to predict students' performance in college. Based on this, the SATs are
    a. achievement tests.
    b. aptitude tests.
    c. tests of multiple intelligence.
    d. tests of interpersonal intelligence.

21. The first important tests of intelligence were developed by
    a. Stern.
    b. Wechsler.
    c. Tversky.
    d. Binet.

22. What would be the IQ, as defined by Stern, of a child with a mental age of 12 and a chronological age of 12?
    a. 100.
    b. 90.
    c. 120.
    d. 200.

23. What may be concluded from the finding that children with higher IQs tend to do better in school than children with lower IQs?
    a. IQ is the only important variable that influences school performance.
    b. Children with high IQs are more valuable students than children with lower IQs.
    c. People with higher IQs will grow up to have more satisfying lives than people with lower IQs.
    d. IQ tests have some validity.

24. An intelligence test that is based on the language and experiences of a particular culture may have a problem with
    a. cultural bias.
    b. being too aptitude focused.
    c. relying too much on heuristic reasoning.
    d. relying too much on working memory.

25. What did Spearman view as a factor that contributed to performance on any intellectual task?
    a. General intelligence.
    b. Fluid intelligence.
    c. Multiple intelligence.
    d. Crystallized intelligence.

26. According to Cattell, which type of intelligence involves information processing?
    a. General intelligence.
    b. Fluid intelligence.
    c. Multiple intelligence.
    d. Crystallized intelligence.

27. Abe is 70 years old. He knows a lot more words than does his 20-year-old granddaughter, Monika, but he does not think as quickly as she does. According to Cattell, Abe may score better than Monika on tests of which type of intelligence?
    a. Fluid intelligence.
    b. Crystallized intelligence.
    c. Musical intelligence.
    d. Intrapersonal intelligence.

28. According to which researcher would a professional athlete be described as being high in a specific type of intelligence?
    a. Binet.
    b. Wechsler.
    c. Cattell.
    d. Gardner.

29. An individual who suffers from autism but is exceptionally gifted in musical abilities is
    a. A savant.
    b. Academically gifted.
    c. High in all of Gardner's intelligences.
    d. High in g.

30. Peter is not only in touch with his own feelings but understands the feelings of others and gets along well with almost everyone he meets. He may be high in which kind of intelligence?
    a. Linguistic.
    b. Crystallized.
    c. Fluid.
    d. Emotional.

31. What is the approach to understanding intelligence that examines what people know and the skills they have for solving problems?
    a. Cognitive approach.
    b. Biological approach.
    c. Psychometric approach.
    d. Deductive approach.

32. Which of the following has been found regarding brain structure and intelligence?
    a. All parts of the brain seem to be equally important for intelligence.
    b. Brain size is in no way related to intelligence.
    c. As of yet, no relationship between brain functioning and intelligence has been found.
    d. The frontal brain regions seem to be particularly associated with intelligence.

33. Which of the following most clearly demonstrates that genes have a role in determining intelligence?
    a. IQs of monozygotic twins are more similar than are IQs of dizygotic twins.
    b. Social class is related to IQ.
    c. Tests may be culturally biased.
    d. IQ scores have risen in the last century.

MATCHING QUESTIONS

Fill in the letter from Column B corresponding to the term that is most associated with the description presented in Column A.

COLUMN A	COLUMN B
____ 1. What we see in the mind's eye when told to think of an object.	A. Deductive reasoning
____ 2. Groupings based on shared properties.	B. Analogy
____ 3. Schema with a clear sequence of events.	C. Emotional
____ 4. Drawing specific conclusions from general premises.	D. Categories
____ 5. Approach to problem solving focusing on how humans make day-to-day decisions.	E. Aptitude
____ 6. Rules of thumb used to solve problems.	F. General intelligence
____ 7. Focusing only on biased evidence that supports one's hypotheses.	G. Counterfactual thinking
____ 8. Imagining outcomes that did not occur.	H. Achievement
____ 9. Changing the way you look at a problem.	I. Prodigy
____ 10. Persisting with a specific method of problem solving.	J. Creative
____ 11. Problem-solving strategy using methods that are for a different problem.	K. Heuristics
____ 12. Test to measure knowledge of an area.	L. Flynn effect
____ 13. Test to predict future performance.	M. Confirmation bias
____ 14. Assessment of intellectual standing compared to peers of the same age.	N. Choice reaction time
____ 15. Factor that contributes to performance on any intellectual task.	O. Restructuring
____ 16. Typical child with exceptional skill in one area.	P. Script
____ 17. Kind of intelligence involved in novel solutions to problems.	Q. Mental age
	R. Mental set
	S. Descriptive
	T. Image

___ 18. Intelligence associated with the ability to control one's mood and reactions even when upset.

___ 19. Selecting as quickly as possible from among various responses.

___ 20. Finding that IQ scores have risen over the past century.

THOUGHT QUESTIONS

1. Describe how the defining attribute model and the prototype model represent how we know that a robin is a bird and an ostrich is a bird.

2. According to Howard Gardner there are seven types of intelligence. For each type of intelligence, identify a highly gifted person. How do these people differ from each other? Are all these people successful? In what ways? What kinds of intelligence would you want to add to Gardner's theory?

APPLICATIONS

Thinking Critically about Mental Maps

A mental map is an internal representation of a geographic area. Gazzaniga and Heatherton propose that mental maps involve both symbolic and analog representations. Symbolic representations do not preserve the visual/spatial characteristics of the area. Rather, symbolic representations include verbal descriptions like *close* or *square*. In contrast, analog representations do maintain the visual/spatial properties of what is represented. This exercise demonstrates some of the factors that may cause distortions in your mental maps.

Draw a map of your campus. Make it as detailed as possible, including things like roads, paths, buildings, and so on. Please do not read the rest of this exercise until you have completed your map!

Compare your map to the actual campus:

- Are there buildings, roads, or landmarks that you left out? If so, do you go to these often?
- Did you tend to line up buildings directly across from each other even if they are actually offset?
- Did you tend to put roads either parallel to each other or at right angles (perpendicular) to each other even though they actually are neither parallel nor perpendicular?
- Did you put buildings with similar functions (for example, dorms) closer to each other than they really are while putting buildings with different functions (such as classrooms as opposed to dorms) farther from each other than is accurate?

Most people make some kinds of systematic errors. Which did you make? Do you think these were spatial errors or symbolic errors? Were the errors important? If you wanted to give a stranger directions to a building on your map, could the stranger use your map to find the building?

Applications of Levels of Analysis: The Framing Effect

In their discussion of problem solving, Gazzaniga and Heatherton present Tversky and Kahneman's research on the framing effect and decision making. According to this research, how a problem is worded influences decision making. For example, which of the following games would you rather play? In game one, you are given $10. Then a coin is tossed. If it is heads, you get to keep the $10. If it's tails, you get an additional $10. In game two, you are given $20. Then a coin is tossed. If it's heads, you keep only $10. If it's tails, you keep $20.

Most people chose game one, even though this is not logical: The outcomes for the games are identical. As described by the text, people display loss aversion: They avoid situations where something seems to be taken from them.

Why does this occur? There is no clear answer, but hypotheses may be made at several levels of analysis. Psychological scientists working at the cultural level may emphasize that we are inundated with materialism. Psychological scientists' hypotheses at the behavioral level may question whether the perceived value of the punishment exceeds the perceived value of the reward. Psychological scientists within the biological category may ask is there something adaptive about avoiding loss.

Research that includes nonhumans may provide some insight into why loss avoidance occurs. Economist Keith Chen has investigated the framing effect and capuchin monkeys. What did he find? Capuchins are just as illogical as humans. They prefer games that avoid loss. What do you think this implies regarding why we avoid loss?

Reference

Dubner, S. J., & Levitt, S. D. (2005). Monkey business: Can capuchins understand money? *New York Times Magazine*, section 6, pp. 30, 32.

WEB SITES

Problem Solving

www.freakonomics.com

Intelligence

(Do not take scores too seriously!)
www.intelligencetest.com
www.iqtest.com/

ANSWER KEY

Fill-in-the-Blank Questions

1. Cognition
2. Analogical
3. Symbolic
4. Concept
5. Defining attribute model
6. Prototype
7. Exemplar
8. Script
9. Reasoning
10. Syllogism
11. Inductive
12. Normative
13. Heuristics
14. Availability
15. Conjunction
16. Confirmation bias
17. Framing
18. Affective forecasting
19. Insight
20. Functional fixedness
21. Intelligence
22. Aptitude
23. Binet
24. 120
25. Valid
26. Crystallized
27. Interpersonal
28. Savants
29. Practical
30. Reaction time
31. Flynn effect
32. Stereotype threat

Multiple-Choice Questions

1. c. Analogical representations share some traits with the objects they represent.

   Incorrect answers:
   a. Symbolic representations are abstract and do not share traits with what they represent.
   b. A deficient representation would be one that does not work well.
   d. A physical representation would be an actual object.

2. a. Symbolic representations are abstract and do not share traits with what they represent.

   Incorrect answers:
   b. A deficient representation would be one that does not work well.
   c. Analogical representations share some traits with the objects they represent.
   d. An image is a kind of analogical representation.

3. a. Categorization is grouping objects together based on shared characteristics.

   Incorrect answers:
   b. Shared knowledge occurs between people.
   c. Defining representation is not a term.
   d. Mental mapping is a form of analogical representation of space.

4. c. The defining attribute model organizes concepts in a hierarchy.

   Incorrect answers:
   a. The prototype model distinguishes between members of a category based on how representative they are of the category.
   b. There is no representativeness model.
   d. There is no availability model.

5. d. According to the prototype model, apples may be seen as more typical fruits than are kiwis.

   Incorrect answers:
   a. All the models of concepts are conceptual models.
   b. The defining attribute model organizes concepts in a hierarchy.
   c. There is no representativeness model.

6. c. Schemas are used to represent broader areas of knowledge.

   Incorrect answers:
   a. A script is a schema with a clear sequence of events.
   b. Validity means that a test is measuring what it is supposed to measure.
   d. Analogies involve comparing concepts or ideas.

7. b. Deductive reasoning starts with general premises. (Mary is a philosopher. Philosophers are fascinating.) Based on these, a conclusion is drawn. (Mary is fascinating.)

   Incorrect answers:
   a. Inductive reasoning starts with specific outcomes. General principles are developed from those.
   c. Analysis reasoning is not a term.
   d. Meta-reasoning is not a term.

8. a. Inductive reasoning starts with specific outcomes (Albert met four people on the swim team who were all smart). General principles are developed from these (All swimmers are smart).

   Incorrect answers:
   b. Deductive reasoning involves drawing a conclusion from general premises.
   c. Analysis reasoning is not a term.
   d. Meta-reasoning is not a term.

9. b. When using the availability heuristic, a decision is based on what is most easily called to mind. It is important to note that the decision is not always correct.

    Incorrect answers:
    a. Confirmation bias occurs when one focuses only on information consistent with one's hypotheses while ignoring inconsistent information.
    c. When using the representativeness heuristic, one makes decisions based on the degree to which a person or object is typical of a category.
    d. According to the framing effect, judgments are affected by how they are worded.

10. c. When using the representativeness heuristic, one makes decisions based on the degree to which a person or object is typical of a category. Stan seems typical of engineers.

    Incorrect answers:
    a. The affective heuristic involves decisions about emotional reactions.
    b. The availability heuristic involves making decisions based on the information that comes most easily to mind.
    d. According to the framing effect, judgments are affected by how they are worded.

11. a. Confirmation bias occurs when one focuses only on information consistent with one's hypothesis while ignoring inconsistent information.

    Incorrect answers:
    b. When using the representativeness heuristic, one makes decisions based on the degree to which a person or object is typical of a category.
    c. The availability heuristic involves making decisions based on the information that comes most easily to mind.
    d. According to the framing effect, judgments are effected by how they are worded.

12. a. The affective heuristic involves decisions about emotional reactions.

    Incorrect answers:
    b. Simulation involves imagining outcomes.
    c. The availability heuristic involves making decisions based on the information that comes most easily to mind.
    d. According to the framing effect, judgments are affected by how they are worded.

13. b. One uses subgoals when one breaks a big problem into smaller problems.

    Incorrect answers:
    a. According to the framing effect, judgments are affected by how they are worded.
    c. Function fixedness involves thinking about objects only in the ways they are typically used.
    d. A mental set involves repeatedly using the same strategy to solve problems.

14. d. Abruptly seeing the solution to a problem reflects sudden insight.

    Incorrect answers:
    a. Functional fixedness involves thinking about objects only in the ways they are typically used.
    b. Affective problem solving is not used in this context.
    c. Counterfactual reasoning involves imagining outcomes that did not occur.

15. d. Marie did not think to use tape on clothing, an unusual use for tape. Being unable to think of unusual uses of objects reflects functional fixedness.

    Incorrect answers:
    a. Counterfactual thinking involves imagining outcomes that did not occur.
    b. The availability heuristic involves making decisions based on the information that comes most easily to mind.
    c. According to the framing effect, judgments are affected by how they are worded.

16. b. Working backward involves solving a problem by starting at the goal and working toward the initial state.

    Incorrect answers:
    a. Using an analogy involves comparing one situation to another situation.
    c. Unconscious processing occurs without awareness.
    d. Deductive reasoning involves drawing a conclusion from general premises.

17. b. Unconscious processing occurs without awareness. It may occur in real-world situations when one has little time to choose between alternatives.

    Incorrect answers:
    a. Working backward involves solving a problem by starting at the goal and working toward the initial state.
    c. A mental set involves repeatedly using the same strategy to solve problems.
    d. Restructuring involves thinking about a problem in a new way.

18. b. Using knowledge to solve problems and adapt to the environment defines intelligence.

    Incorrect answers:
    a. According to the framing effect, judgments are affected by how they are worded.
    c. A heuristic is a rule of thumb used in problem solving.
    d. Insight involves abruptly seeing the solution to a problem.

19. a. Achievement tests assess one's current knowledge in an area.

    Incorrect answers:
    b. Aptitude tests assess potential in an area.
    c. Invalid tests do not measure what they are supposed to measure.
    d. Intelligence tests were developed as aptitude tests to predict school performance.

20. b. SATs are used to assess potential for college work, and so are aptitude tests.

    Incorrect answers:
    a. Achievement tests assess one's current knowledge in an area.
    c. Gardner's theory of multiple intelligences includes linguistic, mathematical/logical, spatial, musical, bodily–kinesthetic, intrapersonal, and interpersonal areas. The SATs measure only linguistic and mathematical knowledge.
    d. Interpersonal intelligence is not assessed by SATs.

21. d. Binet developed the first important test of intelligence.

    Incorrect answers:
    a. Stern developed the Intelligence Quotient (IQ).
    b. Wechsler more recently developed a widely used intelligence test where IQ is determined by how similar your score is to the scores of other people.
    c. Tversky studied problem solving.

22. a. Stern calculated IQ as mental age divided by chronological age multiplied by 100. In the question $12/12 \times 100 = 100$.

    Incorrect answers:
    b. Mental age must be less than chronological age to get an IQ less than 100.
    c. Mental age must be more that chronological age to get an IQ greater than 100.
    d. Mental age must be twice as high as chronological age to get an IQ of 200.

23. d. IQ tests were developed to predict school performance. Valid tests do what they were developed to do. Finding that IQ tests predict school performance indicates that the tests are valid.

    Incorrect answers:
    a. Other influences on school performance include motivation.
    b. IQ does not determine one's value as a person.
    c. Data do not indicate that life satisfaction is related to IQ.

24. a. Because intelligence tests may be heavily influenced by a particular culture's language and values, the tests may be culturally biased.

    Incorrect answers:
    b. Intelligence tests were developed to be aptitude tests.
    c. Intelligence tests do not focus specifically on heuristic use.
    d. Working memory is an important component of intelligence and is therefore included in the tests.

25. a. Spearman proposed that there was a g factor related to general intelligence.

    Incorrect answers:
    b. Cattell distinguished between fluid and crystallized intelligence.
    c. Gardner proposed there are multiple independent intelligences.
    d. Cattell distinguished between fluid and crystallized intelligence.

26. b. According to Cattell, fluid intelligence involves information processing.

    Incorrect answers:
    a. Spearman proposed there was a g factor related to general intelligence.
    c. Gardner proposed there are multiple intelligences.
    d. According to Cattell, crystallized intelligence is knowledge gained through experience.

27. b. Knowledge of vocabulary reflects crystallized intelligence.

    Incorrect answers:
    a. Fluid intelligence involves information processing.
    c. Musical intelligence involves understanding music.
    d. Intrapersonal intelligence involves understanding oneself.

28. d. Gardner includes bodily–kinesthetic intelligence in his theory: A professional athlete would have a high degree of this kind of intelligence.

Incorrect answers:

a. Binet focused on school performance.
b. Wechsler did not include bodily-kinesthetic intelligence.
c. Cattell discussed fluid and crystallized intelligence.

29. a. Individuals with cognitive disabilities in most areas but exceptional skills in one are savants.

Incorrect answers:

b. Academically gifted children do well on IQ tests.
c. The question describes only musical intelligence.
d. People high in g have high general intelligence. This was not described in the question.

30. d. People high in emotional intelligence understand and manage emotional responses in themselves and others.

Incorrect answers:

a. Linguistic intelligence involves use of language.
b. Crystallized intelligence is knowledge gained through experience.
c. Fluid intelligence involves information processing.

31. a. The cognitive approach to intelligence focuses on knowledge and skills.

Incorrect answers:

b. The biological approach to intelligence focuses on biological correlates with intelligence such as the role of genes or the relationship between brain functioning and intelligence.
c. The psychometric approach to intelligence focuses on testing.
d. There is no explicitly deductive approach to intelligence.

32. d. Recent research indicates the frontal lobes are particularly associated with intelligence.

Incorrect answers:

a. Different parts of the brain seem to be important for different kind of skills.
b. Brain size is related to intelligence: People with bigger brains tend to be more intelligent.
c. There are relationships between brain functioning and intelligence.

33. a. Monozygotic twins have identical genes while dizygotic twins do not. If genes play a role in intelligence, then the IQs of monozygotic twins should be most similar.

Incorrect answers:

b. The finding that social class is related to IQ may demonstrate environmental influences in intelligence.

c. Problems with cultural bias in testing are not biologically based.
d. Because human genetics have not changed in the last century, the increase in IQ scores must reflect some kind of environmental or testing effect.

Matching Questions

1. T   Image
2. D   Categories
3. P   Script
4. A   Deductive reasoning
5. S   Descriptive
6. K   Heuristics
7. M   Confirmation bias
8. G   Counterfactual thinking
9. O   Restructuring
10. R   Mental set
11. B   Analogy
12. H   Achievement
13. E   Aptitude
14. Q   Mental age
15. F   General intelligence
16. I   Prodigy
17. J   Creative
18. C   Emotional
19. N   Choice reaction time
20. L   Flynn effect

Thought Questions

1. The defining attribute model represents both robins and ostriches as part of a hierarchal network where animals may be at the top, birds would be linked to animals, and ostriches and robins would be linked to birds. In addition, characteristics of all animals would be linked to animals, characteristics of all birds would be linked to birds, and characteristics specific to robins or ostriches would be linked to them directly. In contrast, the prototype model would identify robins as prototypical birds, whereas ostriches would be nonprototypical.

2. The seven intelligences cited in the textbook are linguistic, mathematical/logical, spatial, musical, bodily–kinesthetic, intrapersonal, and interpersonal. There are many people to choose from to represent each. For example, as a successful politician, Secretary of State Condoleeza Rice must have high interpersonal intelligence. Mozart, who was a child prodigy, had outstanding musical intelligence. Think of your own examples for each category.

CHAPTER 9 | Motivation

GUIDE TO THE READING

Why do we do the things we do? How do we balance what we want with what is socially appropriate? These are the kinds of issues addressed in the study of motivation. The authors describe motivation as that which energizes or stimulates behavior. They then discuss the roles of needs, drives, and arousal in motivating behavior, emphasizing the interaction of biological and psychological states. The human need for social interaction and need for achievement are discussed in some detail. Influences on eating, addiction, and sex are then presented. Throughout the chapter the interplay of biological, psychological, and cultural forces on motivated behavior is emphasized.

How Does Motivation Activate, Direct, and Sustain Behavior?

Gazzaniga and Heatherton describe four qualities of motivational states: They energize behavior, they give behavior direction, they help ensure people persist in a behavior until the goal is reached, and they vary in strength (i.e., some motives are stronger than others). To explain how motivational states accomplish these, the authors discuss needs, drives, and arousal. Biological needs are just that—you must satisfy them to survive (for example, you need food). There are also psychological needs, such as a need to be with other people. Needs first result in arousal, a physiological state. Drives are psychological states that are then activated. These motivate goal-directed behaviors to satisfy the needs.

According to early researcher Clark Hull, as deprivation of a need increases, drive to satisfy that need also increases. However, this is not always the case. For example, people may be motivated by incentives—outside rewards like good grades—rather than by internal needs. In addition, people

seem to be motivated to maintain an optimal level of arousal: neither too little stimulation, which is boring, nor too much stimulation, which is overwhelming. Pleasure may also motivate behavior, with people pursuing behaviors that result in pleasure and avoiding those that result in pain. From an evolutionary perspective this makes sense: Behaviors resulting in pleasure are often adaptive, whereas those resulting in pain are not. Finally, whereas some behaviors are performed because they are extrinsically motivated, or to achieve some external goal, other behaviors are intrinsically motivated. This means they are performed for no obvious external reason.

Why Are Human Beings Social?

Psychological scientists have found that people have a basic need for other people, a need to belong. Because of this need to belong, people become anxious if their social group rejects them. Similarly, anxious people seek the company of others, especially other anxious people. It also appears that people are attuned to cheating by others, and groups will reject cheaters. The need to belong helps account for why most people usually do not selfishly meet their basic needs, but rather do so in socially appropriate ways.

How Do People Achieve Personal Goals?

To achieve a personal goal, Gazzaniga and Heatherton propose that first you should have a good goal: one that is neither too hard nor too easy and is clearly defined. Next you should have both the expectation that you can accomplish the goal (what Bandura called self-efficacy) and the desire to achieve the goal, or achievement motivation. Often achievement of personal goals requires delay of gratification. This means putting off immediate rewards, like going to a party, in favor of long-term rewards, like getting good grades. Self-regulation, or controlling behavior to attain personal goals, is essential for achievement. Recent research indicates that people get better at self-regulation with practice and may be better at regulating themselves in some situations than others. Psychological scientists also find that the frontal lobes are important for self-regulation. The frontal lobes are involved in awareness of social expectations and in the ability to inhibit inappropriate behaviors.

What Determines How We Eat?

Many factors influence eating. Sometimes we eat simply because we are hungry. Sometimes we eat just because it is time to eat. Sometimes we eat because the food tastes good. Not surprisingly, both biology and culture play important roles in eating. What we eat is determined largely by culture and by personal experience. Biology is significant for feeling of hunger. The hypothalamus is the brain structure that integrates information on eating. Stomach distention seems to play some minor role in feelings of hunger. Glucostatic theory proposes there are receptors in the blood that respond to glucose, a sugar. When there is glucose in the bloodstream, animals feel less hungry. According to lipostatic theory there is a set-point for body fat: Animals below their set-point feel hungry. Recent research has focused on the role of leptin, a hormone, in fat regulation.

What Is Addiction?

Although addiction involves physiological dependence, the authors emphasize that addiction may be studied at several levels of analysis. At the social level, the roles of parents, peers, and society in providing models for addiction may be emphasized. At the individual level of analysis, the roles of personal traits, such as sensation seeking, in the development of addictions may be the focus. At the biological level, inherited predispositions for risky behaviors or sensitivity to drugs may be investigated. The authors conclude this section with a discussion of the biological mechanisms and psychological effects of several psychoactive, or mind-altering, drugs, with special focus on alcohol.

What Factors Motivate Sexual Behavior?

Like eating, sex is influenced by biological, individual, and societal variables. The sexual response cycle of excitement, plateau, orgasm, and resolution is one demonstration of the biological role in sexual responding. Current research includes study of hormones and neurotransmitters. Cultural rules also influence behavior. Gender differences in mating behaviors may have both cultural and biological underpinnings.

FILL-IN-THE-BLANK QUESTIONS

1. Maslow's theory is an example of _____ psychology emphasizing people striving to personal fulfillment.

2. _____ is a term used to describe physiological activation.

3. If a behavior consistently reduces drive over time it may become a _____.

4. _____ are external objects that motivate behavior.

5. Janey, a 5-year-old, likes to explore her mother's purse just to see what is in it. She is demonstrating what kind of motivation? _____

6. Rewarding intrinsically motivated behavior may decrease the behavior because it may lessen people's feeling of _____.

7. Dr. Trippe is a psychologist who helps companies train, retain, and motivate employees. Dr. Trippe's training is in _____ psychology.

8. Jemima would never lie to her friends because she is afraid they would stop speaking to her if she did. Jemima's reaction supports _____.

9. When Meagan got an 85 percent on an exam, she was not sure if it was a good grade or not. To find out, she asked her friends what they earned and she found out the class average. Meagan's response supports _____.

10. When one experiences a conflict between meeting one's own needs and cooperating with others, one is faced with a _____.

11. A _____ is a desired outcome.

12. The expectancy that one's efforts will be successful is _____.

13. Luis is very worried about a lot of things. Instead of dealing with his problems he tries to forget them by drinking. He is demonstrating _____.

14. When Cindy looks at a bottle of soda she sees it as pleasantly fizzy, tasty, and sweet. However, she wants to *not* drink the soda, so she changes the way she views it: It becomes brown sludge. Cindy has changed _____ into _____.

15. When animals eat less if given just one type of food but more when presented with a variety of different types of food, they are demonstrating _____.

16. The part of the brain with the greatest influence on eating is the _____.

17. _____ are receptors that monitor the extent to which glucose is taken into a cell.

18. The recently discovered hormone _____ is involved in fat regulation.

19. The need to consume more and more of a drug to have it achieve an effect is called _____.

20. _____ drugs are mind-altering substances.

21. A drug that is similar to stimulants but may also cause slight hallucinations is _____.

22. _____ is the active ingredient in marijuana.

23. For women, but not for men, the more of the hormone _____ they have, the more likely they are to have sexual thoughts and desires.

24. The hormone _____ appears to be important for sexual arousal and orgasm in both men and women.

25. The part of the brain most important for stimulating sexual behavior is the _____.

26. _____ are chemicals detected through the olfactory system that may influence sexual behavior.

27. Cognitive ideas about how sexual episodes should unfold are _____.

28. Differences in what men and women look for when seeking a mate may be explained by _____.

MULTIPLE-CHOICE QUESTIONS

1. Motivational states guide behavior toward satisfying a specific goal. In this sense, motivational states are
   a. energizing.
   b. directive.
   c. persistent.
   d. strong.

2. Because an animal must have water, getting water
   a. satisfies a basic need.
   b. results in self-actualization.
   c. satisfies a habit.
   d. results in a hierarchy.

3. Which of the following most closely reflects self-actualization?
   a. A hungry child getting food.
   b. An animal finding a safe place to shelter.
   c. A baby loving her father.
   d. An artist achieving great art.

4. Joe has not eaten for 20 hours and is now feeling irritable, shaky, and anxious. His lack of eating has most clearly resulted in
   a. arousal.
   b. equilibrium.
   c. homeostasis.
   d. set-point reduction.

5. When Lori went outside into the cold, she started to shiver. The shivering helped to warm her body. Her body's ability to maintain a particular temperature is described by
   a. the negative feedback model.
   b. a habitlike reflex.
   c. self-actualization.
   d. underarousal theory

6. According to Hull, as deprivation of some need increases, what happens to the drive to satisfy it?
   a. Drive increases only until a certain set-point, and then decreases.
   b. Drive increases as deprivation increases.
   c. Drive increases until feedback develops.
   d. Drive increases until an incentive is met.

7. Leo works at two jobs because he wants to earn enough money to buy a new car. In this situation, what is the incentive motivating Leo?
   a. Money to buy the car.
   b. Feelings of satisfaction for a job well done.
   c. Basic hedonism.
   d. Anxiety about not having enough money.

8. According to the Yerkes-Dodson law, who of the following should perform best on an exam?
   a. Anita, who is so anxious she can't eat or sleep.
   b. Joe, who is so relaxed that he does not feel that he has to study.
   c. Maria, who is a little nervous but is studying hard.
   d. Marco, who is so anxious he spelled his name wrong.

9. Charlotte believes in eating good foods, having good sex, and staying happy. She avoids all activities that make her uncomfortable. Her behavior exemplifies
   a. the reality principle.
   b. an optimal level of arousal.
   c. incentive theory.
   d. hedonism.

10. Which neurotransmitter may be increased by the anticipation of sexual activity?
    a. Dopamine.
    b. Serotonin.
    c. GABA.
    d. Hippocampin.

11. Jennine studies hard because her mother gives her $10 for every A she earns. Jennine is influenced by
    a. extrinsic motivation.
    b. intrinsic motivation.
    c. habit.
    d. creativity.

12. Jose, a 10-year-old, loves playing the piano and will play for hours just for his own enjoyment. Based on the research presented in the textbook, what would happen if Jose's mother starts to give him $5 for every hour that he plays?
    a. His playing will increase because the money is a reward.
    b. His playing will increase because the money is an incentive.
    c. His playing will be unaffected because he plays so much already.
    d. His playing will decrease because it was intrinsically motivated initially.

13. When Noreen was ill, she spent a lot of time alone in her room. She found that she became starved for company and was delighted when people visited her. Her reaction reflects
    a. an extrinsic need for hedonism.
    b. a need to belong.
    c. safety needs.
    d. social exclusion theory.

14. A rumor spread among Jodi's friends that she had cheated on a big test. Jodi's friends were angry about the cheating and started to ignore Jodi in school and not invite her out. Jodi became anxious about this and promised her friends she would never cheat again. Jodi's reaction supports
    a. homeostasis theory.
    b. social exclusion theory.
    c. Yerkes-Dodson theory.
    d. hedonism theory.

15. Jason picked up a pizza for himself and his friends. Jason is really hungry and would like to keep half the pizza for himself. However, he knows his friends will be really annoyed if he does so. Jason is facing
    a. a social dilemma.
    b. extrinsic selection.
    c. self-efficacy.
    d. gourmand syndrome.

16. Monica believes that if she studies for her exam, she will do well on it. According to Bandura, Monica is displaying a strong sense of
    a. need.
    b. self-actualization.

    c. self-efficacy.
    d. self-drive.

17. Steve would really like to go to a party on Thursday night, but he studies for an exam instead. He knows that if he studies he will do well and then will have a better chance of getting a good job. Steve is displaying
    a. escapism.
    b. the pleasure principle.
    c. delay of gratification.
    d. deindividuation.

18. To decrease cheating, a teacher puts mirrors around her classroom during exams. This teacher is trying to increase
    a. deindividuation.
    b. hedonism.
    c. excapism.
    d. self-awareness.

19. Tanika would like to turn her TV up loud while her favorite song is being performed, but she resists the temptation to do this because she knows it will disturb the other people in her dorm. The area of the brain most active in regulating her decision is
    a. the hypothalamus.
    b. the hippocampus.
    c. the occipital lobe.
    d. the frontal lobes.

20. When JR eats dinner at his mom's house, he doesn't eat too much of the burger, salad, and potatoes that she serves. However, when he goes to his grandma's he eats a lot of the chicken, burgers, salad, fruit, chips, candy, cake, and pie that she loves to make. JR's increased eating at his grandma's house may reflect
    a. the effects of time on eating.
    b. sensory-specific satiety.
    c. neophobia.
    d. gourmand syndrome.

21. The brain structure with the most influence on eating is the
    a. hypothalamus.
    b. hippocampus.
    c. occipital lobe.
    d. frontal lobes.

22. When Rebecca does not get a particular drug, she gets anxious and tense and suffers cravings. She has also found she needs more and more of this drug to avoid these feelings. Rebecca is probably
    a. only psychologically dependent on the drug.
    b. using the drug to avoid sensation seeking.
    c. addicted to the drug.
    d. intolerant of the drug.

23. Sidney took a psychoactive drug. This means the drug would
    a. definitely cause addiction.
    b. definitely cause physiological dependence.
    c. possibly cause hallucinations.
    d. possibly have only physical, rather than mind-altering, effects.

24. Jim took a drug that increased his heart rate, kept him awake, and made him feel good. The drug he took was probably
    a. marijuana.
    b. a stimulant.
    c. alcohol.
    d. heroin.

25. The research presented in the textbook on the effects of alcohol found that
    a. alcohol interferes with memory and motor skills.
    b. alcohol has no influence on sexual performance.
    c. believing that one drank alcohol has no effect on behavior if no alcohol was actually consumed.
    d. alcohol improves sexual performance.

26. While a couple is kissing, their blood flows to their genitals and they become aroused. According to Masters and Johnson, they are in what stage of the sexual response cycle?
    a. Excitement.
    b. Plateau.
    c. Orgasm.
    d. Resolution.

27. Eleven-year-old Judy is developing pubic hair, breasts, and underarm hair. All these are examples of
    a. abnormal development.
    b. the effects of oxytocin.
    c. the effects of nitric oxide.
    d. secondary sex characteristics.

28. Which neurotransmitter is enhanced by Viagra?
    a. Dopamine.
    b. MDMA.
    c. Nitric oxide.
    d. Sexomine.

29. Cherise comes from a family where girls are expected to be virgins when they marry but boys are expected to get as much experience as they can. Her family's values
    a. reflect a double standard.
    b. are unknown in any culture.
    c. reflect erotic plasticity.
    d. are pheromone based.

MATCHING QUESTIONS

Fill in the letter from Column B corresponding to the term that is most associated with the description presented in Column A.

COLUMN A

____ 1. Developer of the need hierarchy.
____ 2. Psychological states activated to satisfy needs.
____ 3. Tendency for the body to maintain equilibrium.
____ 4. Hypothetical state that indicates homeostasis.
____ 5. Law proposing performance increases with arousal up to a certain point and then decreases.
____ 6. Underlies motivation to seek pleasure and avoid pain.
____ 7. Tendency to generate useful ideas.
____ 8. Motivation to act because of external goals.
____ 9. Basic need for interpersonal attachments.
____ 10. Comparing yourself with others to validate your emotional responses.
____ 11. Process by which people modify their behaviors to reach personal goals.
____ 12. Expectancy that one's efforts will be successful.
____ 13. Desire to do well.
____ 14. Mental state characterized by low self-awareness that may cause people to lose touch with their normal standards of behavior.
____ 15. Putting off immediate rewards in favor of long-term goals.
____ 16. Area of the brain important for self-regulation.
____ 17. A fear of novel things.

COLUMN B

A. Maslow
B. Pleasure principle
C. Achievement motivation
D. Delay of gratification
E. Addiction
F. Extrinsic
G. Cannon
H. Neophobia
I. Social comparison
J. Set-point
K. Homeostasis
L. Alcohol
M. Gourmand syndrome
N. Need to belong
O. Stimulants
P. Sexual response cycle
Q. Deindividuation
R. Self-regulation
S. Creativity
T. Frontal lobes
U. Self-efficacy
V. Yerkes-Dodson
W. Drives

___ 18. Disorder where people are obsessed with fine food.

___ 19. Researcher who proposed hunger is associated with stomach contractions.

___ 20. Physical dependence.

___ 21. Drugs that increase behavioral and mental activity.

___ 22. The most widely abused drug.

___ 23. Predictable pattern of physiological responding during sex.

THOUGHT QUESTIONS

1. List three extrinsically motivated behaviors and three intrinsically motivated behaviors. For each extrinsically motivated behavior describe what could be the external goal. How do these contrast with the goals of the intrinsically motivated behaviors? Should rewards be given to children for performing intrinsically motivated behaviors?

2. Describe a very satisfying meal. Explain from a biological, personal, and cultural perspective why that meal is satisfying.

APPLICATIONS

Thinking Critically about How People View Food

For this exercise you will need to go to an eating establishment on campus: the commons, a snack bar, or the like. First note what foods are available to choose. Are there a lot of choices? Are they healthful choices, like fruits and salads, or less healthful choices like fatty or sweet foods? Next observe what people select to eat. What are the most common choices? Are these healthful or not? Several variables may motivate what people select: choices available, cost, taste, healthfulness, desire to lose weight, desire to gain weight. Which do you think are the most significant influences on people's choices? What data support your conclusions?

Applications of Levels of Analysis: Causes of Evil

People are motivated to fill their biological needs for things like food and water. People are also motivated to fill psychosocial needs for belonging, achievement, and power. Even when these needs are pressing, most people are concerned with how filling their own needs will impact others.

Throughout the chapter, the authors emphasize the balance between meeting one's own needs and meeting the expectations of society. But what happens when people do not care about the consequences to the rest of society?

Evil may be defined as the purposeful hurting of others. Why would people do this? Are they incapable of balancing their needs and the good of society? Psychological scientists may approach this from different levels of analysis. Ge et al. (1996) took a biological perspective. Their data indicated that children might inherit traits from their parents that make them more likely to violate social rules. The *DSM-IV* (the main diagnostic manual used by mental health professionals) approached the issue from the individual level: It describes the behaviors of people with antisocial personality disorder. For example, these people are dishonest, aggressive, and lacking in remorse for wrongs they have committed. From the biological and individual perspective, people who perform evil acts may do so because they cannot or will not take society into account when filling their own needs. Zimbardo (2003), arguing from the social perspective, took a different view. He proposed that biological or psychological characteristics are often not the cause of antisocial behaviors. Rather, Zimbardo argued that in the right context almost anyone can be manipulated into performing acts of evil. For example, in Milgram's (1963) infamous experiments on obedience, otherwise normal people were willing to give intense shocks to a stranger just because an authority told them to do it. (They did not know that no one was really shocked.) From Zimbardo's perspective the need to belong in one social context, such as being accepted by the authority, can lead to behavior that is evil in another social context, such as shocking a stranger. In today's world we see many incidents where innocent people are hurt. Are these acts evil? What is motivating them? Are the perpetrators of the acts incapable of caring about others? Or are they products of a social context that encourages evil?

References

Ge, X., Conger, R. D., Cadoret, R. J., Neiderhiser, J. M., Yates, W., Troughton, E., & Stewart, M. A. (1996). The developmental interface between nature and nurture: A mutual influence model of child antisocial behavior and parent behaviors. *Developmental Psychology, 32(4)*, 574–589.

Milgram, S. (1963). Behavioral study of obedience. *Journal of Abnormal and Social Psychology*, 67, 371–378.

Zimbardo, P. (2003). A situationist perspective on the psychology of evil: Understanding how good people are transformed into perpetrators. In A. Miller (Ed.) *The social psychology of good and evil: Understanding our capacity for kindness and cruelty.* Retrieved September12, 2005, from www.zimbardo.com/downloads/2003%20evil%20chapter.pdf.

WEB SITES

www.socialpsychology.org
http://zimbardo.com

ANSWER KEY

Fill-in-the-Blank Questions

1. Humanistic	14. Hot cognitions into cold cognitions
2. Arousal	15. Sensory-specific satiety
3. Habit	16. Hypothalamus
4. Incentives	17. Glucostats
5. Intrinsic	18. Leptin
6. Personal control	19. Tolerance
7. Industrial and organizational (I-O)	20. Psychoactive
8. Social exclusion theory	21. MDMA (ecstasy)
9. Social comparison theory	22. THC
10. Social dilemma	23. Testosterone
11. Goal	24. Oxytocin
12. Self-efficacy	25. Hypothalamus
13. Escapism	26. Pheromones
	27. Sexual scripts
	28. Sexual strategies theory

Multiple-Choice Questions

1. b. The quality of motivational states that guides the behavior to a goal is directive.

   Incorrect answers:
   a. The energizing quality results in arousal.
   c. The quality of persistence keeps the animal working toward a goal.
   d. Different motives vary in strength.

2. a. Animals must have the basic needs, like the need for water, filled to survive.

   Incorrect answers:
   b. Self-actualization, the top of Maslow's hierarchy, occurs when people live up to their dreams.
   c. A habit is formed when a behavior regularly reduces a drive.
   d. Maslow proposed that people are motivated by a need hierarchy that starts with survival needs and ends with self-actualization.

3. d. Self-actualization, the top of Maslow's hierarchy, occurs when people live up to their dreams.

   Incorrect answers:
   a. Getting food satisfies survival needs.
   b. Finding shelter satisfies safety needs.
   c. Feeling love relates to emotional needs.

4. a. The question describes physiological activation, which is arousal.

   Incorrect answers:
   b. Equilibrium refers to keeping the body in balance.
   c. Homeostasis is the body's ability to maintain equilibrium
   d. Set-point reduction is not a term.

5. a. The negative feedback model describes a way to maintain equilibrium. For example, shivering when cold helps increase body temperature.

   Incorrect answers:
   b. Habits are formed when a behavior reduces drive. No habit is described.
   c. Self-actualization is the top of Maslow's hierarchy.
   d. There is no underarousal theory.

6. b. Hull proposed a straightforward relationship between need and drive: As need increased, drive increased. This view is not entirely correct.

   Incorrect answers:
   a. Hull did not propose that drive decreased if need increased.
   c. Hull did not discuss feedback in this context.
   d. Hull did not discuss incentives.

7. a. Incentives are external objects, like money, that motivate behavior.

   Incorrect answers:
   b. Feelings of satisfaction are internal.
   c. Hedonism, which involves feelings of pleasure, is internal.
   d. Anxiety is internal.

8. c. According to the Yerkes-Dodson law, animals perform best under an optimal level of arousal. Some anxiety for a test may motivate studying.

   Incorrect answers:
   a. Anita's anxiety is causing too much arousal and is interfering with her functioning.
   b. Joe is overly relaxed and so has too little arousal to motivate studying.
   d. Marco's anxiety is causing overarousal and interfering with performance.

9. d. Hedonism involves feelings of pleasure.

   Incorrect answers:
   a. The reality principle was proposed by Freud and involves rational decision making.
   b. The question does not describe an optimal level of arousal for a particular task.
   c. Incentives are external objects that motivate behavior and are not limited to pleasurable sensations.

10. a. Dopamine is related to reward and the anticipation of rewarding activities, like sex.

    Incorrect answers:
    b. Serotonin, a neurotransmitter, may be related to hallucinations.
    c. GABA, a neurotransmitter, may be mimicked by alcohol.
    d. Hippocampin is not a word.

11. a. Extrinsic motivation is based on external goals, like getting money.

    Incorrect answers:
    b. Intrinsically motivated behaviors are performed only for themselves; there is no external goal.
    c. Habits are formed when behavior reduces drive.
    d. Creativity refers to the ability to produce new ideas.

12. d. Jose plays the piano because he loves it: It is an intrinsically motivated behavior. Research indicates that rewarding intrinsically motivated behaviors may actually decrease them.

    Incorrect answers:
    a. His playing will not increase because it is intrinsically motivated.
    b. Money will not work as incentive for this intrinsically motivated behavior.
    c. Research indicates his playing may be affected negatively.

13. b. Humans seem to have a need to be with other people and to belong.

    Incorrect answers:
    a. Hedonism involves feelings of pleasure.
    c. Safety needs include things like finding shelter.
    d. Social exclusion theory refers to people's feelings of anxiety when rejected by a group. Although related to the need to belong, it is not described in the example.

14. b. Social exclusion theory refers to people's anxiety when rejected by a group. People may be rejected for violating rules, like cheating on an exam.

    Incorrect answers:
    a. Homeostasis is the body's ability to maintain equilibrium.
    c. According to the Yerkes-Dodson law, animals perform best under an optimal level of arousal.
    d. Hedonism involves feelings of pleasure; there is no hedonism theory.

15. a. Social dilemmas occur when there is a conflict between social expectations and meeting one's own needs.

Incorrect answers:
b. Extrinsic selection is not a term.
c. Self-efficacy is Bandura's term describing one's expectations that one's actions will be successful.
d. Gourmand syndrome results from brain damage and involves an obsession with fine food.

16. c. Self-efficacy is Bandura's term describing one's expectations that one's actions will be successful.

    Incorrect answers:
    a. A need is a state of deficiency.
    b. Self-actualization, the top of Maslow's hierarchy, occurs when people live up to their dreams.
    d. Self-drive is not a term.

17. c. Delay of gratification involves putting off immediate rewards, like going to a party, in favor of long-term rewards, like getting a good job.

    Incorrect answers:
    a. Escapism involves avoiding self-awareness.
    b. Freud described the pleasure principle as motivating people to seek pleasure and avoid pain.
    d. Deindividuation is a mental state where people have low self-awareness and so may act in a manner inconsistent with their usual values.

18. d. Self-awareness involves consciousness of one's internal states.

    Incorrect answers:
    a. Deindividuation is a mental state where people have low self-awareness and so may act in a manner inconsistent with their usual values.
    b. Hedonism involves feelings of pleasure.
    c. Escapism involves avoiding self-awareness.

19. d. The frontal lobes are important for self-regulation. For example, they are involved in inhibiting inappropriate behavior, such as playing the TV too loudly.

    Incorrect answers:
    a. The hypothalamus is the main brain structure involved in eating.
    b. The hippocampus is important for memory.
    c. The occipital lobes are important for vision.

20. b. Sensory-specific satiety is reflected when animals become full more quickly when eating just one type of food, but will eat more when presented with lots of different foods.

    Incorrect answers:
    a. The effects of time on eating were not described in the question.
    c. Neophobia is fear of new things, and can include new kinds of food.

d. Gourmand syndrome results from brain damage and involves an obsession with fine foods.

21. a. The brain structure with the most influence on eating is the hypothalamus.

    Incorrect answers:
    b. The hippocampus is important for memory.
    c. The occipital lobe is important for vision.
    d. The frontal lobes are important for self-regulation.

22. c. The question describes characteristics of physiological dependence, such as tolerance. Physiological dependence is addiction.

    Incorrect answers:
    a. Because physical symptoms are described, Rebecca is not only psychologically dependent.
    b. Drug users are usually high in sensation seeking, not avoiding sensation seeking.
    d. Needing increasing amounts of a drug describes tolerance; intolerance is not used in this context.

23. c. Psychoactive drugs have mind-altering effects, such as hallucinations.

    Incorrect answers:
    a. Psychoactive drugs may or may not cause addiction.
    b. Physiological dependence is addiction; psychoactive drugs may or may not cause addiction.
    d. By definition, psychoactive drugs cause mind-altering effects.

24. b. Stimulants increase heart rate, wakefulness, and feelings of well-being.

    Incorrect answers:
    a. Marijuana improves mood but also leads to a relaxed state.
    c. In large amounts alcohol may decrease mood, and it does not cause wakefulness.
    d. Heroin results in pleasure and stupor.

25. a. Alcohol has a negative effect on both memory and motor abilities.

    Incorrect answers:
    b. Alcohol interferes with sexual performance.
    c. Believing they have had a drink may make people less inhibited even if they have not actually had any alcohol.
    d. Alcohol interferes with sexual performance.

26. a. Excitement, accompanied by the increase in blood flow to the genitals, is the first stage in Masters and Johnson's sexual response cycle.

    Incorrect answers:
    b. During plateau, the second stage, arousal increases.
    c. During orgasm, the third stage, there are involuntary muscle contractions.
    d. During resolution, the final stage, males enter a refractory period and women don't.

27. d. Secondary sex characteristics reflect the onset of puberty and include breast and pubic hair development.

    Incorrect answers:
    a. These changes at puberty are normal.
    b. Oxytocin, a hormone, is related to sexual arousal and orgasm.
    c. Nitric oxide, a neurotransmitter, is related to sexual stimulation.

28. c. Nitric oxide, a neurotransmitter related to sexual arousal, is enhanced by Viagra, a drug used to treat men who have difficulty maintaining erections.

    Incorrect answers:
    a. Dopamine is apparently not related to Viagra.
    b. MDMA is ecstasy and is not related to Viagra.
    d. Sexomine is a made-up word.

29. a. Cultures, societies, or people with one expectation of appropriate sexual behavior for women and a different expectation for men have a double standard.

    Incorrect answers:
    b. Many cultures have double standards.
    c. Erotic plasticity is the degree to which culture or situation can influence sex drive.
    d. Pheromones are chemicals picked up by the olfactory system that may influence sexual behavior, but their effect is not described here.

Matching Questions

1. A Maslow
2. W Drives
3. K Homeostasis
4. J Set-point
5. V Yerkes-Dodson
6. B Pleasure principle
7. S Creativity
8. F Extrinsic motivation
9. N Need to belong
10. I Social comparison
11. R Self-regulation
12. U Self-efficacy

13. C   Achievement motivation
14. Q   Deindividuation
15. D   Delay of gratification
16. T   Frontal lobes
17. H   Neophobia
18. M   Gourmand syndrome
19. G   Cannon
20. E   Addiction
21. O   Stimulants
22. L   Alcohol
23. P   Sexual response cycle

Thought Questions

1. The extrinsically motivated behaviors are performed for an external goal. For example, if someone is hungry for an apple, that person will search for an apple. Intrinsically motivated behaviors are not performed for an external goal. For example, child who loves to read may read just for pleasure. Research indicates that children should not be given rewards for performing intrinsically motivated behaviors because the rewards may decrease the behaviors.

2. The discussion of biological factors should included glucostatic theory, stomach distention, lipostateic theory, and leptin. The discussion of personal factors should include time and taste, including sensory-specific satiety. It may also include need to belong. Discussion of culture should include the foods accepted in our society.

CHAPTER 10 | Emotions and Health

GUIDE TO THE READING

In Chapter 10 the authors present the current state of psychological science in regard to the topics of emotion and health. Emotions are perplexing in that they nearly defy verbal description, yet everyone understands them. Complex emotions like love have motivated a considerable proportion of the art, literature, and music of our civilization. For all the importance and phenomenological understanding ascribed to these feelings, psychological scientists have come to a reasonable understanding of emotions only recently. Early psychologists often overlooked their role, instead preferring to view the organism as a rational information-processing machine. A more recent evolutionary perspective has proven more fruitful in integrating the motivating and sustaining forces of emotion with animal behavior. In addition, recent advances in behavioral neuroscience have clarified and improved earlier theories. The authors address this topic by considering how emotions are adaptive, how people experience emotions, the neurophysiological basis of emotion, how people cope with stress, and what behaviors affect health.

How Are Emotions Adaptive?

The chapter begins with a consideration of how emotions serve a survival function. Emotions, immediate responses to environmental events, are distinguished from moods, which are diffuse and long-lasting emotional states. The evolutionary basis of emotion is supported by cross-cultural recognition of the facial expression of emotions. The authors present Ekman and Friesen's classic studies in which the facial expressions of anger, fear, disgust, happiness, sadness, and surprise were recognized in diverse cultures. Subsequent research has continued to provide support for the

cross-cultural congruence in identification of facial expressions. While recognition of facial expression appears universal and adaptive, the display rules, or norms, for the exhibition of emotion differ dramatically. The adaptive nature of emotions is also seen in their influence on cognitive functions. They serve as heuristic guides in decision making, capture our attention, and aid memory. They also strengthen interpersonal relations. Even seemingly negative emotions such as guilt, shame, and jealousy strengthen social bonds, renew commitments to relationships, and motivate positive behavior. Embarrassment may help reaffirm close relationships after a transgression.

How Do People Experience Emotions?

The next section looks at attempts to define and quantify the phenomenological experience of emotion. Psychological scientists have agreed on three components that accompany emotions: a subjective experience, physical changes, and cognitive appraisals. There are three main theories of emotion that differ in their emphasis on these components (see Table 10.1).

Table 10.1 THEORIES OF EMOTION

Theory of Emotion	Process of Experiencing Emotion
James Lange	Specific patterns of physical changes give rise to the perception of associated emotions.
Cannon-Bard	Processed in subcortical pathways resulting in two experiences: emotion and physical reaction.
Two-factor	Situation evokes physiological response (arousal) and a cognitive interpretation (emotion label).

The subjective nature of emotions is illustrated by the difficulty in verbally describing them. You know you are having an emotion because you feel it; however, the intensity of the reaction varies. The physiological changes associated with emotion are exemplified by the facial feedback hypothesis, the idea that facially mimicking an emotion will activate the associated emotion. Actors portraying emotions experience similar physiological changes (heart rate, skin temperature) as individuals experiencing the emotion. There also is a cognitive component or labeling of emotion from environmental information. The importance of this process is seen when one actually mislabels or misattributes arousal. Excitation transfer is an example of misattribution in which the arousal from one event is transferred to a new stimulus. The authors give some useful advice in that one should take a date to an arousing movie so that those feelings of arousal might be misattributed to positive emotions about you! Individuals use a variety of emotion regulation processes every day. Humor and distraction are two excellent techniques for regulating negative affect.

What Is the Neurophysiological Basis of Emotion?

Recent advances in behavioral neuroscience have substantially improved our understanding of emotions. It has long been known that emotions are associated with activation in the autonomic nervous system. However, it is now clear that there is tremendous overlap in autonomic activity among the various emotions. James Papez and Paul MacLean contributed much understanding of emotion in their research on the limbic system, a term used for the neural circuit involved in emotional processing. Ironically, two areas they did not deem important—the amygdala and the orbitofrontal cortex—have been found to be highly involved with emotion. The amygdala has been associated with fear conditioning and perception of social stimuli, particularly fearful faces. The orbitofrontal cortex is also involved in the processing of emotional cues, especially those related to interpersonal interactions. It also has been shown that there is a cerebral asymmetry in emotional activation. It appears that right hemisphere activity is associated with negative affect and left hemisphere activity is associated with positive affect.

How Do People Cope with Stress?

The next section of the chapter deals with stress and the emotional/behavioral responses of coping. Hans Selye formulated the general adaptation syndrome (GAS) to describe the stages of physiological coping with stress. He identified a consistent pattern of responding in the alarm stage, resistance stage, and exhaustion stage. Other investigators focused on the particular stressors, or environmental events, that lead to stress and coping. These have been divided into the categories of major life stressors and daily hassles. The field of psychoneuroimmunology has advanced our understanding of how psychological factors can compromise our immune system. Personality traits (such as hostility) have been found to influence the perception of stress. A number of styles for coping with stress have been articulated, including emotion-focused coping, problem-focused coping, and positive reappraisals. One of the most important variables in coping is the use of social support. This seems to help people experience less stress overall as well as lessen the negative effects of the stress that occur (the buffering hypothesis).

What Behaviors Affect Health?

The final section of the chapter addresses behaviors that affect physical health. One highly relevant topic in American society is obesity, which results from genetic predisposition and overeating. The conflict between scientific data on eating and societal views is seen with the stigma of obesity. In addition, extreme standards of thinness that are presented in the media are difficult, if not impossible, for most people to obtain. This can lead to the dangerous and mostly futile behavior of dieting. Fewer than 1 percent of individuals who lose weight are able to maintain their weight loss over five years. Part of this is attributable to the body's tendency to maintain a set-point as a natural defense against weight loss. In addition, chronic dieters or restrained eaters tend to easily abandon their diets and go on bouts of overeating. Chronic dieting and incorporation of unrealistic societal messages can lead to the eating disorders of anorexia nervosa, bulimia nervosa, and binge eating disorder. Smoking and lack of exercise are other common societal ills.

FILL-IN-THE-BLANK QUESTIONS

1. _____ refers to feelings that involve subjective evaluation, physiological processes, and cognitive beliefs.

2. _____ is a pattern of behavioral and physiological responses to events that match or exceed an organism's abilities.

3. _____ is the field of psychological science concerned with the events that impact physical well-being.

4. _____ is a negative emotional state associated with anxiety, tension, and agitation.

5. _____ is a naturally occurring emotional state that usually occurs following social events such as violations of cultural norms, loss of physical poise, teasing, and self-image threats.

6. _____ are a category of disorders such as depression or panic disorder in which individuals experience such strong emotions they can become immobilized.

7. _____ emotions include anger, fear, sadness, disgust, and happiness.

8. _____ emotions include remorse, guilt, submission, and anticipation and are blends of primary emotions.

9. _____ is a term used when an emotion label is derived from the wrong source.

10. _____ is the way in which one thinks about an event.

11. _____ is a simple method of regulating negative emotions that results in an improved immune system and the release of hormones, catecholamines, and endorphins.

12. _____ is a mistaken method of emotion regulation in which individuals attempt not to respond or feel the emotion at all.

13. _____ is a mistaken method of emotion regulation in which individuals think about, elaborate, and focus on the undesired thoughts or feelings, which prolongs the mood.

14. According to Zajonc, _____ emotions occur from cooling the brain.

15. The _____ system was MacLean's term for the extended neural circuit of emotion.

16. _____ syndrome is the term following removal of the amygdala in which animals display hypersexuality and fearless behavior.

17. The _____ hemisphere of the brain is more involved with the interpretation and comprehension of emotional material.

18. A _____ is an environmental event or stimulus that threatens an organism.

19. A _____ response is made by an organism to avoid, escape from, or minimize an aversive stimulus.

20. The _____ response describes the physiological preparation of animals to deal with any attack.

21. The _____ stage of GAS is when an emergency reaction prepares the body to fight or flee.

22. The _____ stage of GAS is when the defenses are prepared for a longer, sustained attack against the stressor.

23. The _____ stage of GAS is when a variety of physiological and immune systems fail.

24. The _____ behavior pattern is characterized by relaxed, noncompetitive, easygoing, and accommodating behavior.

25. The _____ is the body's mechanism for dealing with invading microorganisms, such as allergens, bacteria, and viruses.

26. The field of _____ studies the response of the body's immune system to psychological variables.

27. Coping that occurs before the onset of a future stressor is called _____ coping.

28. _____ is a type of coping that involves taking direct steps to solve a problem.

29. _____ is a cognitive process in which people focus on possible good things in their current situation.

30. _____ refers to having other people who can provide help, encouragement, and advice.

31. Chronic dieters who are prone to excessive eating in certain situations are known as _____.

32. Individuals with _____ have an excessive fear of becoming fat, and as a result they refuse to eat.

33. Individuals with _____ alternate between dieting and binge eating.

MULTIPLE-CHOICE QUESTIONS

1. Jon is on his first date with a woman he really likes. She is being polite, but he wonders how she actually feels about him. Based on research on nonverbal displays of emotion, Jon should look at her _____ for clues about her inner states, moods, and needs.
   a. eyebrows
   b. eyes
   c. cheek muscles
   d. mouth

2. Which of the following basic emotions is most easily recognized in facial expressions across cultures?
   a. Happiness.
   b. Sadness.
   c. Fear.
   d. Disgust.

3. Jean-Claude is at the movies with his girlfriend. Because he lost a bet, they are watching a love story. When the heroine dies at the end of the movie, Jean-Claude feels tears rush to the corners of his eyes. He tries to look away and subtly wipe his eyes because crying would violate the _____ in his culture for how emotions are exhibited by tough guys.
   a. affective standards
   b. mood guidelines
   c. display rules
   d. feelings norms

4. Portia is at the mall when she is asked to evaluate a new soft drink, a combination of vanilla, cherry, and cola. Portia is fairly neutral about the beverage, but she gives it a positive evaluation because she is in a good mood and it is nice to be out of the house. This behavior, in which individuals use their current emotional state to make judgments and appraisals, is predicted by the _____.
   a. affect-as-information theory
   b. somatic marker hypothesis
   c. emotional heuristic theory
   d. affective information guide

5. Which of the following negative emotions is most highly influenced by the social environment?
   a. Fear.
   b. Disgust.
   c. Anger.
   d. Guilt.

6. Which of the following is *not* one of the components of emotion?
   a. Language.
   b. Subjective experience.
   c. Physical changes.
   d. Cognitive appraisal.

7. Leonard was in a car accident and suffered damage to his prefrontal cortex. Suddenly he seemed detached from his problems, and his relationships and job have fallen apart because he does not experience the subjective component of emotions. Leonard most likely suffers from _____.
   a. antisocial personality disorder
   b. affective constriction
   c. alexithymia
   d. asocial traits

8. Excitement is an affective state that can be described by its valence (high pleasantness) as well as its activation (high arousal). This description in which two basic factors of emotion are arranged in a circle around intersections of the core dimensions of affect is an example of a(n) _____.
   a. alexithymic report
   b. circumplex model
   c. phenomenological taxonomy
   d. dysthymic description

9. Augustus is a gloomy, pessimistic individual. He always sees the glass as half empty and generally exhibits an unpleasant affect. Relative to others, Augustus probably shows an increase in which of the following neurotransmitters related to these negative activation states?
   a. Dopamine.
   b. Norepinephrine.
   c. Acetylcholine.
   d. GABA.

10. While Sara was on safari in Africa, the Land Rover in which she was riding was charged by a lion. Before she could even think that she was safe in the car, her heart began pounding and her brain received specific physiological feedback from her body, so she automatically knew she was experiencing fear! This experience supports the _____ theory of emotion.
    a. James-Lange
    b. Cannon-Bard
    c. two-factor
    d. opponent-process

11. Wes was in a really bad mood because he got fired from his job, and he had been frowning all day. That evening his friends were attempting to cheer him up. Finally one friend suggested that if he smiled, the change in his facial expression would produce a corresponding change in his mood. This process the friend suggested is based on which of the following?
    a. The opponent-process theory.
    b. The facial feedback hypothesis.
    c. The emoticon-activation hypothesis.
    d. Two-factor theory.

12. Lenny is at a local comedy club. The comedian is making some cruel jokes about people in a recent tragedy. Lenny is unsure how he feels about this, but everyone around him is laughing hysterically. Because of this environmental influence, he finds the comedian uproariously funny also. Lenny's reaction is best predicted by which theory of emotion?
    a. James-Lange.
    b. Cannon-Bard.
    c. Two-factor.
    d. State-trait.

13. Corey is pumping iron at the gym and really gets her heart rate up. Afterward she is cooling down and doesn't even realize that she is still aroused. Just then she bumps into a guy and notices that she is attracted to

him. Which of the following processes explains why she is highly attracted to this guy she does not even know?
a. State-trait.
b. Adaptation level theory.
c. Excitation transfer.
d. Opponent-process.

14. Klaus is a juror in a high-profile murder case. At one point the defense lawyer states that the victim was a prostitute who was once convicted for spousal abuse. In response to the prosecutor's objections, the judge had this comment stricken from the record and ordered the jurors to ignore it. Despite his best efforts, this is all Klaus can think about for the rest of the day. This common failure of thought suppression is known as the
a. rebound effect.
b. rumination tendency.
c. response modulator.
d. attentional deployment failure.

15. Courtney's roommates are worried about her. She was crushed by the revelation that her boyfriend was cheating on her. She has been miserable and unable to eat or attend classes. Courtney's roommates should recommend which of the following techniques to help her regulate her mood?
a. Thought suppression.
b. Distraction.
c. Rumination.
d. Rebound effect.

16. Several people in the dorms are playing charades. They are showing high levels of arousal acting out the emotions as evidenced by increased heart rate and pupil dilation. Although they may have some differential patterns of responding for the various emotions, there is tremendous overlap in terms of the activity of their
a. parasympathetic nervous system.
b. limbic nervous system.
c. somatic nervous system.
d. autonomic nervous system.

17. According to the textbook, what are the overall findings regarding the use of the polygraph as a lie detector test?
a. It has been found reliable in both criminal and employment situations.
b. It has been found useful to detect lies in employment situations, but it is not allowed in criminal investigations.
c. It has been found useful in detecting lies in criminal investigations, but it has not been found as accurate in detecting lies given during employment interviews.
d. It has not been found to be a reliable lie detector.

18. Niles, a local psychologist, is diagnosed as having brain damage, but he still is performing psychotherapy. However, he can no longer recognize when his clients are experiencing fear or highly intense emotions. Which of the following brain structures is most likely damaged?
a. Amygdala.
b. Hypothalamus.
c. Hippocampus.
d. Medulla.

19. Kathi is watching a television special about puppies and kittens. She thinks they are adorable and feels happy when she watches them. Based on studies of cerebral asymmetry, we would expect an increase in activation in which of the following cortical brain areas?
a. Right prefrontal.
b. Left hemisphere.
c. Anterior parietal.
d. Amygdala.

20. Mike is driving along the interstate when a huge 18-wheeler truck drifts into his lane right in front of him. His heart begins to pound and his blood pressure escalates as he swerves to avoid the truck. At this point Mike is in which stage of the general adaptation syndrome?
a. Alarm.
b. Reactive.
c. Resistance.
d. Exhaustion.

21. Monica is on her way to class when traffic is slowed by an accident. She is already late for class when she finds there are no parking spaces near her building. When she finally arrives at class and gets an annoyed stare from her professor, she finds she has no pen to write with. These stressors that are part of day-to-day irritations are known as
a. major life stressors.
b. daily hassles.
c. eustress.
d. petit stressors.

22. Lori is a busy person, and she always speed-walks through campus, never stopping to talk to people. When she does stop to talk, she speaks rapidly and interrupts the other person constantly. She also is frustrated and hostile, especially when waiting in line or competing with other students. Lori can best be described as having which type of personality?
a. Type A.
b. Type B.
c. Type C.
d. Hardy.

23. Which of the following is *not* one of the types of lymphocytes?
    a. B cells.
    b. C cells.
    c. T cells.
    d. Natural killer cells.

24. Xavier has four exams and a paper due in the next week. He also has an athletic event and a party that he should attend. He constructs a schedule that will allow him to get his work done as well as meet his social obligations. This evaluation of response options and potential coping behaviors is an example of
    a. primary appraisals.
    b. secondary appraisals.
    c. emotion-focused behaviors.
    d. positive reappraisals.

25. Raoul is trying to get a class he needs to graduate next December, and he just found out that it won't be offered until next spring. Although he is upset, he realizes that there is nothing he can do about it and that the situation is out of his control. So he just gripes about it to his friends, who comfort him and tell him they will all have a good time next year anyhow. What course of action is Raoul taking to deal with his stress?
    a. Thought suppression.
    b. Anticipatory coping.
    c. Problem-focused coping.
    d. Emotion-focused coping.

26. Melinda was upset about the grade she received in her psychology course. The combination of exams and papers resulted in an 89.6 percent average. However, her professor refused to round this number up and gave her a B rather than an A. She was whining about the unfairness of it all when a student came by crying because she had flunked out of school. Oh well, she thought, at least I am not in that situation! This is an example of the positive reappraisal process of
    a. downward comparisons.
    b. creation of positive events.
    c. Pollyanna thinking.
    d. delusional thinking.

27. Meg, a hard-working CEO, is committed to her work and family. She enjoys the challenges she experiences in her job and in her personal life. She has a sense of being in control of her life and of her destiny. Overall, she doesn't experience much stress despite her busy life. Meg is high in the personality characteristic of
    a. realistic pessimism.
    b. neuroticism.
    c. hardiness.
    d. extraversion.

28. Alex is having a tough time at home with his wife and children. He comes into work every day and shares many of these interactions with his colleagues, who offer sympathy, advice, and support. The fact that this social support actually lessens the negative effects of stress is an example of the
    a. resilience phenomenon.
    b. buffering hypothesis.
    c. familial intervention theory.
    d. dampening phenomenon.

29. Albert's physician is concerned about Albert's weight. He wonders whether Albert would qualify as obese so that he might receive insurance reimbursement for his treatment. His physician computes a ratio of Albert's body weight to his height in a measure known as the
    a. actuarial cutoff technique.
    b. body mass index.
    c. weight-density indicator.
    d. scale of morbid obesity.

30. Which of the following eating disorders is the most potentially deadly?
    a. Anorexia nervosa.
    b. Bulimia nervosa.
    c. Bulimarexia.
    d. Binge eating disorder.

31. Larry is an adolescent who desperately wants to fit in with the crowd. He takes up smoking because he incorrectly believes that this behavior is common among his peer group. This overestimation of the number of adolescent and adult smokers is known as the
    a. false-consensus effect.
    b. multiple-hit phenomenon.
    c. reward gradient effect.
    d. partial reinforcement extinction effect.

MATCHING QUESTIONS

Fill in the letter from Column B corresponding to the term that is most associated with the description presented in Column A.

Column A	Column B
____ 1. Feelings that are immediate responses to environmental events.	A. Charles Darwin
	B. Blushing
____ 2. Diffuse and long-lasting emotional state.	C. Negative emotion
____ 3. *Expression of Emotion in Man and Animals.*	D. James-Lange
	E. Daily hassles
____ 4. Govern how and when emotions are exhibited.	F. Fight-or-flight
	G. Primary appraisal

____ 5. Gut feeling.

____ 6. Turning red as a nonverbal apology for interpersonal errors.

____ 7. A sign of passion and commitment to the relationship when faced with a rival.

____ 8. Theory that emotion is the result of perceiving specific patterns of bodily responses.

____ 9. Theory of emotion that posits that information from an emotion-producing stimulus is processed subcortically.

____ 10. Theory of emotion that proposes a situation evokes both a physiological response and a cognitive interpretation, or emotion label.

____ 11. Results from warming the brain.

____ 12. Electronic instrument that assesses body's physiological response to questions.

____ 13. Physiological preparation of animals to deal with any attack.

____ 14. Females respond to stress by protecting and caring for offspring and forming social alliances.

____ 15. Consistent pattern of responses to stress: alarm, resistance, exhaustion.

____ 16. Changes that strain central areas of people's lives.

____ 17. Day-to-day irritations and annoyances.

____ 18. Specialized white blood cells that make up the immune system.

____ 19. Protein molecules that attach themselves to foreign agents and mark them for destruction.

____ 20. Decide whether a stimulus is stressful, benign, or irrelevant.

H. Cannon-Bard
I. Two-factor
J. Affect
K. Mood
L. Polygraph
M. General adaptation syndrome
N. Antibodies
O. Major life stressors
P. Lymphocytes
Q. Tend-and befriend
R. Display rules
S. Jealousy
T. Somatic marker

THOUGHT QUESTIONS

1. Many college students report that their lives are very stressful, and they predict that they are much more stressed than were their grandparents. With the many time-saving devices invented in the last two generations, what factors might account for this increase in perceived stress?

2. Imagine that you have a good friend that you believe is suffering from an eating disorder, yet that friend denies it. How would you determine whether it was time for that friend to seek help? If the friend refused to go for help, what would you do?

APPLICATIONS

An Activity to Demonstrate the Universality of Basic Emotions

Your textbook cites the research that the six basic emotions (anger, disgust, fear, joy, sadness, and surprise) are recognized in virtually all cultures. A simple activity will demonstrate the innate nature of these feelings. Get a group of three friends to play "Emotion Charades." The rest of the group can observe. Write each of the basic emotions on an index card and show it to the three "actors." Have the actors think about and silently portray these emotions. See who in the group can recognize the emotion first. Have the three actors hold their expression of emotion and look for similarities in their facial features. Be sure to alternate actors and observers. Try to identify the characteristics for each emotion (e.g., disgust is wrinkled nose, anger is furrowed brow). A digital camera is also excellent for capturing the similarities in these expressions.

Along with the basic emotions, try to portray the complex emotions. Also talk about gender and cultural differences in display rules.

Research on the Societal Causes of Eating Disorders

Most students have heard a bit about the causes of eating disorders. They actually are a complex disorder that is intertwined with one's sense of self, one's community, and one's family. Anorexia nervosa is quite difficult to treat and is potentially lethal. There are a number of potential causes including cognitive deficiencies and ego disturbances, cultural and power factors, perceptual problems, and family issues in communication. It is simplistic to just say it is the way the media and society put pressure on women to be thin.

However, three recent research findings demonstrate just how strong and potentially toxic those messages can be. Studies done by the authors of the study guide (BB, EAS), found that middle school students who had more media exposure (e.g., television, magazines) endorsed more characteristics of restrained eating. Another study found that simply watching 30 seconds of a dieting commercial substantially (negatively) altered women's views toward themselves. Finally, the island of Fiji was one of the last areas of the world to get satellite television. Your textbook identifies this area as one of the places that continues to value a larger body shape. However, within six months of receiving satellite television (much of it American) there were reports of symptoms of restrained eating and subclinical eating disorders.

Obviously this is a small and selective sample of research. But the evidence is beginning to mount that exposure to our popular culture can encourage the development of eating disorders.

WEB SITES

Stress Management

http://ub-counseling.buffalo.edu/stressmanagement.shtml
http://cehs.unl.edu/stress

Health Psychology

www.health-psych.org

Stop Smoking

www.cancer.org/docroot/PED/ped_10.asp

Eating Disorders

www.anad.org
www.something-fishy.org
www.sjmcmd.org/eatingdisorders

ANSWER KEY

Fill-in-the-Blank Questions

1. Emotion
2. Stress
3. Health psychology
4. Guilt
5. Embarrassment
6. Mood disorders
7. Primary
8. Secondary
9. Misattribution of arousal
10. Cognitive framing
11. Humor
12. Thought suppression
13. Rumination
14. Positive
15. Limbic
16. Kluver-Bucy
17. Right
18. Stressor
19. Coping
20. Fight-or-flight
21. Alarm
22. Resistance
23. Exhaustion
24. Type B
25. Immune system
26. Psychneuroimmunology
27. Anticipatory
28. Problem-focused coping
29. Positive reappraisal
30. Social support
31. Restrained eaters
32. Anorexia nervosa
33. Bulimia nervosa

Multiple-Choice Questions

1. d The lower part of the face is more important in communicating emotion.

   Incorrect answers:
   a. The lower part of the face is more important in communicating emotion.
   b. The lower part of the face is more important in communicating emotion.
   c. The lower part of the face is more important in communicating emotion.

2. a Happiness was most clearly identified across cultures.

   Incorrect answers:
   b. Happiness was most clearly identified across cultures.
   c. Happiness was most clearly identified across cultures.
   d. Happiness was most clearly identified across cultures.

3. c Display rules govern how and when emotions are exhibited.

   Incorrect answers:
   a. Affective standards is a made-up term.
   b. Mood guidelines is a made-up term.
   d. Feelings norms is a made-up term.

4. a The affect-as-information theory posits that people use their current emotional state to make judgments and appraisals.

   Incorrect answers:
   b. The somatic marker hypothesis states that gut feelings influence self-regulatory actions and decisions.
   c. Emotional heuristic theory is a made-up term.
   d. Affective information guide is a made-up term.

5. d. Of the negative emotions, guilt is unique in being highly influenced by the social environment.

   Incorrect answers:
   a. Of the negative emotions, guilt is unique in being highly influenced by the social environment.
   b. Of the negative emotions, guilt is unique in being highly influenced by the social environment.
   c. Of the negative emotions, guilt is unique in being highly influenced by the social environment.

6. a. The components of emotion are subjective experience, physical changes, and cognitive appraisal.

   Incorrect answers:
   b. The components of emotion are subjective experience, physical changes, and cognitive appraisal.
   c. The components of emotion are subjective experience, physical changes, and cognitive appraisal.
   d. The components of emotion are subjective experience, physical changes, and cognitive appraisal.

7. c. Alexithymia is the disorder in which people do not experience the subjective component of emotions.

   Incorrect answers:
   a. Antisocial personality disorder is when individuals are unaffected by societal rules.
   b. Affective constriction is a made-up term.
   d. Asocial traits is a made-up term.

8. b. Circumplex model is the description in which two basic factors of emotion are arranged in a circle around intersections of the core dimensions of affect.

   Incorrect answers:
   a. Alexithymia is the disorder in which people do not experience the subjective component of emotions.
   c. Phenomenological taxonomy is a made-up term.
   d. Dysthymic description is a made-up term. Dysthymia is chronic mild symptoms of depression.

9. b. Negative activation states are associated with an increase in norepinephrine.

   Incorrect answers:
   a. Positive activation states are associated with an increase in dopamine.
   c. Negative activation states are associated with an increase in norepinephrine.
   d. Negative activation states are associated with an increase in norepinephrine.

10. a. The James-Lange theory states that felt emotion is the result of perceiving specific patterns of bodily responses.

    Incorrect answers:
    b. The Cannon-Bard theory asserts that emotion-producing stimuli from the environment elicit both an emotional and a physical reaction.
    c. The two-factor of emotion proposes that a situation evokes both a physiological response, such as arousal, and a cognitive interpretation.
    d. The opponent-process theory states that an affective state is followed by an equal and opposite affective state.

11. b. The facial feedback hypothesis states that if you mold the facial muscles to mimic an emotional state, you activate the associated emotion.

    Incorrect answers:
    a. The opponent-process theory states that an affective state is followed by an equal and opposite affective state.
    c. The emoticon-activation hypothesis is a made-up term.
    d. The two-factor of emotion proposes that a situation evokes both a physiological response, such as arousal, and a cognitive interpretation.

12. c. The two-factor of emotion proposes that a situation evokes both a physiological response, such as arousal, and a cognitive interpretation.

    Incorrect answers:
    a. The James-Lange theory states that felt emotion is the result of perceiving specific patterns of bodily responses.
    b. The Cannon-Bard theory asserts that emotion-producing stimuli from the environment elicit both an emotional and a physical reaction.
    d. State-trait refers to short-term and long-term nature of a variable.

13. c. Excitation transfer is a form of misattribution in which residual physiological arousal caused by one event is transferred to a new stimulus.

    Incorrect answers:
    a. State-trait refers to short-term and long-term nature of a variable.
    b. Adaptation level theory is a made-up term.
    d. The opponent-process theory states that an affective state is followed by an equal and opposite affective state.

14. a. The rebound effect is when people think more about something after thought suppression than before.

Incorrect answers:
   b. Rumination is thinking about, elaborating, and focusing on undesired thoughts or feelings, which prolongs the negative mood.
   c. Response modulator is a made-up term.
   d. Attentional deployment failure is a made-up term.

15. b. Distraction is the best way to avoid the problems of suppression or rumination.

   Incorrect answers:
   a. Thought suppression often leads to a rebound effect.
   c. The opponent-process theory states that an affective state is followed by an equal and opposite affective state.
   d. The rebound effect is when people think more about something after thought suppression than before.

16. d. Emotions tend to overlap in their pattern of autonomic nervous system activity.

   Incorrect answers:
   a. The parasympathetic nervous system is responsible for relaxing us after sympathetic activation.
   b. The limbic system is a collection of structures in the midbrain.
   c. The somatic nervous system is responsible for motor movement.

17. d. The polygraph has not been found to be a reliable lie detector.

   Incorrect answers:
   a. The polygraph has not been found to be a reliable lie detector.
   b. The polygraph has not been found to be a reliable lie detector.
   c. The polygraph has not been found to be a reliable lie detector.

18. a. The amygdala is involved with the recognition of fearful faces and intense emotions.

   Incorrect answers:
   b. The hypothalamus controls eating, drinking, and motivated behavior.
   c. The hippocampus is involved with emotional memory.
   d. The medulla is involved with breathing and heartbeat.

19. b. Greater activation of the left hemisphere is associated with positive affect.

   Incorrect answers:
   a. Great activation of the right prefrontal cortex is associated with negative affect.

   c. Greater activation of the left hemisphere is associated with positive affect.
   d. The amygdala is involved with the recognition of fearful faces and intense emotions.

20. a. In the alarm stage, an emergency reaction prepares the body to fight or flee.

   Incorrect answers:
   b. Reactive is not a stage of the general adaptation syndrome.
   c. During the resistance stage, the defenses are prepared for a longer, sustained attack against the stressor.
   d. In the exhaustion stage, a variety of physiological and immune systems fail.

21. b. Daily hassles are small, day-to-day irritations and annoyances.

   Incorrect answers:
   a. Major life stressors are changes or disruptions that strain central areas of people's lives.
   c. Eustress is a term for beneficial amounts of stress.
   d. Petit stressors is a made-up term.

22. a. The Type A behavior patterns describes competitive, achievement-oriented, aggressive, hostile, time-pressed, impatient, and confrontational people.

   Incorrect answers:
   b. The Type B behavior pattern describes a relaxed, noncompetitive, easygoing, accommodating person.
   c. There is no Type C personality.
   d. Hardiness is a personality trait that enables people to perceive stressors as controllable challenges.

23. b. The three types of lymphocytes are B cells, T cells, and natural killer cells.

   Incorrect answers:
   a. The three types of lymphocytes are B cells, T cells, and natural killer cells.
   c. The three types of lymphocytes are B cells, T cells, and natural killer cells.
   d. The three types of lymphocytes are B cells, T cells, and natural killer cells.

24. b. If the stimulus is deemed stressful, people use secondary appraisals to evaluate response options and choose coping behaviors.

   Incorrect answers:
   a. People use primary appraisals to decide whether the stimulus is stressful, benign, or irrelevant.
   c. Emotion-focused coping involves trying to prevent having an emotional response to a stressor.

d. Positive reappraisals are a cognitive process in which people try to perceive positive things in their current situation.

25. d. Emotion-focused coping involves trying to prevent having an emotional response to a stressor.

   Incorrect answers:
   a. Thought suppression involves purposefully not thinking about an event.
   b. Anticipatory coping occurs before the onset of a future stressor.
   c. Problem-focused coping involves taking direct steps to solve the problem.

26. a. Downward comparison is the positive reappraisal process when people compare themselves to those who are worse off.

   Incorrect answers:
   b. Creation of positive events is the positive reappraisal process of infusing ordinary events with positive meaning.
   c. Pollyanna thinking is a made-up term.
   d. Delusional thinking is characterized by false beliefs that are inconsistent with reality.

27. c. Hardiness is a personality trait that enables people to perceive stressors as controllable challenges.

   Incorrect answers:
   a. Realistic pessimism is a made-up term.
   b. Neuroticism is a personality trait that includes anxiousness, worry, and poor coping with environmental stressors.
   d. Extraversion is a personality trait that includes sociability, assertiveness, and attention to the environment.

28. b. The buffering hypothesis is the idea that other people can provide direct support in helping individuals cope with stressful events.

   Incorrect answers:
   a. Resilience phenomenon is a made-up term.
   c. Familial intervention theory is a made up term.
   d. Dampening phenomenon is a made-up term.

29. b. The body mass index is a ratio of body weight to height used to measure obesity.

   Incorrect answers:
   a. Actuarial cutoff technique is a made-up term.
   c. Weight-density indicator is a made-up term.
   d. Scale of morbid obesity is a made-up term.

30. a. Anorexia nervosa has a mortality rate of 15 to 20 percent.

Incorrect answers:
b. Although bulimia nervosa is associated with serious health problems, it is seldom fatal.
c. Bulimarexia is an older term for a combination of anorexia nervosa and bulimia nervosa. Anorexia nervosa has a mortality rate of 15 to 20 percent.
d. Anorexia nervosa has a mortality rate of 15 to 20 percent.

31. a. The overestimation of the number of adolescent and adult smokers is known as the false consensus effect.

Incorrect answers:
b. Multiple-hit phenomenon is a made-up term.
c. Reward gradient relates to the idea that we respond to short-term reinforcers (even those that are harmful) more than long-term reinforcers.
d. The partial reinforcement extinction effect is that partial reinforcement is more persistent and resistant to extinction than continuous reinforcement.

Matching Questions

1. J   Affect
2. K   Mood
3. A   Charles Darwin
4. R   Display rules
5. T   Somatic marker
6. B   Blushing
7. S   Jealousy
8. D   James-Lange
9. H   Cannon-Bard
10. I   Two-factor
11. C   Negative emotion
12. L   Polygraph
13. F   Fight-or-flight
14. Q   Tend-and-befriend
15. M   General adaptation syndrome
16. O   Major life stressors
17. E   Daily hassles
18. P   Lymphocytes
19. N   Antibodies
20. G   Primary appraisal

Thought Questions

1. Answers will vary, but most students will identify that their stressors are different from those of their grandparents. Interestingly, they believe that earlier stressors of day-to-day survival were easier than those of a fast-paced society and increased expectations. Of course, you can point out that multitasking and personal expectations are self-inflicted stressors. It also seems we are

bombarded with news from around the world, most of which is negative. Students need to realize that this is not an accurate portrayal of daily life for most of the world. Finally, one should point out that much of the time we have saved with new inventions has been reinvested in entertainment. Ask yourself how much time you spend daily at the computer, cell phone, and television. One wonders if we have freely given away a more leisurely, stress-free lifestyle.

2. Answers will vary, but students should look at assessing the problem in a similar way that professionals do: What percentage of weight has been lost? How much does weight loss occupy the person's thoughts and activities? How much does it interfere with the person's life? What health symptoms are accompanying these behaviors? Students need to realize that eating disorders create serious health complications and that anorexia nervosa is potentially fatal. Secrecy and denial often are part of these behaviors; however, friends cannot sit back and let the behavior continue. Friends need to educate themselves by talking to a local professional (perhaps someone from the university counseling center) and/or visiting some of the Web sites we have recommended. In a caring way, you will need to let this person know of your concerns. This may be through individual appeals, family involvement, or group/friend intervention. Whatever the path, it is something that must be done. Get as much help as you can!

CHAPTER 11 | Human Development

GUIDE TO THE READING

This chapter focuses on how individuals change physiologically, cognitively, and socially with age. The authors address key questions about the nature of development. What are the roles of nature and nurture? To what degree is development hardwired, and to what degree is it influenced by the environment? How do both the physical and social environment shape who we are? The authors follow the course of development from the womb to old age. The discussion of infancy includes changes in neurology, the role of attachment, and perceptual processes. The authors then focus on the development of cognition, including Piaget's theory of cognitive development, more recent research modifying his theory, and the development of language. A discussion of social development in children and adolescent follows, emphasizing development of identity and moral development. The chapter ends with discussion of social and cognitive issues in adulthood.

What Shapes a Child?

Across the world, babies make their first social smile at about six weeks, sit up before they walk, and make eye contact with others shortly after birth. The tremendous consistency found for some skills in all healthy children suggests that genes control the speed and order of development. However, the role of genes is affected by environmental influences starting in the womb. Nature, the genes, and nurture, the environment, work together to form people.

In the womb, although genes govern prenatal development, the environment can influence the work of the genes. For example, teratogens—outside agents such as disease, drugs, or alcohol—cause abnormal prenatal development. At birth, healthy babies not only have many sensory abilities and reflexes, but also their brains continue to go through an enormous amount of growth. The authors describe two important aspects of early brain growth: the maturation of specific brain regions, and the continued development of communication between different brain areas. The environment continues to influence neurological development through infancy and childhood. Humans appear to have sensitive periods—times during which they more easily acquire specific skills such as language. Children exposed to an inadequate environment during this time will not appropriately develop the skill.

Social development is also influenced by nature and nurture. According to Bowlby, attachment, the strong connection between people, serves an adaptive function by keeping caregivers and babies in close proximity to each other and so helps keep the baby safe. Mary Ainsworth described different styles of attachment. It is believed that both the child's biology and the child's environment influence attachment.

How Do Children Learn about Their Worlds?

Babies first learn about the world through their perceptual systems. Researchers learned that babies prefer bold black and white patterns to gray ones, that adultlike acuity (distance vision) is not developed for about a year, and that babies see depth some time in the first six months. Babies' hearing has been studied in the womb!

To describe how children learn, Jean Piaget proposed one of the most important theories of cognitive development. He described four stages during which significant skills were developed: the sensorimotor stage, the preoperational stage, the concrete operational stage, and the formal operational stage. More recent researchers have addressed the limitations of Piaget's theory, finding, for example, that infants have more innate abilities than Piaget thought.

For humans more than for any other animal, language is a significant means through which to learn. The basic components of language, the course of language acquisition, and theories emphasizing biological and cultural bases for language acquisition are presented.

How Do Children and Adolescents Develop Their Identities?

Identity development—understanding who you are and what you want to be—is a significant component of social development. One important component of identity development involves gender. Individuals develop a gender identity, or how they think of themselves as male or female. Individuals also acquire gender roles, or the behaviors that differ between males and females. Gender schemas, our individual cognitive representations of male and female, profoundly influence gender identity. The authors emphasize the influences of interpersonal interactions, situations, culture, and biology on the development of gender identity.

The relative importance of peers and parents in the formation of identity garners much research. Judith Harris proposed that parents have little influence on their children's personality. Other researchers have been critical of this, showing that both peers and family exert lasting influences on children and adolescents.

The authors present two specific areas of identity development: moral development and race and ethnicity. Lawrence Kohlberg's stage theory of moral development, the research on moral emotions, and the biological basis of morality are presented. The authors describe some of the many variables that may influence the complicated process of racial and ethnic identity development.

What Brings Meaning to Adulthood?

People do not stop changing at age 20, but rather continue to develop. Gazzaniga and Heatherton first describe Erik Erikson's theory of adult development. They then describe the transitions that influence many adults: career, marriage, and children. The authors emphasize that many elderly people are productive and happy despite the inevitable biological changes. The section ends with a discussion of cognitive changes associated with aging. Mental processing speed generally slows, and short-term memory tasks become more difficult. However, people who remain mentally active may continue to increase their specific knowledge, or crystallized intelligence, throughout their lives.

FILL-IN–THE-BLANK QUESTIONS

1. _____ is concerned with age-related changes in physiology, cognition, and social behavior.

2. _____ refers to the maturation of skills and abilities that allow people to interact with others.

3. _____ and _____ work together to make people the way they are.

4. _____ is one of the most common teratogens, and causes low birth weight, face and head abnormalities, slight mental retardation, and behavioral and cognitive problems.

5. _____ is when the synaptic connections that are frequently used are preserved, and those that are not decay and disappear.

6. A _____ is a developmental stage during which young animals are able to acquire specific skills and knowledge.

7. _____ is a strong, intimate, emotional connection between people that persists over time and across circumstances.

8. Harry Harlow showed that _____ is *not* the basis for attachment.

9. A child who is not upset when his mother leaves him in a new environment and then ignores her when she returns is displaying _____ attachment.

10. The hormone _____ is related to social behaviors, including infant–caregiver attachment.

11. _____ refers to a person's typical mood, activity level, and emotional reactivity.

12. The _____ is the tendency of humans to pay more attention to novel stimuli.

13. A child who understands objects only by grasping or sucking them is in which of Piaget's stages? _____

14. _____ is the understanding that an object continues to exist even when it is hidden from view.

15. Seven-year-old Mary knows that a short fat glass and a tall thin one contain the same amount of water, but Mary cannot yet think abstractly. She is in which of Piaget's stages? _____

16. Modern research showed that object permanence occurs _____ than Piaget had thought.

17. Freud referred to the inability to remember events from early childhood as _____.

18. Not knowing where you learned something is called _____.

19. _____ is knowing that other people have mental states and using that knowledge to infer what another person is thinking or feeling.

20. Piaget labeled being unable to see from another person's point of view_____.

21. The word *cat* is an example of a/n _____.

22. _____ is the system of rules used to combine words into phrases and phrases into sentences.

23. _____ argued that language must be governed by "universal grammar."

24. The finding that children deprived of exposure to language early in development are unlikely to develop normal language indicates there may a _____ for language acquisition.

25. _____ teaches an association between letters and their sounds.

26. Your idea of yourself as male or female is your _____.

27. _____ are behaviors that differ between men and women because of cultural influences, expectation, or learning.

28. Kohlberg's _____ level are responses that center around complex reasoning about abstract principals and values.

29. Empathy, sympathy, guilt, and shame are all _____.

30. Damage to the _____ seems to be associated with problems with moral and social reasoning.

31. Studying how people develop over the entire course of life reflects a _____ perspective.

32. The brain condition which is a progressive deterioration of thinking, memory, and behavior is called _____.

33. _____ intelligence is the ability to process new general information that does not requires specific knowledge.

MULTIPLE-CHOICE QUESTIONS

1. Meagan was conceived one month ago. She is now in the stage in which the internal organs and the nervous system begin to form. She is a(n)
   a. fetus.
   b. embryo.
   c. critical period.
   d. scheme.

2. Harold's mother was very stressed while she was pregnant with him. This stress resulted in his having lower birth weight than he would have had otherwise. The influence Harold's mother's stress had on his development exemplifies the effects of
   a. genes.
   b. the cultural environment.
   c. the physical environment.
   d. the FAS environment.

3. Which of the following is *not* an agent that can cause abnormal development in the womb?
   a. Viruses.
   b. Bacteria.
   c. Drugs.
   d. Milk.

4. During infancy synaptic connections that are not used decay and disappear. This is termed:
   a. myelination.
   b. the rooting reflex.
   c. dendritic release.
   d. synaptic pruning.

5. Who popularized the importance of attachment serving to motivate infants and caregivers to stay in close contact?
   a. Konrad Lorenz.
   b. Mary Ainsworth.
   c. John Bowlby.
   d. Noam Chomsky.

6. Joey walked through a park shortly after some ducklings hatched. He was surprised when the ducklings followed him wherever he went. The ducklings were demonstrating
   a. imprinting.
   b. bonding.
   c. anxiety.
   d. orienting reflex.

7. In his experiment with infant rhesus monkeys, Harry Harlow found that the infants preferred a surrogate mother who
   a. made monkeylike noises.
   b. provided food.
   c. fought off threats.
   d. was soft.

8. Samuel, a 1-year-old, was happy playing in the doctor's office while his mother was nearby. When she had to step out for just a second he started to cry. His mother quickly came back, and he ran to her smiling. Samuel was probably displaying which style of attachment?
   a. Avoidant attachment.
   b. Secure attachment.
   c. Anxious attachment.
   d. Ambivalent attachment.

9. Baby Aretha is generally happy and easygoing. In contrast, baby Diane is often fussy and hard to calm. These babies clearly have different
   a. temperaments.
   b. parents.
   c. attachment objects.
   d. learning histories.

10. According to the text, what may be concluded about whether divorce harms children?
    a. Children always do better if their parents stay together.
    b. There are no negative effects associated with divorce.
    c. There is nothing more harmful to a child's emotional well-being than divorce.
    d. Parental conflict may produce more negative outcomes than divorce.

11. Based on the research on babies' vision, which of the following is a three-month-old most likely to look at?
    a. A complex design in shades of gray.
    b. Bold black and white patterns.
    c. A picture across the room rather than a pattern that is closer.
    d. A picture painted with pale pastel colors.

12. A group of fetuses was read the *The Cat in the Hat*. After birth the babies altered their sucking to turn on tapes playing *The Cat in the Hat*. This research indicates that
    a. babies can understand simple books even before they are born.
    b. babies' sensory systems are completely developed before birth.
    c. babies can hear before birth and have some memory of what they heard.
    d. babies are as competent as older children in recognizing stories.

13. Which of the following is *not* one of Piaget's stages of development?
    a. Concrete operational.
    b. Sensorimotor.
    c. Preoperational.
    d. Sensory operational.

14. After Jenny's brother hides her bear under a blanket, Jenny does not seem to know the bear still exists. Jenny has not yet acquired what?
    a. Theory of mind.
    b. Object permanence.
    c. Accommodation.
    d. Orienting reflex.

15. Five-year-old Jared is upset when his sister gets a tall thin glass of juice when he gets a short wide one. Jared's mom tries to explain there is the same amount of juice in both cups, but Jared does not believe her. Jared is probably in which of Piaget's stages?
    a. Preoperational.
    b. Concrete operational.
    c. Formal operational.
    d. Postformal operational.

16. If a child thinks a tall thin glass has more juice than a short wide glass when both in fact have the same amount, the child is having problems with
    a. object permanence.
    b. conservation.
    c. abstract thinking.
    d. dialectic thinking.

17. Further research into the mental capacities of young children showed that Piaget
    a. overestimated children's abilities.
    b. was correct in his theories.
    c. underestimated children's abilities.
    d. did not describe conservation.

18. Carl went into the hospital when he was 2 years old for an operation. He has no memory of this, probably reflecting
    a. preoperational thought.
    b. learning amnesia.
    c. infantile amnesia.
    d. repression.

19. Three-year-old Stephie was told by her brother that she could watch TV. When Stephie's dad saw her watching TV, and he asked her who said she could watch, Stephie could not remember. Her forgetting is an example of
    a. source amnesia.
    b. infantile amnesia.
    c. repression.
    d. short-term memory dysfunction.

20. When talking on the phone with his grandpa, 3-year-old Ben nodded when asked if his mom was at home. Ben did not realize that his grandpa could not see him. According to Piaget, Ben is reflecting
    a. a fully developed theory of mind.
    b. formal thought.
    c. conservation.
    d. egocentrism.

21. The sound of the "R" in the word *rat* is called a
    a. morpheme.
    b. syntax.
    c. pragmatic.
    d. phoneme.

22. "Eat soup. All gone." would be an example of
    a. a theory named for Roger Brown.
    b. ASL.
    c. teratogenic speech.
    d. telegraphic speech.

23. Who argued that language must be governed by "universal grammar"?
    a. Lev Vygotsky.
    b. Noam Chomsky.
    c. Nim Chimpsky.
    d. Roger Brown.

24. Who developed the first major theory that emphasized the role of social and cultural context in cognition and language development?
    a. Lev Vygotsky.
    b. Noam Chomsky.
    c. Laura Ann Petitto.
    d. Roger Brown.

25. Robin, a deaf child, was born to deaf parents who used American Sign Language to communicate with each other and with Robin. Based on the research, Robin will acquire language
    a. faster than hearing children of hearing parents.
    b. slower than hearing children of hearing parents.
    c. at a rate identical to hearing children of hearing parents.
    d. in a manner totally different from children who can hear.

26. Ms. Smith teaches her students to read by focusing on meaning and understanding of how words are connected in sentences. She is using which approach to teaching reading?
    a. Schema.
    b. Whole language.
    c. Syntax.
    d. Phonics.

27. Whether people think of themselves as male or female reflects their
    a. gender.
    b. gender role.
    c. gender schema.
    d. gender identity.

28. What are the cognitive structures that influence how people perceive the behaviors of females and males?
    a. Gender.
    b. Gender role.
    c. Gender schema.
    d. Gender identity.

29. Adolescents often question who they are because of three changes. Which of the following is *not* one of them?
    a. Heightened pressure to prepare for the future and to make career choices.
    b. Addressing the conflict of generativity versus stagnation.
    c. Changing physical appearance.
    d. More sophisticated cognitive abilities.

30. Who tested moral reasoning skills in children?
    a. Judith Harris.
    b. Lev Vygotsky.
    c. Erik Erikson.
    d. Lawrence Kohlberg.

31. If asked whether it was wrong for a man to steal a drug to save his dying wife, a child who responded "He shouldn't steal the drug because it is wrong to steal, so everyone will think he is a bad person" is at which moral level?
    a. Conventional.
    b. Preconventional.
    c. Social disapproval.
    d. Postconventional.

32. When asked to sort pictures of people, 5-year-old Sally puts all the pictures of Asian people in one pile and all the pictures of Caucasian people in another pile. Three-year-old Matt cannot do this: He does not see the difference between Asians and Caucasians. What may we conclude from this?
    a. Matt is unable to form ethnic categories.
    b. Matt is concrete operational.
    c. Sally has stereotypes based on race.
    d. Sally has a clear ethnic identity.

33. Who proposed a theory of development that emphasizes age-related psychological processing and their effects on social functioning across the life span?
    a. Sigmund Freud.
    b. Lev Vygotsky.
    c. Erik Erikson.
    d. Lawrence Kohlberg.

34. Yolanda, aged 84, spends most of her time taking care of her flowers and talking with her two best friends. She avoids going places or seeing people she does not like. Yolanda's behavior supports Carstensen's ideas on
    a. socioemotional selectivity theory.
    b. identity versus role confusion.
    c. postformal thought.
    d. dementia.

MATCHING QUESTIONS

Fill in the letter from Column B corresponding to the term that is most associated with the description presented in Column A.

Column A

____ 1. The study of changes in physiology, cognition, and social behavior over the life span.

____ 2. The maturation of skills or abilities that enable people to live in the world with other people.

____ 3. Personal beliefs about whether one is male or female.

____ 4. The second stage in Piaget's theory of cognitive development, when children think symbolically about objects, but reason is based on appearance rather than logic.

____ 5. The time in which certain experiences must occur for normal brain development.

____ 6. When a person remembers an event but cannot remember where they encountered the information.

____ 7. The process by which a schema is adapted to incorporate a new experience that does not easily fit into an existing schema.

____ 8. The tendency of children to speak using rudimentary sentences that are missing words and grammatical markings but do follow a logical syntax.

____ 9. A strong emotional bond that persists over time and across circumstances.

____ 10. Environmental agents that harm the embryo or fetus.

____ 11. The behaviors associated with men and women because of cultural influence or learning.

Column B

A. Source amnesia
B. Gender schemas
C. Teratogens
D. Gender identity
E. Object permanence
F. Gender
G. Gender roles
H. Developmental psychology
I. Attachment
J. Sensorimotor stage
K. Critical period
L. Theory of mind
M. Schemas
N. Accommodation
O. Social development
P. Orienting reflex
Q. Telegraphic speech
R. Synaptic pruning
S. Preoperational stage
T. Infantile amnesia

____ 12. Hypothetical cognitive structures that help us perceive, organize, process, and use information.

____ 13. The first stage in Piaget's theory of cognitive , influence when infants acquire information about the world through their senses and respond reflexively.

____ 14. A process whereby the connections in the brain that are frequently used are preserved, and those that are not are lost.

____ 15. The understanding that an object continues to exist even when it is out of sight.

____ 16. The term used to describe the ability to explain and predict other people's behavior as a result of recognizing their mental state.

____ 17. The inability to remember events from early childhood.

____ 18. Cognitive structures that influence how people perceive the behaviors of males and females.

____ 19. The tendency for humans to pay more attention to novel stimuli.

____ 20. A term that refers to the culturally constructed differences between males and females.

THOUGHT QUESTIONS

1. Imagine that you are interested in writing children's books. You wish to write one book that will be engaging to children about 3 years old. You want the other book to appeal to 10-year-olds. Given the cognitive and social abilities of these age groups, what will your books be like?

2. According to Erikson, middle-aged adults, such as the parents of most typically aged college students, are in the stage of generativity versus stagnation. Describe the

characteristics of an individual who is successfully dealing with this stage. Give specific examples of what this adult may be doing.

APPLICATIONS

Thinking Critically about How Gender Roles are Presented on TV

Gender roles are behaviors that differ between men and women. The textbook discusses how parents, teachers, and the media may all influence what roles children believe are appropriate for males or females. Television may be an important source of information for children on appropriate gender role behavior. But how do children's TV shows present gender roles?

Pick at least two TV shows that target young children for their audience. Pick shows that vary in some manner. For example, one show may be a cartoon, the other a comedy. One show may target preschoolers, the other late elementary school aged children. One show may be on commercial TV, the other may be on public television. Next decide how you will evaluate the presentation of gender roles. First you might want to count the number of male and female characters. Then you may note whether the characters were good or bad, whether the characters accomplished their goals or whether they had to be helped or rescued, and what kinds of jobs the characters had. After you decide on what you will measure, develop some hypotheses about what you expect to find. Why do you hold these hypotheses? Now watch the TV shows and collect your data. What did you find? Was it what you expected? Why or why not? What do you think children's TV shows are teaching children about gender roles?

Applications of the Levels of Analysis: Middle Schoolers

For many children the transition to middle school is not easy. Their stress increases while their grades decrease. Why this occurs is not entirely known, but all three categories of analysis—biological, individual, and social—seem to have a role in explaining this transition. How is a middle school student different from an elementary school student biologically? Middle school students are not just bigger—they are often in the midst of puberty. Puberty, the biological changes that result in sexual maturation, includes increases in hormone production, development of secondary sex characteristics, and marked increases in height and weight. How do middle school students differ from elementary students on the level of the individual? According to Piaget, middle school students are starting to move from concrete operational thought to formal operational thought. They are starting to be able to generate hypotheses and think of possible outcomes. They may apply these cognitive skills not just in school but also to their personal lives. How do middle school students differ from elementary school students on a social level? Many children are increasingly influenced by peers as they move into middle school. Not only may the older student differ from the younger, but the school environment may also differ. For the first time students may have many different teachers, each with their own expectations. To sum up the middle school experience, children may be coping with changing moods and new body shapes as a result of puberty. They may be dealing with newly developing but not yet fully formed cognitive skills. And they are dealing with a new environment and new social expectations. Clearly middle school students could benefit from support from both parents and teachers when facing these transitions.

Reference

Eccles, J. S. (2004). Schools, academic motivation, and stage–environment fit. In R. M. Lerner & L. Steinberg (Eds.) *Handbook of adolescent psychology* (2nd ed., pp. 125–153). Hoboken, NJ: Wiley.

WEB SITES

Parenting

www.parenting.org

Language Acquisition

www.carla.umn.edu

Aging

www.aoa.gov
www.ncoa.org

ANSWER KEY

Fill-in-the-Blank Questions

1. Developmental psychology
2. Social development
3. Nature (genes), nurture (environment)
4. Alcohol
5. Synaptic pruning
6. Critical period
7. Attachment
8. Food
9. Avoidant
10. Oxytocin
11. Temperament
12. Orienting reflex
13. Sensorimotor
14. Object permanence
15. Concrete operational
16. Earlier

17. Infantile amnesia
18. Source amnesia
19. Theory of mind
20. Egocentrism
21. Morpheme
22. Syntax
23. Noam Chomsky
24. Sensitive period
25. Phonics
26. Gender identity
27. Gender roles
28. Postconventional
29. Moral emotions
30. Prefrontal cortex
31. Lifespan
32. Dementia
33. Fluid

Multiple-Choice Questions

1. b. For the first two months the developing human is an embryo. This is when the internal organs begin to develop.

    Incorrect answers:
    a. After the first two months the developing human is called a fetus.
    c. A critical period is a stage during which animals are able to acquire a new behavior.
    d. A scheme is a conceptual model of how the world works.

2. c. Harold's mother's hormones were influenced by stress and are part of Harold's physical environment.

    Incorrect answers:
    a. The question described environmental, not genetic, influences.
    b. The question described a physical, not a cultural, influence.
    d. "FAS environment" is not a term.

3. d. Milk does not cause abnormalities in prenatal development.

    Incorrect answers:
    a. Viruses can cause abnormal development.
    b. Bacteria can cause abnormal development.
    c. Drugs can cause abnormal development

4. d. The decay and disappearance of synaptic connections that are not used is called synaptic pruning.

    Incorrect answers:
    a. Myelination involves wrapping neurons in a fatty sheath that increases the speed of neural transmission.
    b. The rooting reflex is when newborns turn toward and suck objects near their mouth.
    c. "Dendritic release" is not a term.

5. c. John Bowlby popularized the importance of attachment.

    Incorrect answers:
    a. Konrad Lorenz studied imprinting.

    b. Mary Ainsworth developed the Strange Situation to study styles of attachment.
    d. Noam Chomsky developed a theory of language acquisition.

6. a. Imprinting occurs when an animal follows an object.

    Incorrect answers:
    b. Bonding is used to describe attachment relationships but does not necessarily involve following the attachment object.
    c. Anxiety involves distress.
    d. The orienting reflex is demonstrated by increased attention to a novel stimulus.

7. d. Harlow found the baby monkeys preferred the soft cloth mother.

    Incorrect answers:
    a. He did not study noises.
    b. The baby monkeys did not prefer the mother who gave them food.
    c. None of the mothers fought off threats.

8. b. Securely attached babies will be upset when their mothers leave and happy when their mothers return.

    Incorrect answers:
    a. Avoidant children are not upset when their mother leaves and often ignore her when she returns.
    c. Anxious–ambivalent (not anxious) attachment is reflected by the child clinging to the mother in the strange situation, becoming very upset when she leaves, and acting both positively (e.g., running to her) and negatively (e.g., hitting her) when she returns.
    d. Anxious–ambivalent (not ambivalent) attachment is reflected by the child clinging to the mother in the strange situation, becoming very upset when she leaves, and acting both positively (e.g., running to her) and negatively (e.g., hitting her) when she returns.

9. a. A person's typical mood, activity level, and emotional reactivity describes their temperament.

    Incorrect answers:
    b. Siblings may have different temperaments.
    c. Attachment objects are not described in the question.
    d. Temperament does not seem to be based on learning history.

10. d. In the "Thinking Critically" section, evidence is presented that parental conflict may be worse for children than divorce.

Incorrect answers:
a. Because conflict may be worse than divorce, children may not do better if their parents stay together.
b. The text describes a number of negative outcomes associated with divorce.
c. Many things may be more harmful than divorce.

11. b. Babies prefer bold black and white patterns.

Incorrect answers:
a. Babies do not see shades of gray as well as they see black and white.
c. Babies' distance vision is not good, so they will not see objects across the room well.
d. Babies cannot see pale pastel colors well.

12. c. After birth, babies who had been read *The Cat in the Hat* before birth modified their sucking to turn on tapes playing *The Cat in the Hat.*

Incorrect answers:
a. There is no evidence that the babies understood what they had been read.
b. Babies' sensory systems are not completely developed before birth: This study investigated only one system, hearing.
d. Babies and older children were not compared in this study.

13. d. Piaget's stages are sensorimotor, preoperational, concrete operational, and formal operational.

Incorrect answers:
a. Concrete operations is one of Piaget's stages.
b. Sensorimotor is one of Piaget's stages.
c. Preoperational is one of Piaget's stages.

14. b. Understanding that objects continue to exist even when hidden is object permanence.

Incorrect answers:
a. Theory of mind involves understanding that other people have mental states and inferring what another person may be thinking or feeling.
c. Accommodation is a Piagetian term describing changing schemes to fit new experiences.
d. The orienting reflex is demonstrated by increased attention to a novel stimulus.

15. a. In the preoperational stage children fail conservation tasks such as the one described in the question.

Incorrect answers:
b. Concrete operational children can conserve.
c. Formal operational children can conserve.
d. Postformal thought was not discussed in this context.

16. b. When children can conserve, they realize that the quantity of a substance does not change even if its appearance changes.

Incorrect answers:
a. Understanding that objects continue to exist even when hidden is object permanence.
c. According to Piaget, abstract thinking develops in formal operations and involves deductive logic.
d. Dialectic thinking was not discussed in this context.

17. c. Recent researchers found that Piaget underestimated the abilities of young children.

Incorrect answers:
a. Piaget did not overestimate the abilities of young children.
b. Piaget was not correct in his theories.
d. Piaget did describe conservation.

18. c. Infantile amnesia was used by Freud to refer to people's inability to recall events that occurred before they were about 3 years old.

Incorrect answers:
a. Preoperational thought is a Piagetian stage where thinking is symbolic but not logical.
b. "Learning amnesia" is not a term.
d. Repression was used by Freud to describe forcing information from consciousness.

19. a. Forgetting where you learned something is source amnesia.

Incorrect answers:
b. Infantile amnesia was used by Freud to refer to people's inability to recall events that occurred before they were about 3 years old.
c. Repression was used by Freud to describe forcing information from consciousness.
d. "Short term memory dysfunction" is not a term.

20. d. Piaget described children as egocentric when they were unable to see things from another person's point of view.

Incorrect answers:
a. Theory of mind is the ability to infer what another person is thinking or feeling.
b. Formal thought is characterized by the ability to think abstractly.
c. When children can conserve, they realize that the quantity of a substance does not change even if its appearance changes.

21. d. Phonemes are language sounds.

    Incorrect answers:
    a. Morphemes are the smallest units of language that have meaning.
    b. Syntax is the system of rules for combining words into sentences.
    c. Pragmatic means practical.

22. d. Telegraphic speech follows syntactic rules but includes only basic words.

    Incorrect answers:
    a. Roger Brown studied telegraphic speech, but it was not named for him.
    b. ASL stands for American Sign Language.
    c. "Terotogenic speech" is not a term.

23. b. Noam Chomsky's theory focused on universal grammar.

    Incorrect answers:
    a. Lev Vygotsky developed the first major theory of language emphasizing social and cultural context.
    c. Nim Chimpsky, a chimp, was taught ASL to see if he would use language in the same way as humans.
    d. Roger Brown studied telegraphic speech.

24. a. Russian psychologist Lev Vygotsky developed the first major theory of language emphasizing social and cultural context.

    Incorrect answers:
    b. Noam Chomsky's theory focused on universal grammar.
    c. Laura Ann Petitto was a researcher who worked with a chimp, Nim Chimpsky, to see if he would use language in the same way as humans.
    d. Roger Brown studied telegraphic speech.

25. c. Deaf children of deaf parents will acquire language at the same rate as will hearing children of hearing parents.

    Incorrect answers:
    a. Deaf children of deaf parents do not acquire language faster than hearing children.
    b. Deaf children of deaf parents do not acquire language slower than hearing children.
    d. Deaf children of deaf parents acquire language similarly to hearing children.

26. b. The whole language approach to reading focuses on meaning and understanding of how words are connected in sentences.

    Incorrect answers:
    a. Schemas are ways of thinking.

    c. Syntax is a system of rules for putting words together to form sentences.
    d. The phonics method of teaching reading focuses on language sounds.

27. d. Gender identity refers to how one thinks of oneself as male or female.

    Incorrect answers:
    a. Gender describes differences between males and females.
    b. Gender roles are behaviors that differ between males and females.
    c. Gender schema are cognitive structures related to our ideas of male and female.

28. c. Gender schemas are the cognitive structures that influence how we perceive the behaviors of males and females.

    Incorrect answers:
    a. Gender describes differences between males and females.
    b. Gender roles are behaviors that differ between males and females.
    d. Gender identity is one's sense of self as male or female.

29. b. According to Erikson, generativity versus stagnation is the crisis faced by people in middle adulthood.

    Incorrect answers:
    a. Adolescents do face heightened pressure to prepare for the future.
    c. Physical appearance does change in adolescence, contributing to issues with identity.
    d. Cognitive skills also change in adolescence and contribute to issues with identity.

30. d. Lawrence Kohlberg studied moral reasoning in children.

    Incorrect answers:
    a. Judith Harris studied the influence of parents and peers on personality.
    b. Lev Vygotsky studied cognition and language.
    c. Erik Erikson studied development through the lifespan.

31. a. This is a conventional response because it focuses on other people's approval.

    Incorrect answers:
    b. Preconventional responses focus on self-interest.
    c. Social disapproval is not one of Kohlberg's stages.
    d. The postconventional stage focuses on abstract principles.

32. a. Young children can not sort people into categories based on race.

Incorrect answers:
b. Although Piaget's stages are not discussed in this context, based on his age and his inability to form ethnic categories, Matt is probably preoperational.
c. Although Sally could sort based on race, there was no information provided to indicate she had developed stereotypes.
d. There was no indication of what Sally's ethnicity was or if she had an ethnic identity.

33. c. Erik Erikson developed this lifespan theory.

Incorrect answers:
a. Freud, whose theory is described in another chapter, did not have a lifespan theory of development.
b. Lev Vygotsky studied cognition and language.
d. Kohlberg studied moral reasoning.

34. a. According to Carstensen's socioemotional selectivity theory, older adults focus on emotionally rewarding goals.

Incorrect answers:
b. According to Erikson, identity versus role confusion is the primary crisis of adolescence.
c. Postformal thought was not discussed in this context.
d. Dementia is progressive deterioration of thinking, memory, and behavior.

Matching Questions

1. H   Developmental psychology
2. O   Social development
3. D   Gender identity
4. S   Preoperational stage
5. K   Critical period
6. A   Source amnesia
7. N   Accommodation
8. Q   Telegraphic speech
9. I   Attachment
10. C   Teratogens
11. G   Gender roles
12. M   Schemas
13. J   Sensorimotor stage
14. R   Synaptic pruning
15. E   Object permanence
16. L   Theory of mind
17. T   Infantile amnesia
18. B   Gender schemas
19. P   Orientating reflex
20. F   Gender

Thought Questions

1. Three-year-olds have very different cognitive skills, language skills, and social skills than do 10-year-olds. To write engaging books for these age groups consider Piaget's stages, language development, and social development. For example, 3-year-olds are probably preoperational, whereas 10-year-olds are concrete operational. The language skills of 3-year-olds are not as developed as those of 10-year-olds. Three-year-olds are still very attached to their parents; 10-year-olds, though still attached to their parents, are spending increasing time with peers.

2. According to Erikson, people successfully address this stage when they are generative. This means that they feel they produce something of value or give back something to society. People accomplish this in many different ways: jobs, families, scientific contributions, and art are just some forms of generativity.

CHAPTER 12 | Personality

GUIDE TO THE READING

Chapter 12 addresses the issue of personality, one of the oldest topics in psychology. It seems to be a fundamental aspect of human nature to speculate about why each of us is unique and what made us that way. Investigators have long debated what personality is, the correct way to study it, and how individual personality interacts with the broader social environment. The authors summarize the four traditional approaches to understanding personality (psychodynamic, trait, humanistic, cognitive-social) and the methods of personality assessment associated with each. Recent advances in the area of behavioral neuroscience have contributed greatly to our understanding of the individual person. Many of our traits have a strong genetic component, and these tendencies are relatively stable from infancy through adulthood. But although genetics and neurochemistry may set the framework for our tendencies, our interactions with the environment finalize this process based on our selections of which traits and skills are adaptive.

How Have Scientists Studied Personality?

The initial section of the chapter reviews what personality is and the four traditional approaches for studying it. Although researchers have disagreed about specific aspects, there is relative agreement that the term *personality* refers to a person's characteristics, emotional responses, thoughts, and behaviors that are relatively stable over time and across circumstances. Psychodynamic theorists, beginning with Freud, have proposed that unconscious forces influence behavior. Freud developed a topographical model of the mind in which there are three levels of mental awareness: conscious, preconscious, and unconscious. Freud described how thinking and behavior develop in five psychosexual stages (oral, anal, phallic, latency, genital) based on children's interactions with their parents. Finally, he proposed a structural model of personality in which three dynamic processes (id, ego, superego) struggle to meet basic needs in the context of interaction with the social environment. Despite the many criticisms of Freudian theory, it served as a springboard for much of the theorizing and research of the past century.

Humanistic personality theorists objected to the determinism of Freudian (and later behavioral) models. They emphasized personal experience, or phenomenology, and the fulfillment of human potential (self-actualization). Recently this has led to the positive psychology movement and the scientific investigation of positive aspects of humanity. Trait theorists propose that individuals differ on broad personality dispositions. Factor analysis of these traits has led to a number of different solutions, but in the last 20 years many personality psychologists have endorsed the five-factor theory of personality. The Big Five, as they are known, are extraversion, neuroticism, conscientiousness, agreeableness, and openness to experience. Finally, cognitive-social theories of personality have integrated the findings of learning theory with the idea that beliefs, expectancies, and interpretations also influence the exhibition of behavior.

Table 15.1 TRADITIONAL APPROACHES TO THE STUDY OF PERSONALITY

Theoretical Approach	View of Personality
Psychodynamic	Result of unconscious conflicts, usually developed in childhood.
Humanistic	Result of striving for fullest human potential (self-actualization).
Trait	Reflected in variations of broad human dispositions.
Cognitive–social	Integration of learning history and cognitive expectancies and beliefs.

How Is Personality Assessed and What Does It Predict?

The next section of the chapter deals with the assessment of personality. Idiographic approaches to understanding personality address individuals and the characteristics that make them unique. Common techniques in this approach are case studies and psychobiography. Nomothetic approaches focus on characteristics that are common among all people but which vary for individuals. Traditionally, assessment tools have been divided into projective and objective measures. Projective measures, such as inkblots and the Thematic Apperception Test, are based on psychodynamic theory. That is, it is hypothesized if you are presented with an ambiguous stimulus, you will project your unconscious conflicts onto that stimulus. Recent developments in these techniques have been more empirically based. Objective measures are more direct and usually consist of behavioral observations or self-report questionnaires (e.g., the NEO personality inventory).

Walter Mischel initiated a turning point in personality study with his 1968 proclamation that the traits assessed by such measures did a poor job of predicting behavior. His theory of situationism suggested that the interpersonal environment had a much greater influence on behavior, which calls into question whether the construct of personality even exists. The result of this work led to much research and today's idea of interactionism, which maintains that behavior is the result of both broad dispositions and the unique situation.

What Is the Biological Basis of Personality?

Research into the biological basis of personality has done much to illuminate many of the classic questions of personality (e.g., Does personality exist? Can personality change?). It is now evident that personality is strongly rooted in neurophysiology, and roughly half the variance in personality traits is accounted for by genetic influences. Biological differences in personality, referred to as *temperaments*, are evident in very young children and often persist throughout the life span, regardless of parental upbringing. The temperamental trait of introversion/extraversion has been strongly linked to neurophysiology. Introverts have an active behavioral inhibition system that leads them to avoid social situations in which they anticipate possible negative outcomes. Extraverts have a stronger behavioral approach system and are influenced more by the possibility of rewards than punishments. The results of these investigations suggest that people are different because of differing physiology. These preferences also likely reflect what has been adaptive for us over the course of human evolution.

Can Personality Change?

Sigmund Freud proposed that the personality is basically fixed by the age of 5. This infuriated people in Western cultures because it contradicted the possibility for change and improvement that is part of our mythology. Research in temperament suggests that these early tendencies do play a pervasive and influential role in adulthood. A meta-analysis of 150 studies on personality change indicated that there is a possibility for change in childhood, but personality become very stable by middle age. Part of the debate concerns the definition of *personality*. Our basic tendencies, which are highly determined by biological processes, tend to be stable. Our characteristic adaptations may vary in novel situations, but it is argued that our core dispositions do not change. Still, we maintain the possibility of a quantum change or personality transformation, but this results only from an extreme negative affect (hitting rock bottom) and/or a trigger event. A final finding that certain personality traits are strongly related to neurochemistry (e.g., hostility and serotonin) and can be manipulated leads to a host of ethical questions. If thousands of years of human evolution have led us to vary on the trait of sociability, should we take a pill that instantly would make us more sociable? Is it adaptive to make everyone more cooperative and less hostile?

FILL-IN-THE-BLANK QUESTIONS

1. _____ refers to a person's characteristics, emotional responses, thoughts, and behaviors that are relatively stable over time and across circumstances.

2. A _____ is the dispositional tendency to act in a certain way over time and across circumstances.

3. The _____ is the Freudian term for the process that directs people to seek pleasure and avoid pain.

4. The energy that drives the pleasure principle is called _____.

5. The _____ is the Freudian conflict in which boys develop an unconscious conflict to kill their fathers and marry their mothers.

6. The _____ is the Freudian term for the ego that involves rational thought and problem solving.

7. _____ are unconscious mental strategies the mind uses to protect itself from conflict and distress.

8. _____ approaches to personality emphasize personal experiences, belief systems, and human potential.

9. _____ refers to the subjective human experience.

10. The _____ encourages the use of science to study the positive aspects of humanity.

11. _____ is a general term for how much happiness and satisfaction people have in their lives.

12. _____ is the tendency to assume that personality characteristics go together, and therefore to make predictions about people based on minimal evidence.

13. _____ is Kelly's term for people's understanding of their circumstances.

14. According to Mischel's _____, people's responses in a given situation are influenced by how they encode or perceive the situation, their affective response to the situation, the skills and competencies they have to deal with challenges, and their anticipation of the outcomes that their behavior will produce.

15. _____ are traits that are particularly descriptive of individuals as compared to others.

16. _____ are traits that people consider less personally descriptive or not applicable at all.

17. The _____ is a reconstructive and imaginative process in which people link together personal motives, goals, and beliefs with events and people and the circumstances in which they find themselves.

18. The method of _____ uses personal life stories to develop and test theories about human personality.

19. _____ focus on the characteristics that are common among all people, but on which people vary.

20. The _____ requires people to sort 100 statements printed on cards into nine piles according to what extent the statement is descriptive of them.

21. _____ is a trait referring to how much excitement you seek out of life.

22. _____ are trait theorists who believe that behavior is jointly determined by situations and underlying dispositions.

23. _____ are described as general tendencies to feel or act in certain ways.

24. _____ refers to the overall amount of energy and behavior a person exhibits.

25. _____ refers to the general tendency to affiliate with others.

26. _____ children react to new situations or strange objects by becoming startled and distressed.

27. The _____ regulates cortical arousal or alertness.

28. The _____ consists of the brain structures that lead organisms to approach stimuli in pursuit of rewards.

29. The _____ consists of the brain structures that are sensitive to punishment and therefore inhibit behavior that might lead to danger of pain.

30. The _____ system locks a person into the strategy chosen, to the exclusion of others that might have been pursued under different circumstances.

31. _____ are dispositional traits that are determined to a great extent by biological processes.

32. _____ are the adjustments people make to situational demands, which tend to be consistent because they are based on skills, habits, and roles.

MULTIPLE-CHOICE QUESTIONS

1. Randall has been highly disruptive in college. His poor grades and antisocial behavior have eventually led him to be expelled. His therapist explains to his parents that Randall is unconsciously acting out because he did not want to attend college. The therapist is taking a _____ approach to understanding personality.
   a. psychodynamic
   b. trait
   c. cognitive-social
   d. humanistic

2. Which of the following is *not* one of the levels of mental awareness in Freud's topographical model of the mind?
   a. Conscious.
   b. Preconscious.
   c. Subconscious.
   d. Unconscious.

3. Julie is introduced to her biological mother, who abandoned her as an infant. As they shake hands Julie says, "It's nice to beat you." This Freudian slip is an example of information at the _____ level being accidentally revealed.
   a. conscious
   b. preconscious
   c. subconscious
   d. unconscious

4. Which of the following is *not* one of Freud's psychosexual stages of development?
   a. Oral.
   b. Anal.
   c. Castration.
   d. Latency.

5. As a baby, Dave did not receive sufficient gratification from his mother. Now, as an adult, he smokes, drinks excessively, and constantly chews on his fingernails. According to Freud, Dave's behavior is a result of

   _____.
   a. fixation
   b. projection
   c. identification
   d. compression

6. Alexander sees a new CD that he really wants. Part of him thinks about just stealing it when the salesperson's head is turned, but part of him feels guilty for thinking in such a selfish, antisocial way. Finally Alexander decides to do a few extra jobs to earn the money for the CD. Which Freudian personality structure is guiding his behavior?
   a. Id.
   b. Libido.
   c. Ego.
   d. Superego.

7. Eileen's son is applying for college. He really wants to go to one of the military academies but unfortunately gets rejected. When he gets his rejection letters he states, "I didn't want to go there anyway, those guys are just a bunch of jarheads, and their parents probably paid someone to get them in!" This represents the defense mechanism of
   a. denial.
   b. rationalization.
   c. repression.
   d. projection.

8. Pete gets turned down for the convenience store employee of the month because he did not turn in the guy who was stealing breath mints. Rather than beat his employer with a stale hoagie, Pete tells everyone what a great guy he is and how he only is trying to help him improve. This represents which ego defense mechanism?
   a. Projection.
   b. Denial.
   c. Sublimation.
   d. Reaction formation.

9. Holly tries to do her best at everything. Even though she may fail periodically, her boyfriend, Sven, sticks with her in all her endeavors. According to Rogers, Sven is demonstrating _____ toward Holly.
   a. unconditional love
   b. reciprocal determinism
   c. unconditional positive regard
   d. self-efficacy

10. Ginger's friends are trying to figure out why she would humiliate herself as a stripper at a local cabaret. They finally agree on a type/trait approach to understanding personality. Which of the following explanations best represents that approach?
    a. She is unconsciously trying to get back at her parents who were rather repressed in the area of sexuality.
    b. At her stable core, Ginger is just an exhibitionist.
    c. She has received attention (i.e., reinforcement) for this behavior.
    d. She is trying to fulfill her potential and sees clothing as an artificial societal constraint.

11. Which of the following is *not* a level of Eysenck's hierarchical model of personality?
    a. Specific response.
    b. Habitual response.
    c. Superordinate .
    d. Emotional stability.

12. Which of the following is *not* a superordinate trait in Eysenck's hierarchical model of personality?
    a. Neuroticism.
    b. Introversion–extraversion.
    c. Emotional stability.
    d. Psychoticism.

13. Which of the following is *not* one of the basic traits of the five-factor personality theory?
    a. Extraversion.
    b. Psychoticism.
    c. Neuroticism.
    d. Agreeableness.

14. Tyshawn gets a 75 on his first psychology exam. He decides that he will have to study harder to receive the A he desires for the class. Tyshawn is exhibiting a(n) _____ locus of control.
    a. internal
    b. external
    c. efficacious
    d. utilitarian

15. Professor Perez is trying to figure out why John is consistently disruptive during her lectures. John not only laughs throughout the class but also points and throws unmentionable items up at the stage! Professor Perez finally decides that John has been inadvertently rewarded with attention for his rude behavior, and he expects to be rewarded for it in the future. Which theory of personality does her approach most closely resemble?
    a. Psychodynamic.
    b. Humanistic.
    c. Trait.
    d. Cognitive-social.

16. Latasha is doing a case study about Karen Horney, a famous personality theorist. Latasha is investigating her background and how it contributed to her ideas about human behavior. Latasha is using a(n) _____ approach to understanding personality.
    a. idiographic
    b. nomothetic
    c. individual
    d. stratified

17. Tiffany is developing a scale called the California Conscientiousness Chart. She is hoping to describe people on this trait ranging from low to high. Tiffany is using a(n) _____ approach to understanding personality.
    a. idiographic
    b. person-centered
    c. nomothetic
    d. psychobiographical

18. Juan was trying his luck as a painter. One day in frustration he just tossed some different paints on the blank canvas in no particular order. When he showed his "masterpiece" to his friends, they began describing the ambiguous splotches according to their personal needs, conflicts, hopes, and fears. Unknowingly, Juan had created a _____ test.
    a. thematic apperception.
    b. projective.
    c. Minnesota Multiphasic Personality Inventory.
    d. subliminal perception.

19. Andrea is in treatment when her therapist decides to do some additional personality assessment. Andrea takes a test in which she is shown an ambiguous picture and asked to tell a story about it. Andrea likely has taken a

    _____.
    a. Thematic Apperception Test
    b. Rorschach inkblot Test
    c. Millon personality inventory
    d. NEO personality inventory

20. Ramone is administering a self-report questionnaire to his client to learn more about his personality. Ramone is using a(n) _____ measure of personality.
    a. subjective
    b. objective
    c. projective
    d. multimodal

21. Paul is taking a self-report questionnaire designed to assess the Big Five personality traits. Paul is most likely taking the _____.
    a. NEO personality inventory
    b. Minnesota Multiphasic Personality Inventory

c. California Q-sort
d. Millon Clinical Multiaxial Inventory

22. Wes takes a personality test when he applies for a job at a local prison, and he scores well. However, his answers do not really reflect his behavior and his personality differs drastically from one situation to the next. His behavior relative to his measured traits supports Mischel's idea that
    a. prospective employees must be retested several times to get a true picture of their personality.
    b. behaviors are determined to a much greater extent by situations than by personality traits.
    c. only projective personality tests (which cannot be faked) give a true picture of individual's traits.
    d. several personality tests must be used to reliably predict behavior in a particular situation.

23. Which of the following statements best describes the relation between the trait of self-monitoring and the consistency of personality?
    a. People who are high in self-monitoring alter their behavior to match the situation, so they exhibit low levels of consistency.
    b. People who are high in self-monitoring alter their behavior to match the situation, so they exhibit high levels of consistency.
    c. People who are low in self-monitoring are less able to alter their self-presentation to match situations, so they exhibit low levels of consistency.
    d. People who are low in self-monitoring are less able to alter their self-presentation to match situations, so their personalities are relatively unpredictable.

24. According to twin studies, genetic influence accounts for approximately what percentage of the variance in personality traits?
    a. 0–10%.
    b. 10–20%.
    c. 20–40%.
    d. 40–60%.

25. Emily is an expressive child. The slightest offense can cause her to cry, and she is easily frightened by new situations. Emily is high in the temperament of
    a. affectivity.
    b. activity level.
    c. sociability.
    d. emotionality.

26. Cindy is doing a research study on the effects of caffeine on various behaviors. Cindy finds that several of her participants are very arousable or reactive to the caffeine. These individuals likely fit which of the following trait categories?
    a. Introverts.

b. Extraverts.

c. Sensation seekers.

d. Sociopaths.

27. Dan lives an exciting lifestyle. He likes to go bungee jumping and parachuting on a waveboard. Dan seeks arousal through adventures and new experiences. He is easily bored and used to escape this boredom through the use of drugs and alcohol. Dan is high in the arousal-based trait of

   a. sociopathy.

   b. psychopathy.

   c. extraversion.

   d. sensation seeking.

28. Drew the extravert loves to gamble. He is more influenced by the possibility of winning the big pot than he is by the constant punishment of losing his money. Which of the following neurological systems has the greatest affect on Drew?

   a. Behavioral approach system.

   b. Behavioral inhibition system.

   c. Ascending reticular activating system.

   d. Early experiential calibration system.

29. Farrah is in a relationship with a man who is demeaning and abusive. In response to her confrontation he tells her, "I can change!" According to a meta-analysis of 150 studies on personality change, personality becomes more stable by

   a. age 5.

   b. adolescence.

   c. young adulthood.

   d. middle age.

30. Which of the following is not one of the levels of personality as classified by Dan McAdams?

   a. Dispositional traits.

   b. General typologies.

   c. Personal concerns.

   d. Life narratives.

31. Following a divorce from an oppressive spouse, Rebecca took on an entirely new look. She suddenly became outgoing and sociable, enrolled for evening classes at a local university, signed on for a travel club, and dressed in a more flamboyant manner. Her friends said it was like she acquired a new personality. This transformation is known as a(n)

   a. butterfly effect.

   b. affective blossoming.

   c. quantum change.

   d. trigger event.

32. Hannah is a hostile young woman. In response to complaints from family and friends, she enrolls in a clinical trial to test a new medication that might reduce her hostility. Hannah's medication will likely focus on which of the following neurotransmitters?

   a. Norepinephrine.

   b. Y-aminobutyric acid (GABA).

   c. Serotonin.

   d. Dopamine.

MATCHING QUESTIONS

Fill in the letter from Column B corresponding to the term that is most associated with the description presented in Column A.

COLUMN A

____ 1. Mask used by actors in Greek and Roman theater.

____ 2. Individual's characteristics, emotional responses, thoughts, and behaviors that are relatively stable across time.

____ 3. Theory of personality that unconscious forces influence behavior.

____ 4. Psychic force that can be satisfied by seeking pleasure and avoiding pain.

____ 5. Freudian model of the mind that divided awareness into conscious, preconscious, and unconscious levels.

____ 6. Level of mental awareness in which people are aware of their thoughts.

____ 7. Level of mental awareness in which people are unaware of thought content, but it can easily be brought into awareness.

____ 8. Level of mental awareness that contains material that the mind cannot easily retrieve.

____ 9. Freudian stages of development.

____ 10. Psychosexual stage in which libido is suppressed or channeled into schoolwork and friendships.

COLUMN B

A. Personality

B. Topographical

C. Unconscious

D. Broaden-and-build

E. Self-actualization

F. Superego

G. Anal-retentive

H. Arousability

I. Rorschach

J. Fully functioning person

K. Conscious

L. Persona

M. Psychodynamic

N. Life instinct

O. Personality types

P. Person-centered

Q. Psychosexual

R. Self-efficacy

S. Factor analysis

T. Preconscious

U. Ego

V. Id

W. Latency

X. Genital

___ 11. Psychosexual stage in which adolescents or adults work to attain mature attitudes about sexuality and adulthood.

___ 12. Personality that is stubborn and overly regulating due to strict toilet training.

___ 13. Freudian personality structure that acts on impulses and desires.

___ 14. Freudian personality structure that tries to satisfy the id and the superego.

___ 15. Freudian personality structure that internalizes societal and parental standards of conduct.

___ 16. Fulfilling one's individual potential for personal growth through greater self-understanding.

___ 17. Rogers's approach to personality.

___ 18. Rogers's term for adult with healthy self- esteem from receiving unconditional positive regard.

___ 19. Theory that positive emotions prompt people to consider novel solutions to problems.

___ 20. Discrete categories into which we place people.

___ 21. Procedure for grouping items together based on their similarities.

___ 22. Belief that one can achieve a specific outcome.

___ 23. Test in which person describes an apparently meaningless inkblot.

___ 24. Reactivity to stimuli.

THOUGHT QUESTIONS

1. The authors state that virtually everyone has an implicit theory of personality; that is, they have some idea of what traits and behaviors go together based on their experiences. Let us make this theory more explicit. Of the four models given (psychodynamic, humanistic, trait, cognitive-social), which do you think provides the best understanding of human personality? Try to iden-

tify the experiences in your life that led you to support one model and to discount the others.

2. Suppose you found out that someone you were dating had modified his or her personality through neurochemical means. Your friend states that he or she is less hostile and more sociable when taking the medication. How would you feel about this? Would you encourage your friend to continue with it? How would you determine whether the medication was necessary? What other options would you have for personality change?

APPLICATIONS

An Internet Application for Assessing Your Personality

Although dozens of Web sites offer free personality tests with all the reliability and validity of your daily horoscope, a few sites that can be worthwhile. One such site is Personality Online (www.personalityonline.com). They are fully willing to admit that some of their scales are fluff and just for entertainment. However, they try to keep up with more "serious" tests that have some research validation. The site requires that you register with them (for free), but after that you have relatively complete access to the site and its various assessment scales. They also have links to other personality-oriented Web sites, a discussion about the various theories of personality, and the opportunity for a professional consultation about your personality scores (we recommend that you skip that). Try to apply what you learned in the chapter to the scales they are offering.

Six Basic Questions about Human Nature That All Personality Theories Must Address

In his textbook on personality, Duane Schultz (2004) indicated that all personality theories varied along certain critical dimensions. To understand the similarities and dissimilarities among the theories, you should understand where each theory stands along the dimensions of six basic questions regarding human nature. Ultimately, your beliefs about these dimensions are used to answer the question "Who am I?" A paraphrasing of the dimensions is as follows:

1. *Free will versus determinism:* Are we basically free to choose our actions, or are we determined by outside forces?

2. *Nature versus nurture:* In terms of these deterministic forces, are we more influenced by what we are born with (nature) or by our environmental experiences (nurture)?

3. *Childhood versus later experiences:* Are our personalities basically fixed by the age of 5 (as Freud hypothesized) or can they change throughout the life span as a result of our experiences?

4. *Unique versus universal:* Do we all develop in relatively different fashions under differing timelines (unique), or does our development reflect rather similar issues and stages for everyone (universal)?

5. *Hedonistic versus self-actualization:* This issue regards our motivations. Do we basically seek pleasure and attempt to avoid pain (hedonistic), or are we motivated to fulfill our fullest human potential (self-actualization)?

6. *Good versus evil:* At our very core, are we basically good individuals or are we pretty much evil?

Try to assess each of the theories presented in the textbook (i.e., psychodynamic, humanistic, trait, cognitive-social) along these dimensions. For example, the psychodynamic theory might be 95 percent determinism (maybe more) and 5 percent free will. Avoid using the easy scoring of 50–50. Take a stand in one direction, even if just a little. Also, assess your beliefs along each of these dimensions. This should help you understand your answer to Thought Question #1.

WEB SITES

Personality Assessment

www.personalityonline.com
http://discoveryourpersonality.com

Personality Disorders

www.isspd.com

Psychodynamic Theories

www.freud.org.uk

ANSWER KEY

Fill-in-the-Blank Questions

1. Personality
2. Personality trait
3. Pleasure principle
4. Libido
5. Oedipus complex
6. Reality principle
7. Defense mechanisms
8. Humanistic
9. Phenomenology
10. Positive psychology movement
11. Subjective well-being
12. Implicit personality theory
13. Personal constructs
14. Cognitive-affective personality system
15. Central traits
16. Secondary traits
17. Life story
18. Psychobiography
19. Nomothetic approaches
20. California Q-sort
21. Sensation-seeking
22. Interactionists
23. Temperaments
24. Activity level
25. Sociability
26. Inhibited
27. Ascending reticular activating system
28. Behavioral approach system
29. Behavioral inhibition system
30. Early experiential calibration
31. Basic tendencies
32. Characteristic adaptations

Multiple-Choice Questions

1. a. The central premise of the psychodynamic theory of personality is that unconscious forces, such as wishes and motives, influence behavior.

   Incorrect answers:
   b. Trait approaches to personality describe broad behavioral dispositions.
   c. Cognitive-social theories reflect learning and cognitive processes.
   d. Humanistic approaches emphasize integrated personal experience.

2. c. Subconscious is *not* one of the levels of mental awareness in Freud's topographical model of the mind. Conscious, preconscious, and unconscious are the levels of mental awareness in Freud's topographical model of the mind.

   Incorrect answers:
   a. Conscious, preconscious, and unconscious are the levels of mental awareness in Freud's topographical model of the mind.
   b. Conscious, preconscious, and unconscious are the levels of mental awareness in Freud's topographical model of the mind.
   d. Conscious, preconscious, and unconscious are the levels of mental awareness in Freud's topographical model of the mind.

3. d. The unconscious mind contains wishes, desires, and motives that are associated with conflict, anxiety, or pain.

   Incorrect answers:
   a. At the conscious level, people are aware of their thoughts.
   b. The preconscious consists of content that is not currently in awareness but could easily be brought into awareness.
   c. The subconscious is not one of the levels of mental awareness in Freud's topographical model of the mind.

4. c. Castration is *not* one of Freud's psychosexual stages of development. Oral, anal, and latency are stages of Freud's psychosexual model of development.

    Incorrect answers:
    a. Oral, anal, and latency are stages of Freud's psychosexual model of development.
    b. Oral, anal, and latency are stages of Freud's psychosexual model of development.
    d. Oral, anal, and latency are stages of Freud's psychosexual model of development.

5. a. Freud stated that people become fixated at a stage during which they have received excessive parental restriction or indulgence; excessive pleasure via the mouth is characteristic of fixation at the oral stage.

    Incorrect answers:
    b. Projection is an ego defense mechanism in which one attributes unacceptable material to others.
    c. Identification is an ego defense mechanism and a way of coping with the Oedipus Complex by mimicking the same-sex parent.
    d. Compression is not a term in Freud's model.

6. c. The ego uses problem solving to satisfy the wishes of the id while being responsive to the dictates of the superego.

    Incorrect answers:
    a. The id operates according to the pleasure principle, acting on impulses and desires.
    b. The libido is not a Freudian personality structure.
    d. The superego acts as a brake on the id and internalizes societal and parental standards of conduct.

7. b. Rationalizations are excuses by which one blames situational factors over which you have little control.

    Incorrect answers:
    a. Denial is a failure to attend to any external danger or problem.
    c. Repression is the involuntary removal of a traumatizing event from consciousness.
    d. Projection is an ego defense mechanism in which one attributes unacceptable material to others.

8. d. Reaction formation occurs when people ward off an uncomfortable thought about the self by embracing its opposite.

    Incorrect answers:
    a. Projection is an ego defense mechanism in which one attributes unacceptable material to others.
    b. Denial is a failure to attend to any external danger or problem.

    c. Sublimation is channeling one's libidinal energy into more socially acceptable pursuits.

9. c. Unconditional positive regard is when individuals are accepted, loved, and prized no matter how they behave.

    Incorrect answers:
    a. Unconditional love is not a term in Rogers's model.
    b. Reciprocal determinism is the interaction among the person, behavior, and the environment.
    d. Self-efficacy is the belief that one can achieve a specific outcome.

10. b. Type and trait approaches to personality describe people by general behavioral dispositions such as exhibitionism.

    Incorrect answers:
    a. The central premise of the psychodynamic theory of personality is that unconscious forces, such as wishes and motives, influence behavior.
    c. Cognitive-social theories reflect learning and cognitive processes.
    d. Humanistic approaches emphasize integrated personal experience.

11. d. Emotional stability is *not* a level of Eysenck's hierarchical model of personality. Specific response, habitual response, trait, and superordinate are levels of Eysenck's hierarchical model of personality.

    Incorrect answers:
    a. Specific response, habitual response, trait, and superordinate are levels of Eysenck's hierarchical model of personality.
    b. Specific response, habitual response, trait, and superordinate are levels of Eysenck's hierarchical model of personality.
    c. Specific response, habitual response, trait, and superordinate are levels of Eysenck's hierarchical model of personality.

12. a. Neuroticism is *not* a superordinate trait in Eysenck's hierarchical model of personality. Introversion–extraversion, emotional stability, and psychoticism are superordinate traits in Eysenck's hierarchical model of personality.

    Incorrect answers:
    b. Introversion–extraversion, emotional stability, and psychoticism are superordinate traits in Eysenck's hierarchical model of personality.
    c. Introversion–extraversion, emotional stability, and psychoticism are superordinate traits in Eysenck's hierarchical model of personality.

d. Introversion–extraversion, emotional stability, and psychoticism are superordinate traits in Eysenck's hierarchical model of personality.

13. b. Psychoticism is *not* one of the basic traits of the five-factor personality theory. The basic traits of the Big Five are extraversion, neuroticism, conscientiousness, agreeableness, and openness to experience.

    Incorrect answers:
    a. The basic traits of the Big Five are extraversion, neuroticism, conscientiousness, agreeableness, and openness to experience.
    c. The basic traits of the Big Five are extraversion, neuroticism, conscientiousness, agreeableness, and openness to experience.
    d. The basic traits of the Big Five are extraversion, neuroticism, conscientiousness, agreeableness, and openness to experience.

14. a. Individuals with an internal locus of control believe that their efforts (e.g., studying) will bring about positive outcomes.

    Incorrect answers:
    b. People with an external locus of control believe that rewards are the result of forces beyond their control.
    c. Efficacious is not a locus of control.
    d. Utilitarian is not a locus of control.

15. d. Cognitive-social theories reflect learning and cognitive processes.

    Incorrect answers:
    a. The central premise of the psychodynamic theory of personality is that unconscious forces, such as wishes and motives, influence behavior.
    b. Humanistic approaches emphasize integrated personal experience.
    c. Type and trait approaches to personality describe people by general behavioral dispositions such as exhibitionism.

16. a. Idiographic approaches focus on individual lives and how various characteristics are integrated into unique persons.

    Incorrect answers:
    b. Nomothetic approaches focus on characteristics that are common among all people, but on which people vary.
    c. Individual is not an approach to studying personality.
    d. Stratified is not an approach to studying personality

17. c. Nomothetic approaches focus on characteristics that are common among all people, but on which people vary.

    Incorrect answers:
    a. Idiographic approaches focus on individual lives and how various characteristics are integrated into unique persons.
    b. Idiographic approaches are person-centered in that they focus on individual lives and how various characteristics are integrated into unique persons.
    d. The method of psychobiography uses personal life stories to develop and test theories about human personality.

18. b. Projective measures are tools that attempt to delve into the realm of the unconscious by presenting people with ambiguous stimuli and asking them to describe the stimulus items or tell stories about them.

    Incorrect answers:
    a. In the Thematic Apperception Test, a person is shown an ambiguous picture and asked to tell a story about it.
    c. The Minnesota Multiphasic Personality Inventory is a true/false objective measure of personality.
    d. Subliminal perception is not a personality measure.

19. a. In the Thematic Apperception Test, a person is shown an ambiguous picture and asked to tell a story about it.

    Incorrect answers:
    b. In the Rorschach Inkblot Test, people look at an apparently meaningless inkblot and describe what it might be.
    c. The Millon personality inventory (MCMI) is an objective measure of personality.
    d. The NEO personality inventory is an objective measure of personality.

20. b. Objective measures of personality are straightforward assessments, usually made by self-report questionnaires or observer ratings.

    Incorrect answers:
    a. There are no subjective measures of personality; however, virtually all tests require people to make subjective judgments.
    c. Projective measures are tools that attempt to delve into the realm of the unconscious by presenting people with ambiguous stimuli and asking them to describe the stimulus items or tell stories about them.
    d. Multimodal is a style of therapy that looks at the individual from different perspectives.

21. a. The NEO personality inventory consists of 240 items designed to assess the Big Five personality traits.

   Incorrect answers:
   b. The Minnesota Multiphasic Personality Inventory is a true/false objective measure of personality traits used in clinical assessment.
   c. The California Q-sort requires people to sort 100 statements printed on cards into 9 piles according to what extent the statement is descriptive of them.
   d. The Millon personality inventory (MCMI) is an objective measure of personality traits used in clinical assessment.

22. b. Mischel proposed the theory of situationism, the idea that behaviors are determined to a much greater extent by situations than by personality traits.

   Incorrect answers:
   a. Mischel proposed the theory of situationism, the idea that behaviors are determined to a much greater extent by situations than by personality traits.
   c. Mischel proposed the theory of situationism, the idea that behaviors are determined to a much greater extent by situations than by personality traits.
   d. Mischel proposed the theory of situationism, the idea that behaviors are determined to a much greater extent by situations than by personality traits.

23. a. People who are high in self-monitoring alter their behavior to match the situation, so they exhibit low levels of consistency.

   Incorrect answers:
   b. People who are high in self-monitoring alter their behavior to match the situation, so they exhibit low levels of consistency.
   c. People who are high in self-monitoring alter their behavior to match the situation, so they exhibit low levels of consistency.
   d. People who are high in self-monitoring alter their behavior to match the situation, so they exhibit low levels of consistency.

24. d. According to twin studies, genetic influence accounts for 40–60 percent of the variance in personality traits, including the Big Five.

   Incorrect answers:
   a. According to twin studies, genetic influence accounts for 40–60 percent of the variance in personality traits, including the Big Five.

b. According to twin studies, genetic influence accounts for 40–60 percent of the variance in personality traits, including the Big Five.
c. According to twin studies, genetic influence accounts for 40–60 percent of the variance in personality traits, including the Big Five.

25. d. Emotionality describes the intensity of emotional reactions, or how easily and frequently people become aroused or upset.

   Incorrect answers:
   a. Affectivity is not a type of temperament.
   b. Activity level refers to the overall amount of energy and behavior a person exhibits.
   c. Sociability refers to the general tendency to affiliate with others.

26. a. Introverts tend to be more arousable or reactive to stimuli at all levels of intensity.

   Incorrect answers:
   b. Extraverts tend to be less arousable or reactive to stimuli at all levels of intensity.
   c. Sensation seekers are similar to extraverts and less arousable or reactive to stimuli at all levels of intensity.
   d. Sociopaths are individuals with no conscience. They tend to have low reactivity, particularly to punishment or avoidance learning.

27. d. Sensation seekers are easily bored and pursue arousal through adventures and new experiences.

   Incorrect answers:
   a. Sociopaths are individuals with no conscience.
   b. Psychopaths are individuals with no conscience.
   c. Extraverts seek new situations and new emotional experiences.

28. a. Extraverts are highly affected by the behavioral approach system, so they are more influenced by rewards than punishments.

   Incorrect answers:
   b. Introverts are highly affected by the behavioral inhibition system, so they are more influenced by punishments than rewards.
   c. The ascending reticular activating system controls arousal and alertness.
   d. The early experiential calibration system locks a person into the strategy chosen, to the exclusion of others that might have been pursued under different circumstances.

29. d. A meta-analysis of 150 studies on personality change indicated that personality does change some in childhood, but it becomes more stable by middle age.

Incorrect answers:

a. A meta-analysis of 150 studies on personality change indicated that personality does change some in childhood, but it becomes more stable by middle age.

b. A meta-analysis of 150 studies on personality change indicated that personality does change some in childhood, but it becomes more stable by middle age.

c. A meta-analysis of 150 studies on personality change indicated that personality does change some in childhood, but it becomes more stable by middle age.

30. b. General typologies is not one of the levels of personality as classified by Dan McAdams.

Incorrect answers:

a. The three levels of personality according to McAdams are dispositional traits, personal concerns, and life narratives.

c. The three levels of personality according to McAdams are dispositional traits, personal concerns, and life narratives.

d. The three levels of personality according to McAdams are dispositional traits, personal concerns, and life narratives.

31. c. A quantum change is a transformation of personality that is sudden, profound, and enduring.

Incorrect answers:

a. The butterfly effect is a made-up term.

b. Affective blossoming is a made-up term.

d. A trigger event is something that often results in a quantum change.

32. c. Low levels of serotonin are associated with hostility, aggressiveness, and criminality.

Incorrect answers:

a. Norepinephrine is associated with physiological arousal.

b. GABA is the primary inhibitory neurotransmitter.

d. Dopamine is often associated with reward areas in the brain.

Matching Questions

1. L   Persona
2. A   Personality
3. M   Psychodynamic
4. N   Life instinct
5. B   Topographical
6. K   Conscious
7. T   Preconscious
8. C   Unconscious
9. Q   Psychosexual
10. W   Latency
11. X   Genital
12. G   Anal-retentive
13. V   Id
14. U   Ego
15. F   Superego
16. E   Self-actualization
17. P   Person-centered
18. J   Fully functioning person
19. D   Broaden-and-build
20. O   Personality types
21. S   Factor analysis
22. R   Self-efficacy
23. I   Rorschach
24. H   Arousability

Thought Questions

1. Answers will vary, but students should try to identify their experiences that fit or do not fit each of the models. For example, if they can identify specific issues early in childhood that might have impacted their unconscious needs and motives, then they should endorse the psychodynamic model. Similarly, if they do not like the deterministic aspects of the psychodynamic and trait models and feel as if they are motivated to fulfill their fullest potential, then they should agree with the humanistic model. Students who see situations and the environment as being as important as inborn traits will follow the cognitive-social theories.

2. Answers will vary, but students should realize the association between neurotransmitter systems (e.g., serotonin) and personality traits such as hostility. The necessity for the medication could be addressed by the degree of impairment exhibited initially. Students might propose methods of personality change from other theories (e.g., psychodynamic, humanistic, cognitive-social). The potential for change would also depend on the age of the person, with greater stability being exhibited at middle age. The phenomenon of quantum change usually occurs in response to extreme negative affect and/or a trigger event.

CHAPTER 13 | Disorders of Mind and Body

GUIDE TO THE READING

In Chapter 13 the authors explain how certain behaviors come to be classified as mental disorders and consider the cognitive, situational, and biological context in which these behaviors occur. The designation of behavior as "abnormal" or as a "mental disorder" is invariably a cultural judgment. In addition, within American culture, the labeling of someone with a mental disorder results in stigma. After the chapter introduction, the authors look at common categories of mental disorders (anxiety, mood, schizophrenia, personality, childhood) and their causes. Recent advances from behavioral neuroscience have helped us understand both normal and abnormal human behaviors.

How Are Mental Disorders Conceptualized and Classified?

The chapter begins with a consideration of how disorders are conceptualized and classified. Again, abnormality is a cultural judgment, and particular behaviors may be seen as deviant in one society but unremarkable in another. In American society the symptoms of a disorder must interfere with at least one aspect of a person's life—such as work, social relations, and self-care. Health care professionals use the *Diagnostic and Statistical Manual of Mental Disorders (DSM-IV)* to identify psychological disorders. The *DSM* has been around for more than 50 years, and in its current fourth edition, psychopathology is described in terms of observable symptoms. Individuals are diagnosed on a multiaxial scale, including clinical syndromes, personality disorders, general medical conditions, psychosocial stressors, and global assessment of functioning. However, the *DSM-IV* gives little information about the cause, prognosis, or treatment of disorders.

The authors review some classic models of psychopathology (psychoanalytic, family systems, sociocultural, cognitive-behavioral). Most ideas of cause involve multiple factors and incorporate some aspect of the diathesis-stress model. This is the idea that disorders are the result of an underlying predisposition (diathesis) that is made evident by environmental stress.

Finally, the authors look at the differences between the psychological concept of mental disorders and legal concept of insanity. Most people mistakenly believe that the insanity defense is a common strategy to avoid criminal prosecution. In actuality, competency to stand trial is a more common area in which one's mental functioning comes into question.

Can Anxiety Be the Root of Seemingly Different Disorders?

The next section begins the consideration of specific psychological disorders. The anxiety disorders are characterized by excessive anxiety in the absence of true danger. Within this category, the phobias involve excessive fear of a specific object or situation. Most students will be familiar with specific phobias (e.g., claustrophobia, acrophobia, hydrophobia) that involve discrete events or objects. Most students also will have empathy for the social phobias that involve the fear of being negatively evaluated by others, fear of public speaking, and fear of eating in front of others.

Individuals with generalized anxiety disorder are constantly anxious and worry about trivial matters. Panic disorder involves sudden and overwhelming attacks of terror and often results in agoraphobia, the fear of being in a public situation from which escape is difficult. Obsessive-compulsive disorder (OCD) involves intrusive thoughts that are dealt with through maladaptive, repetitive actions. Numerous theories have been proposed to explain the anxiety disorders, and they certainly involve the cognitive misperceptions of actual danger. Recent advances in neurophysiology have related OCD to dysfunction in the caudate nucleus.

Are Mood Disorders Extreme Manifestations of Normal Mood?

The mood disorders, which involve extreme emotions, include one of the most common diagnostic categories—major depression. Individuals with this disorder show symptoms such as depressed mood, loss of interest in pleasurable activities, weight changes, sleep disturbances, difficulty concentrating, guilt, and suicidal ideation. A milder form of depression, dysthymia, involves depressed mood for at least two years. Moods can also swing from depression to mania, as is seen in bipolar disorder, or from mild depression to hypomania, as is seen in cyclothymia. A strong genetic component has been implicated in bipolar disorder. A genetic component has been found for major depression also, but it is not as strong.

Major depression has been linked to the neurotransmitters norepinephrine and serotonin. Indeed, medications such as Prozac that selectively increase serotonin have had a huge impact on treatment since the early 1990s. Depression has also been associated with maladaptive cognitions (e.g., Beck's cognitive triad), errors in logic, and learned helplessness. Finally, life stressors can precipitate an episode of major depression; however, the effects of these events can be attenuated by the presence of close friends.

Is Schizophrenia a Disorder of Mind or Body?

Schizophrenia is one of the most devastating of all the mental disorders in terms of its effect on the victim and family. Although it often is erroneously referred to as "split personality," the splitting in schizophrenia is between thought and emotion. Schizophrenia is a psychotic disorder, characterized by alterations in thought, perceptions, or consciousness. The rate of schizophrenia in the population is about 1 percent and has remained relatively stable across time and among cultures. Although the *DSM-IV* lists various subtypes of schizophrenia (paranoid, disorganized, catatonic, undifferentiated, residual), they can also be classified by positive and negative symptoms. The positive symptoms of schizophrenia involve excesses of behavior and include delusions, hallucinations, and loosening of associations. The negative symptoms of schizophrenia involve deficits in functioning and include isolation, withdrawal, and apathy. Schizophrenia has a strong biological component, and the positive symptoms often are dramatically reduced by antipsychotic medication. Unfortunately, the negative symptoms tend to persist, which has led investigators to hypothesize that this form of schizophrenia is related to structural brain abnormalities. One recent hypothesis regarding the cause of schizophrenia is that it is related to a slow-acting virus that causes evident symptoms when an individual reaches young adulthood.

Are Personality Disorders Truly Mental Disorders?

The personality disorders are a controversial category of disorders marked by inflexible and maladaptive ways of interacting with the world. Although the *DSM-IV* lists three categories of personality disorder by general behavior (odd/eccentric, dramatic/emotional/erratic, anxious/fearful), there is considerable overlap among the traits in the individual disorders. This has led to a reduction in reliability of diagnosis. Two of the personality disorders that have received considerable research investigation are borderline personality disorder and antisocial personality disorder.

Borderline personality disorder is characterized by a poor sense of self, emotional instability, and impulsivity. These individuals can be very dramatic and exhibit self-mutilation or suicidal behaviors. Borderline personality disorder has been linked to low serotonin levels and a history of physical and/or sexual abuse. Individuals with antisocial personality disorder demonstrate little empathy for others or remorse for their self-gratifying behaviors. This disorder is seen frequently in prison populations and has been related to low levels of arousal, poor response to punishment, and deficits in frontal lobe functioning.

Should Childhood Disorders Be Considered a Unique Category?

The final category, childhood disorders, remains controversial because children show varied rates of development. What is seen as abnormal at one stage may be normal at another. Autism is a severe childhood disorder characterized by deficits in social interaction, impaired communication, and restricted interests. It is hard to believe that not long ago this disorder was associated with poor parenting; today it is understood to have a largely biological cause. Genetic and neurochemical research appears to have tremendous promise in improving our understanding and treatment of autistic behaviors.

Attention-deficit/hyperactivity disorder (ADHD) has received considerable research and media attention in recent years. ADHD children are characterized by restlessness, inattention, and impulsivity. The unfortunate aspect of these symptoms is that they are associated with academic, social, and vocational underachievement. ADHD has been related to poor parenting and sociocultural factors; however, there also is a clear genetic component. Noted deficits in functioning in the frontolimbic system and basal ganglia provide potential areas for future treatments.

FILL-IN-THE-BLANK QUESTIONS

1. _____ is a sickness or disorder of the mind.

2. The _____ is the probable outcome of a disorder.

3. The _____ is based on the idea that the behavior of an individual must be considered within a social context, in particular the family.

4. The _____ view psychopathology as the result of the interaction between individuals and their cultures.

5. The central principle of the _____ approach is that abnormal behavior is learned.

6. The field of _____ involves the application of psychological science to the criminal justice system.

7. _____ crime scenes are those in which the murderer was acting in a rage, suggesting some prior relationship with the victim.

8. _____ crime scenes are those in which the victim appears simply to have been used so that the murderer could achieve other aims, such as obtaining money or sex.

9. _____ are characterized by excessive anxiety in the absence of true danger.

10. A _____ is a fear of a specific object or situation.

11. _____ sufferers experience attacks of terror that are sudden and overwhelming.

12. _____ are particular acts that the OCD patient feels driven to perform over and over again.

13. _____ is a fear of enclosed spaces.

14. _____ is a category of disorders characterized by extreme emotions.

15. _____ is a mood disorder characterized by severe negative moods and a lack of interest in pleasurable activities.

16. _____ is a form of depression that is not severe enough to be diagnosed as major depression.

17. _____ are characterized by elevated mood, increased activity, diminished need for sleep, grandiose ideas, racing thoughts, and extreme distractibility.

18. _____ are less extreme than manic episodes; these are often characterized by heightened creativity and productivity.

19. _____ disorder is when people fluctuate between major depression and hypomania.

20. Beck noted that depressed people often make _____, such as overgeneralizing based on single events, magnifying the seriousness of bad events, and personalizing, or taking responsibility for, bad events in the world that have little to do with them.

21. _____ is a psychotic disorder characterized by alterations in thoughts, perceptions, or consciousness.

22. _____ of schizophrenia are those that involve deficits in functioning such as apathy, lack of emotion, and slowed speech and movement.

23. _____ are false personal beliefs based on incorrect inferences about external reality.

24. The false belief that objects, events, or other people have particular significance to an individual is known as a delusion of _____.

25. The false belief that one has great power, knowledge, or talent is known as a delusion of _____.

26. _____ are perceptions with no clear external cause.

27. _____ is a category of mental disorders marked by inflexible and maladaptive ways of interacting with world.

28. _____ is characterized by identity, affective, and impulse disturbances.

29. _____ is characterized by deficits in social interaction, impaired communication, and restricted interests.

30. _____ is high-functioning autism, in which children of normal intelligence have specific deficits in social interaction, such as having an impoverished theory of mind.

31. _____ is a symptom of autism in which children may replace *I* with *you*.

32. Children with _____ are restless, inattentive, and impulsive.

MULTIPLE-CHOICE QUESTIONS

1. Emil uses the most common psychological text in the United States to diagnose Sybil. The book he is using is known as the
   a. *Minnesota Multiphasic Personality Inventory (MMPI).*
   b. *Diagnostic and Statistical Manual of Mental Disorders (DSM-IV).*
   c. *Mental Health Guide Book (MHGB).*
   d. *International Classification of Diseases (ICD-10).*

2. When Sybil is being diagnosed, she is not given one label but is rated on factors, such as clinical syndromes, personality disorders, and psychosocial stressors. This is the case because the *DSM-IV* employs a _____ system to classify disorders.
   a. multivariate
   b. cross-cut
   c. multiaxial
   d. diathesis-stress

3. According to Freudian psychoanalytic theory, mental disorders are mostly due to _____ that date back to childhood.
   a. incorrect learning experiences
   b. unconscious conflicts
   c. blocked self-actualization strivings
   d. maladaptive cognitions

4. Kramer has a family history of psychotic behavior. However, he does not exhibit these symptoms until he goes through an extremely stressful period with his mother and girlfriend. This interaction of factors that causes Kramer's difficulties is representative of the _____ model of mental disorders.
   a. diathesis-stress
   b. interactive
   c. synergistic
   d. cognitive-behavioral

5. The current definition of _____ states that a person is not responsible if, at the time of the crime, a mental illness or defect led to a lack of capacity to appreciate the criminality of the act or to an inability to conform to the requirements of the law.
   a. schizophrenia
   b. psychoticism
   c. insanity
   d. psychopath

6. Robert has been charged with a felony. He and his attorney are considering using insanity as a defense in the case. In what percentage of felony indictments is an insanity plea made?
   a. 50%.
   b. 25%.
   c. 10%.
   d. 1%.

7. The issue of whether a defendant can understand the legal proceedings and contribute to his own defense is known as
   a. the insanity defense.
   b. competency to stand trial.
   c. civil commitment.
   d. criminal commitment.

8. Ever since Adam fell off the top bunk at camp when he was 12 years old, he has had a fear of heights. Because of this fear, he refuses to climb the Empire State building, go out on his balcony, or ever sleep on the top bunk again. What type of disorder is he experiencing?
   a. Specific phobia.
   b. Social phobia.
   c. Xenophobia.
   d. Agoraphobia.

9. Theresa has been dreading her oral presentation in her public speaking class. As she rushes through her material, she suddenly begins to shake tremendously and becomes fearful of saying something silly to the class. Finally, it gets so bad she is unable to continue. Theresa is suffering from
   a. social phobia.
   b. mixed anxiety disorder.
   c. agoraphobia.
   d. simple phobia.

10. Rebecca notices that her roommate, Tabitha, freaks out when a professor tells her that she needs to study a little more. Rebecca also notices that Tabitha is constantly worried about her relationship with her boyfriend, even though it is a wonderful, loving one. Because of this constant worry that is not linked to an identifiable source, Rebecca thinks Tabitha suffers from
    a. phobic disorder.
    b. panic disorder.
    c. generalized anxiety disorder.
    d. obsessive-compulsive disorder.

11. Amber can't seem to go anywhere and has become a prisoner of her own dorm room. She no longer shops at the mall or goes to the movies, and she is in constant fear of having a panic attack in front of others. Amber's intense fear of public places in which escape would be difficult is referred to as
    a. agoraphobia.
    b. xenophobia.
    c. ophidiophobia.
    d. triskaidekophobia.

12. When Monica leaves for work in the morning, she checks three times to see if her curling iron is off and then checks the coffee maker three times. Next she checks the locks to the house three times before finally leaving. Monica is likely suffering from
    a. obsessive-compulsive disorder.
    b. repetition disorder.
    c. somatoform disorder.
    d. dissociative disorder.

13. Which of the following choices can be considered an obsession related to obsessive-compulsive disorder?
    a. Washing one's hands 15 times before leaving the bathroom after each use.
    b. A baseball player banging his shoes in the dirt before hitting.
    c. Thinking about how you might have left your door unlocked before class.
    d. Cutting your food into even-numbered amounts before eating.

14. Jack suffers from constant fears of contamination and washes his hands repetitively to calm his anxieties. The part of the basal ganglia that seems most associated with this behavior is the
    a. substantia nigra.
    b. caudate nucleus.
    c. locus coeruleus.
    d. mesolimbic system.

15. Rita has been suffering from ever-increasing panic attacks. She worries about either doing something impulsive or going crazy. Which of the following disorders is she likely to develop if these episodes are not treated?
    a. Generalized anxiety disorder.
    b. Acute stress disorder.
    c. Agoraphobia.
    d. Social phobia.

16. One week, Katy was so happy to be a college student. She excitedly told her entire family how much fun she was having, and she decided that she was going to have as much fun as possible while in college. Now, two weeks later, Katy has trouble getting out of bed in the morning and is even thinking about dropping out of school. This drastic change in mood is characteristic of the disorder currently known as
    a. bipolar disorder.
    b. unipolar disorder.
    c. manic depression.
    d. schizophrenia.

17. Patty cycles through about two months of major depression, two months of relative normality, and two months of mania. Her specific *DSM-IV* diagnosis is
    a. bipolar I disorder.
    b. bipolar II disorder.
    c. unipolar mood disorder.
    d. cyclothymia.

18. Elaine suffers from mild affective swings characteristic of a mood disorder. She experiences both hypomania and mild depression. Elaine would be diagnosed with
    a. bipolar I disorder.
    b. bipolar II disorder.
    c. dysthymia.
    d. cyclothymia.

19. William lives in a city in the northern United States. He finds that he becomes depressed every winter when the days become shorter and there is little sunlight. William likely suffers from
    a. Unipolar disorder.
    b. Dysthymia.
    c. Seasonal affective disorder.
    d. Autumnal melancholia.

20. Which of the following is *not* part of Beck's cognitive triad of depression?
    a. Learned helplessness.
    b. Negative thoughts about the self.
    c. Negative thoughts about the situation.
    d. Negative thoughts about the future.

21. After studying for hours and still failing the first two exams in his anthropology class, Jay has given up studying for the class completely. He feels that he has no control whatsoever when it comes to this class, and he is bound to fail despite his level of studying. Jay's expectation of failure and the resulting apathy and depression are examples of
    a. dysthymic cognitions.
    b. self-perpetuating style.
    c. melancholia.
    d. learned helplessness.

22. Matt was diagnosed as having paranoid schizophrenia. He has delusions of the world being taken over by giant lizards and hallucinations of insects crawling over him. Matt's schizophrenic behaviors are an example of which type of symptom?
    a. Negative symptoms.
    b. Positive symptoms.
    c. Flattened affect.
    d. Mood disorders.

23. Pete was sitting in his psychology class when he thought he saw an individual staring at him from the outside. He began to notice those around him acting oddly, and he felt he was being watched every place he went. He even checked the phones in his apartment because he believed they were tapped. Pete was having which type of delusion?
    a. Persecution.
    b. Reference.
    c. Grandeur.
    d. Somatic.

24. The stress of school has pushed Ginger over the edge into exhibiting some schizophrenic symptoms. When asked a question about the Scantron sheet during the exam, she replies, "When a sperm and egg come

together, they make a beautiful baby." This represents the category of symptoms known as
a. loosening of associations.
b. disturbance in thought content.
c. perceptual disturbances.
d. affective symptoms.

25. Amy has been admitted to a prestigious graduate school on the East Coast. However, the housing situation at the school is so bad that Amy deteriorates into speaking in clang association to her professors. Which of the following represents what she most likely said?
a. How are *you* today? How are you *today*? How *are* you today?
b. School rule, fool, tool, drool, ghoul, jewel, *cool toadstool*!!
c. Fred blue hammer Tar Heel Jordan basketball Tobacco Road!
d. I am so tired of *dregling* for *parsingian* apartments!

26. April's personality has begun to closely resemble those of some of the most notorious murderers of the past few decades. She has become very manipulative and self-serving. She feels sorry for nothing and seems to lack a conscience. April suffers from the disorder currently known as _____ personality.
a. psychopathic
b. sociopathic
c. antisocial
d. narcissistic

27. Heather has shown symptoms of autism since she was a little girl. She now is exhibiting the speech symptom of echolalia. Which of the following represents what she would most likely say?
a. How are *you* today? How are you *today*? How *are* you today?
b. School rule, fool, tool, drool, ghoul, jewel, *cool toadstool*!!
c. Fred blue hammer Tar Heel Jordan basketball Tobacco Road!
d. I am so tired of *dregling* for *parsingian* apartments!

28. Mara was highly upset at not being named athlete of the week in the local college newspaper. The stress of this crushing blow caused her to relapse into catatonic schizophrenic behavior. Which of the following symptoms is Mara most likely to exhibit?
a. She giggles hebephrenically and smears her feces on the wall of the lobby.
b. She believes that her coach has talked the newspaper editor into writing bad things about her in the paper.

c. She curls up in the corner by the candy machine and exhibits mutism.
d. She shows a lot of prominent schizophrenic symptoms that do not clearly fit any one pattern.

29. Dr. Beck, a psychology professor, is beginning to display delusions of control. Which of the following symptoms is he most likely exhibiting?
a. He thinks his students are plotting to steal his children because they are sick of their pictures in the lectures.
b. He believes that he will be named teacher of the year by the American Psychological Association.
c. He thinks the neurotransmitters in his brain are being influenced by a supercomputer housed in the administration building.
d. He believes, while watching *No Doubt* videos, that Gwen Stefani is sending him coded messages that she wants to go on a date with him.

30. Nancy was watching *Friends* reruns on television, when she falsely believed that Joey (one of the actors) turned to her and said "How you doin'?" She did not find it odd that a television actor was hitting on her from her TV, and they continued to flirt until the show was over. Nancy is suffering from delusions of
a. control.
b. reference.
c. specificity.
d. somatization.

MATCHING QUESTIONS

Fill in the letter from Column B corresponding to the term that is most associated with the description presented in Column A.

Column A	Column B
____ 1. Process of examining a person's mental functions and psychological health.	A. Mental status exam
____ 2. Brief evaluation given in the ER to determine whether person has a mental disorder.	B. Dissociative identity disorder
____ 3. Most common method of psychological assessment.	C. Histrionic, narcissistic, borderline, antisocial
____ 4. One of the first persons to propose a classification system for mental disorders.	D. Tourette's disorder
	E. Streptococcal infection

_____ 5. Interviews in which the topics of discussion vary.

_____ 6. Interviews that use standardized questions that are asked in the same order each time.

_____ 7. Most widely used questionnaire for psychological assessment.

_____ 8. Occurrence of two or more distinct personalities in the same individual.

_____ 9. Person moves to a new city and assumes a new identity.

_____ 10. Focuses on how physiological factors, such as genetics, contribute to mental illness.

_____ 11. Environmental factor that can trigger OCD.

_____ 12. Anxiety disorder that results from untreated panic attacks.

_____ 13. Psychological scientist who gave a personal account of bipolar disorder in *An Unquiet Mind*.

_____ 14. False belief that others are spying on or trying to harm you.

_____ 15. False belief that you have committed a terrible sin.

_____ 16. Personality disorders in which one displays odd or eccentric behavior.

_____ 17. Personality disorders characterized by dramatic, emotional, and erratic behaviors.

_____ 18. Personality disorders characterized by anxious or fearful behaviors.

_____ 19. Repeated regurgitation and rechewing of partially digested food.

_____ 20. Recurrent motor and vocal tics that cause marked distress or impairment.

F. Rumination disorder
G. Assessment
H. Kraepelin
I. Structured
J. Delusion of guilt
K. Avoidant, dependent, obsessive-compulsive
L. Kay Redfield Jamison
M. Clinical interview
N. Biological perspective
O. Delusion of persecution
P. Paranoid, schizoid, schizotypal
Q. Fugue state
R. MMPI
S. Unstructured
T. Agoraphobia

THOUGHT QUESTIONS

1. Although the syndrome of ADHD has been around for quite some time, its prevalence seems to have exploded in recent years. Speculate as to possible biological and cultural reasons for this increase.

2. As is evident from the text, the fourth edition of the *Diagnostic and Statistical Model of Mental Disorder (DSM-IV)* is based on a medical model. That is, the manual describes symptoms that are then lumped into a syndrome. We assume that these syndromes have a cause or etiology as well as a prognosis and treatment. This is very consistent with how Emil Kraepelin conceptualized mental disorders when he was in Leipzig with Wundt.

    Imagine, however, that a different model had influenced the conceptualization of mental disorders. For example, what if we focused on the sociocultural model as the most influential for etiology, prognosis, and treatment? How would this influence our methods of diagnosis, assessment, and treatments?

APPLICATIONS

An Activity to Explicate One's Model of Abnormality

Identify whether the following vignettes represent abnormal behavior. Provide reasons for your opinions. Then give a definition of *abnormal behavior*.

1. A 22-year-old man is currently unable to maintain any type of employment. He was always in special education classes in school, and his IQ score is significantly below average.

2. A 37-year-old artist is totally devoted to her work. She is independently wealthy and does not like to be around other people. She has her small house staff bring her everything she needs. She has not left her home in five years.

3. A first-year college student maintains religious beliefs that do not allow her to wear makeup; however, her two roommates do. She tries to avoid them and is uncomfortable when she is around them.

4. A 35-year-old man is sexually excited by the sight of a woman's high-heeled shoes. He does not desire to date others, and these fantasies are his only sexual outlet. He takes a job as a shoe salesman.

5. A woman becomes depressed every month before her menstrual cycle begins. She usually is ineffective at her job during these times and is difficult to get along with. Often she yells at her husband and children.

6. Two 27-year-old gay men have been living together for four years. They report a very close monogamous relationship and are distressed about recent sodomy laws. They are considering adopting a child.

7. A man stands on the sidewalk near a large store handing out $100 bills. He explains that he just finished a business deal that will make him a lot of money and he would like to share his wealth with those who are less fortunate.

8. A minister's wife reports that she frequently talks to God and that many times she has heard his "still small voice." She reports some marital difficulties and states that God has told her to take her children out of the home and move to the church's headquarters in Wyoming.

9. A 37-year-old woman has been married since she was 17. Her life revolves around her husband, and she has no independent friends or hobbies. Her husband has engaged in numerous extramarital affairs and is often verbally abusive to her. Her friends tell her to leave this man, but she reports that she enjoys her life with him because she loves him.

10. A mother and father are engaged in a biter divorce struggle in which they use their 8-year-old daughter as a pawn. The mother and father are tormenting the girl, demanding that she decide with whom she wishes to live. She has begun to withdraw from her friends at school and has recently wet her bed.

Abnormal Behavior: An Activity to Assess Popular Views of Mental Disorders

This exercise is based on common diagnostic controversies still evident in the clinical literature. Whether each of the cases would be considered abnormal has changed over time. The purpose of the exercise is to see whether you are consistent in applying your implicit rules of abnormality and to sensitize you to the difficulties of these judgments. Labeling a behavior as abnormal is always a societal judgment that is influenced by one's culture and values.

To assess how people view mental disorders, assemble a group of friends for the following activity. Try to come up with a list of psychological disorders in the chapter that are represented in television and/or the movies (e.g., schizophrenia in *A Beautiful Mind*). When you have your list of movies and TV shows, try to determine whether the media has a sympathetic and helpful version of the disorder or whether it has belittled and sensationalized the individual for entertainment. If you were from another planet and this was your only exposure to our mental health system, would you

be willing to publicly reveal a psychological disorder and seek treatment? Why or why not?

WEB SITES

General Mental Health

www.apa.org
www.webmd.org
http://psychcentral.com

Anxiety Disorders

http://anxiety.psy.ohio-state.edu

Mood Disorders

www.psycom.net/depression.central.html

Schizophrenia

www.schizophrenia.com

Personality Disorders

www.isspd.com

Childhood Disorders

www.adhd.com

ANSWER KEY

Fill-in-the-Blank Questions

1. Psychopathology
2. Prognosis
3. Family systems model
4. Sociocultural model
5. Cognitive-behavioral
6. Forensic psychology
7. Expressive
8. Instrumental
9. Anxiety disorders
10. Phobia
11. Panic disorder
12. Compulsions
13. Claustrophobia
14. Mood disorders
15. Major depression
16. Dysthymia
17. Manic episodes
18. Hypomanic episodes
19. Bipolar II
20. Errors in logic
21. Schizophrenia
22. Negative symptoms
23. Delusions
24. Reference
25. Grandeur
26. Hallucinations
27. Personality disorders
28. Borderline personality disorder
29. Autism
30. Asperger's syndrome
31. Pronoun reversal
32. Attention-deficit/hyperactivity disorder

Multiple-Choice Questions

1. b. The *DSM-IV* is the standard diagnostic text in the field of psychology and psychiatry; it is now in its fourth edition.

   Incorrect answers:
   a. The *Minnesota Multiphasic Personality Inventory (MMPI)* is an objective personality measure.
   c. The *Mental Health Guide Book (MHGB)* is a made-up term.
   d. The *International Classification of Diseases (ICD-10)* is used worldwide, but it is not the standard text in the United States.

2. c. The *DSM-IV* employs a multiaxial system to classify disorders. Patients are not given a single label but rather are classified in terms of a set of clinically important factors.

   Incorrect answers:
   a. Multivariate refers to having multiple variables.
   b. Cross-cut is a made-up term.
   d. Diathesis-stress is a diagnostic model that proposes that disorders develop when an underlying vulnerability is coupled with a precipitating event.

3. b. According to Freudian psychoanalytic theory, mental disorders are mostly due to unconscious conflicts that date back to childhood.

   Incorrect answers:
   a. Incorrect learning experiences are the causal mechanisms in the behavioral (cognitive-social) model of abnormality.
   c. Blocked self-actualization strivings are the causal mechanisms in the humanistic model of abnormality.
   d. Maladaptive cognitions are the causal mechanisms in the cognitive-social model of abnormality.

4. a. Diathesis-stress is a diagnostic model that proposes that disorders develop when an underlying vulnerability is coupled with a precipitating event.

   Incorrect answers:
   b. There is no interactive model of abnormality.
   c. There is no synergistic model of abnormality.
   d. The cognitive-behavioral model focuses on maladaptive cognitions and improper learning as the causes of abnormal behavior.

5. c. The current definition of insanity states that a person is not responsible if, at the time of the crime, a mental illness or defect led to a lack of capacity to appreciate the criminality of the act or to an inability to conform to the requirements of the law.

Incorrect answers:
a. Schizophrenia is a thought disorder characterized by a loss of reality.
b. Psychoticism is a psychological trait; insanity is a legal term.
d. Psychopath is a term for an individual with no conscience.

6. d. The insanity plea is used in only 1 percent of felony indictments.

   Incorrect answers:
   a. The insanity plea is used in only 1 percent of felony indictments.
   b. The insanity plea is used in only 1 percent of felony indictments.
   c. The insanity plea is used in only 1 percent of felony indictments.

7. b. The issue of whether a defendant can understand the legal proceedings and contribute to his own defense is known as competency to stand trial.

   Incorrect answers:
   a. The current definition of insanity states that a person is not responsible if, at the time of the crime, a mental illness or defect led to a lack of capacity to appreciate the criminality of the act or to an inability to conform to the requirements of the law.
   c. Civil commitment is the process of involuntarily committing individuals to mental institutions.
   d The issue of whether a defendant can understand the legal proceedings and contribute to his own defense is known as competency to stand trial.

8. a. Specific phobias are fears of particular objects or situations such as heights (acrophobia).

   Incorrect answers:
   b. Social phobia is a fear of being negatively evaluated by others.
   c. Xenophobia is a fear of strangers.
   d. Agoraphobia is a fear of being in situations in which escape is difficult or impossible.

9. a. Social phobia is a fear of being negatively evaluated by others and includes a fear of public speaking.

   Incorrect answers:
   b. There is no mixed anxiety disorder.
   c. Agoraphobia is a fear of being in situations in which escape is difficult or impossible.
   d. Simple phobia is an earlier term for specific phobia. It is no longer used in the diagnostic manual.

10. c. Generalized anxiety disorder is characterized by constant worry that is not linked to an identifiable source.

Incorrect answers:
a. A phobic disorder refers to a fear of a specific object or situation.
b. Panic disorder is an anxiety disorder characterized by sudden, overwhelming attacks of terror.
d. Obsessive-compulsive disorder is an anxiety disorder characterized by frequent intrusive thoughts and compulsive actions.

11. a. Agoraphobia is a fear of being in situations in which escape is difficult or impossible.

Incorrect answers:
b. Xenophobia is a fear of strangers.
c. Ophidiophobia is a fear of snakes.
d. Triskaidekophobia is a fear of the number 13.

12. a. Obsessive-compulsive disorder is an anxiety disorder characterized by frequent intrusive thoughts and compulsive actions.

Incorrect answers:
b. There is no repetition disorder.
c. Somatoform disorder is the category that involves a loss or alteration of physical functioning with no organic cause that is made worse by psychological factors.
d. Dissociative disorder is the category that involves a loss or alteration in ordinary consciousness (e.g., multiple personality).

13. c. Obsessions are frequent intrusive thoughts.

Incorrect answers:
a. Obsessions are frequent intrusive thoughts; compulsions are repetitive acts.
b. Obsessions are frequent intrusive thoughts; compulsions are repetitive acts.
d. Obsessions are frequent intrusive thoughts; compulsions are repetitive acts.

14. b. The caudate nucleus is the part of the basal ganglia that seems most associated with OCD.

Incorrect answers:
a. The caudate nucleus is the part of the basal ganglia that seems most associated with OCD.
c. The locus coeruleus has been implicated in panic disorder.
d. The caudate nucleus is the part of the basal ganglia that seems most associated with OCD.

15. c. Agoraphobia is often the result of untreated panic attacks.

Incorrect answers:
a. Agoraphobia is often the result of untreated panic attacks.
b. Agoraphobia is often the result of untreated panic attacks.
d. Agoraphobia is often the result of untreated panic attacks.

16. a. Those who are diagnosed with bipolar disorder have periods of major depression but also experience episodes of mania.

Incorrect answers:
b. Unipolar depression is another name for major depression.
c. Manic depression is the earlier name for bipolar disorder.
d. Schizophrenia is a mental disorder characterized by alteration in perceptions, emotions, thoughts, or consciousness.

17. a. Bipolar I disorder is characterized by alternating episodes of major depression and mania.

Incorrect answers:
b. Bipolar II disorder is characterized by fluctuations between major depression and hypomania.
c. Unipolar mood disorder refers to consistent depression.
d. Cyclothymia is when individuals experience hypomania and mild depression.

18. d. Cyclothymia is when individuals experience hypomania and mild depression.

Incorrect answers:
a. Bipolar I disorder is characterized by alternating episodes of major depression and mania.
b. Bipolar II disorder is characterized by fluctuations between major depression and hypomania.
c. Dysthymia is a form of depression that is not severe enough to be diagnosed as major depression.

19. c. Seasonal affective disorder results in periods of depression corresponding to the shorter days of winter in the northern latitudes.

Incorrect answers:
a. Unipolar mood disorder refers to consistent depression.
b. Dysthymia is a form of depression that is not severe enough to be diagnosed as major depression.
d. Autumnal melancholia is a made-up term.

20. a. Beck's cognitive triad of depression includes negative thoughts about the self, situation, and future; learned helplessness is not part of this.

    Incorrect answers:
    b. Beck's cognitive triad of depression includes negative thoughts about the self, situation, and future.
    c. Beck's cognitive triad of depression includes negative thoughts about the self, situation, and future.
    d. Beck's cognitive triad of depression includes negative thoughts about the self, situation, and future.

21. d. People suffering from learned helplessness come to expect that bad things will happen over which they will have little control.

    Incorrect answers:
    a. Dysthymic cognitions would be thoughts that are mildly depressed.
    b. Self-perpetuating style is a made-up term.
    c. Melancholia is a characteristic of depression.

22. b. Positive symptoms of schizophrenia involve excesses of behavior (e.g., delusions, hallucinations).

    Incorrect answers:
    a. The negative symptoms of schizophrenia are marked by deficits in functioning such as apathy, lack of emotion, and slowed speech and movement.
    c. Flattened affect refers to a restricted range of emotional expression.
    d. Mood disorders reflect extreme emotions.

23. a. Delusions of persecution involve the belief that others are persecuting, spying on, or trying to harm oneself.

    Incorrect answers:
    b. A delusion of reference is the belief that objects, events, or other people have particular significance to them.
    c. A delusion of grandeur is the belief that one has great power, knowledge, or talent.
    d. A somatic delusion refers to a false belief about bodily processes.

24. a. Loosening of associations is a symptom of schizophrenia in which individuals shift between seemingly unrelated topics as they speak.

    Incorrect answers:
    b. Disturbance in thought content is a symptom of schizophrenia related to delusions or false beliefs.
    c. Perceptual disturbances refers to the schizophrenic symptom of hallucinations.

d. Affective symptoms are the emotional symptoms of schizophrenia (e.g., flattening, restricted, inappropriate).

25. b. Clang associations are a schizophrenic symptom involving the stringing together of words that rhyme but have no other apparent link.

    Incorrect answers:
    a. Echolalia is the repetition of words or phrases.
    c. Loosening of associations is a symptom of schizophrenia in which individuals shift between seemingly unrelated topics as they speak.
    d. Neologisms is a schizophrenic symptom in which individuals make up new words.

26. c. Antisocial personality disorder is marked by a lack of empathy and remorse.

    Incorrect answers:
    a. Psychopath is an older term for an individual with no conscience.
    b. Sociopath is an older term for an individual with no conscience.
    d. Narcissistic personality disorder refers to individuals who are excessively self-absorbed.

27. a. Echolalia is the repetition of words or phrases, sometimes including an imitation of the intonation and sometime using a high-pitched monotone.

    Incorrect answers:
    b. Clang associations are a schizophrenic symptom involving the stringing together of words that rhyme but have no other apparent link.
    c. Loosening of associations is a symptom of schizophrenia in which individuals shift between seemingly unrelated topics as they speak.
    d. Neologisms is a schizophrenic symptom in which individuals make up new words.

28. c. Catatonic schizophrenia is characterized by extreme motor immobility, negativism, mutism, bizarre movement, and/or echolalia.

    Incorrect answers:
    a. Disorganized schizophrenia involves disorganized speech, disorganized behavior, and inappropriate or flat affect.
    b. Paranoid schizophrenia involves preoccupation with delusions or auditory hallucinations.
    d. Undifferentiated schizophrenia involves the prominent symptoms but does not fit any of the subtypes.

29. c. Delusions of control are the false belief that one's thoughts and behaviors are being controlled by external forces.

Incorrect answers:

a. Delusions of persecution are the false belief that others are persecuting, spying on, or trying to harm them.

b. Delusions of grandeur are the false belief that one has great power, knowledge, or talent.

d. Delusions of reference are the false belief that objects, events, or other people have particular significance.

30. b. Delusions of reference are the false belief that objects, events, or other people have particular significance.

Incorrect answers:

a. Delusions of control are the false belief that one's thoughts and behaviors are being controlled by external forces.

c. There are no delusions of specificity.

d. There are no delusions of somatization.

Matching Questions

1. G   Assessment
2. A   Mental status exam
3. M   Clinical interview
4. H   Kraepelin
5. S   Unstructured
6. I   Structured
7. R   MMPI
8. B   Dissociative identity disorder
9. Q   Fugue state
10. N   Biological perspective
11. E   Streptococcal infection
12. T   Agoraphobia
13. L   Kay Redfield Jamison
14. O   Delusion of persecution
15. J   Delusion of guilt
16. P   Paranoid, schizoid, schizotypal
17. C   Histrionic, narcissistic, borderline, antisocial
18. K   Avoidant, dependent, obsessive-compulsive
19. F   Rumination disorder
20. D   Tourette's disorder

Thought Questions

1. Answers will vary but, as with all disorders, greater awareness of it leads to improved diagnosis. In addition, students might consider the American cultural phenomenon of having both parents in the workforce. More students are being placed in structured day care settings at an earlier age and are expected to follow rules and behave cooperatively with others. Similarly, class sizes in school have increased appreciably so that two or three disruptive children represent a significant problem. Poor parenting has been related to ADHD, and students might relate this to the breakup of the traditional family and high divorce rates. Overall, the pace of life has quickened in society, and exposure to rapid information media (e.g., television versus books) may reduce attention spans. Finally, students might speculate as to biological reasons that contribute to the underarousal of frontal lobes seen in ADHD. Undetected environmental toxins from an industrialized society are a possible culprit.

2. Answers will vary, but students should see how much the medical model has influenced our ideas of diagnosis and treatment. From this model, we focus on the individual whose disorder is caused by some sort of pathological process (either biological or environmental). Treatment is often biological and focused on eliminating the "disease." From a sociocultural model, we would focus much more on the context (both interpersonal and environmental). Instead of the individual being ill, you could identify pathological environments. There would be less focus on medication to cure the individual and more on changing the environment to be more healthful and productive. More focus might be given to community support processes as well as possible preventive mechanisms.

CHAPTER 14 | Treating Disorders of Mind and Body

GUIDE TO THE READING

The penultimate chapter of the book presents the findings from psychological science as they apply to psychotherapy. The placement of this chapter toward the end of the text is appropriate because empirically based psychotherapy is an integration of the information learned in previous chapters. The authors present the basic principles of the major approaches to treatment and identify the common factors that enhance all treatments. Then they present research findings on the most successful treatments for anxiety, mood, schizophrenic, personality, and childhood disorders. In some cases one approach to treatment has shown to be superior, whereas in others multiple approaches may be equally effective. For some disorders the prognosis for improvement remains poor. Regardless of technique, social context and familial influences play a major role in therapeutic success. Effective psychotherapy is an ongoing process that combines the art of a caring therapist and the most recent findings from psychological science.

How Is Mental Illness Treated?

The first section of the chapter presents the principles of the major approaches to treatment. Historically, much of what was done in psychotherapy was based on the practitioner's theoretical orientation. One's views about the causes of psychological disorders heavily influenced one's approach and the techniques used.

Psychodynamic therapists employ free association and dream analysis to achieve insight about unconscious influences. Humanistic therapists use reflective listening as in client-centered therapy to facilitate greater self-understanding and personal growth. Behavioral therapists use specific techniques such as social skills training and systematic desensitization to produce more adaptive behavior through the principles of operant and classical conditioning. Cognitive-behavioral therapy (CBT) incorporates these learning principles while addressing the faulty cognitions that lead to maladaptive behaviors and emotions.

Practitioners from different theoretical approaches use the social support and interpersonal learning found in group therapy to address their clients' issues. The systems approach to psychotherapy considers that one's individual problems arise in a larger family context and that one must address how the family interacts to achieve a more durable result. Finally, biological therapies recognize that some psychological disorders result from abnormalities in neural and bodily processes. They attempt to change these processes, most commonly through the use of psychotropic medications such as antianxiety drugs, antidepressants, and antipsychotics.

It is noteworthy that numerous research studies have found these approaches to be effective. It is equally interesting that, overall, no one approach has been found to be clearly superior to the others. Part of this may be attributable to the fact that some common factors contribute to the effectiveness of all approaches despite the specific techniques used. Common factors include a strong relationship between the therapist and client and the powerful emotional reaction of confession (i.e., catharsis).

What Are the Most Effective Treatments?

The next section presents research findings on what the most effective treatments are for anxiety, mood, and schizophrenic disorders. One of the major changes in psychological treatment in recent years has been the shift of therapists from an allegiance to one approach to the more eclectic use of multiple approaches, depending on the person and problem. For specific phobias, behavioral techniques based on exposure (e.g., systematic desensitization) are the treatment of choice. CBT and medication (e.g., imipramine) have been found useful in the treatment of panic disorder. For those who have panic disorder with agoraphobia, the combination of CBT and drugs is significantly better than either treatment alone. CBT and medication (e.g., clomipramine) have also been helpful in the treatment of obsessive-compulsive disorder (OCD). Exposure and response prevention are the critical components of the behavioral intervention for OCD. There are multiple effective treatments for the mood disorders. For depression, several classes of medication have been found to be effective including monoamine oxidase (MAO) inhibitors, tricyclics, and selective serotonin reuptake inhibitors (SSRIs). The SSRIs, including Prozac, are used more frequently because they tend to cause fewer side effects. For depression, results from cognitive behavioral therapy and treatment with medication are equal, which gives clients a choice based on individual preference. CBT attacks the distorted cognitions that result in negative mood. Some recent studies suggest that combining CBT and antidepressants is more effective than either approach alone.

Phototherapy, exposure to high-intensity light, is effective in the treatment of seasonal affective disorder. For more severe treatment-resistant forms of depression, electroconvulsive therapy (ECT) has been a last resort. More recently, transcranial magnetic stimulation (TMS) has been proposed as an alternative to ECT and medication. Thus far it appears that TMS is more effective for nonpsychotic depression, whereas ECT is more effective for psychotic depression. For individuals with bipolar disorder, the choice of treatment is clear—the drug lithium has far surpassed other approaches.

Psychotropic medications have been found to be the most effective treatment for schizophrenia. Traditional antipsychotics (e.g., chlorpromazine, haloperidol) work by blocking dopamine receptors. Unfortunately, they result in significant side effects (e.g., tardive dyskinesia) and change only the positive symptoms of schizophrenia. Newer antipsychotics (e.g., clozapine) address the positive and negative symptoms of schizophrenia. The efficacy of these drugs improves substantially when combined with family support, social and self-care skills training, and cognitive interventions.

Can Personality Disorders Be Treated?

Because personality disorders are, by definition, chronic maladaptive ways of interacting with the world, they are extremely difficult to treat. Individuals with these disorders tend to see the environment rather than their own behaviors as the cause of their problems; thus they are unmotivated to change. Treatment for two well-researched personality disorders is presented.

Dialectical behavior therapy (DBT) has been the most successful treatment program to date for borderline personality disorder. In DBT the therapist targets the client's most extreme and dysfunctional behaviors, explores past traumatic experiences that may be at the root of emotional problems, and facilitates the development of self-respect and independent problem solving. Despite many varied attempts, little has been found to help individuals with antisocial personality disorder. One can hope for a reduction in antisocial behaviors after age 40, perhaps due to a reduction in biological drives. It appears that efforts in this area are better spent in prevention and support for the individual's family.

How Should Childhood Disorders Be Treated?

The final section of the chapter looks at treatments for two of the childhood disorders. Although autism is considered a biological disorder, biological interventions have been largely ineffective. Autistic children seem to benefit the most from highly structured behavioral therapies based on principles of operant conditioning; however, the long-term prognosis for autism remains poor. More options are available for children with attention-deficit/hyperactivity disorder (ADHD). Pharmacological treatment (e.g., methylphenidate) is beneficial for many; however, its use has sparked much controversy. As with most medications, Ritalin is not a magic bullet that removes all problems. Its effect is significantly enhanced when children also receive some type of behavior modification. Recent research indicates that medication plus behavioral therapy is more effective in treating ADHD than either treatment approach alone.

FILL-IN-THE-BLANK QUESTIONS

1. _____ is the generic name given to formal psychological treatment.

2. _____ reflect the medical approach to illness and disease.

3. _____ is the treatment of mental disorders by the use of medications that affect brain or bodily functions.

4. _____ is a psychoanalytic technique in which the therapist interprets the hidden meaning of dreams.

5. _____ is the goal of some types of therapy; it is the personal understanding of one's psychological processes.

6. _____ is an empathetic approach to therapy that encourages people to fulfill their individual potentials for personal growth through greater self-understanding.

7. _____ is a brief client-centered therapy approach for problem drinkers; its success is attributed to the warmth shown the client.

8. _____, based on operant conditioning, rewards desired behaviors and ignores or punishes unwanted behaviors.

9. _____ is a behavioral therapy designed to teach and reinforce appropriate interpersonal behavior.

10. _____ is a treatment technique in which the therapist acts out the appropriate behavior and encourages the client to imitate it.

11. _____ is a treatment in which patients are encouraged to express their emotions and explore interpersonal experiences.

12. Many behavioral therapies for phobia include _____, in which the client is repeatedly exposed directly to the anxiety-producing stimulus or situation.

13. _____ is a therapy technique in which clinicians help their patients recognize maladaptive thought patterns and replace them with ways of viewing the world that are more in tune with reality.

14. Albert Ellis introduced _____, in which therapists act as teachers who explain and demonstrate more adaptive ways of thinking and behaving.

15. Perhaps the most widely used version of cognitive therapy is _____, which incorporates techniques from behavioral therapy and cognitive therapy to correct faulty thinking and change maladaptive behaviors.

16. _____ includes making critical comments about the patient, being hostile toward him or her, and being emotionally overinvolved.

17. _____ are drugs that act on the brain to affect mental processes.

18. _____, commonly called tranquilizers, are used for the short-term treatment of anxiety.

19. _____, also known as neuroleptics, are used to treat schizophrenia and other disorders that involve psychosis.

20. _____ is the side effect of some traditional antipsychotics that produces the involuntary twitching of muscles, especially in the neck and face.

21. _____, one of the more recently developed antipsychotics, is significantly different in that it acts not only on dopamine receptors but also on serotonin, norepinephrine, acetylcholine, and histamine.

22. Drugs that work to prevent seizures, called _____, are also used to regulate moods in bipolar disorder.

23. In systematic desensitization therapy, the client first makes a _____, a list of situations in which fear is aroused, in ascending order.

24. _____ is a tricyclic antidepressant that prevents panic attack.

25. The drug of choice for OCD is the potent serotonin reuptake inhibitor _____.

26. Many patients with seasonal affective disorder respond favorably to _____, in which patients are exposed to a high-intensity light source for a period each day.

27. _____ is a treatment for depression in which an electromagnetic coil is placed on the scalp and transmits pulses of high-intensity magnetism.

28. _____ is a psychosurgical procedure in which nerve-fiber pathways in the prefrontal cortex are severed.

29. _____ is the most successful treatment to date for borderline personality disorder; it combines elements of the behavioral, cognitive, and psychodynamic approaches.

30. _____ is a central nervous system stimulant used to treat ADHD.

MULTIPLE-CHOICE QUESTIONS

1. According to a recent study, there are approximately _____ approaches to psychotherapy.
   a. 5
   b. 50
   c. 100
   d. 400

2. While Joann is therapist shopping, she tries a clinical psychologist who describes herself as eclectic. This means that her therapist
   a. uses a combination of cognitive and behavioral approaches.
   b. does not use techniques from any of the major approaches.
   c. tries mostly new experimental techniques that have been supported by empirical research.
   d. uses a mix of techniques based on what she believes is best for the client's particular condition.

3. Marika is a therapist who specializes in the techniques of psychoanalysis. What is her goal for psychotherapy sessions?
   a. Uncover unconscious feelings and drives that give rise to maladaptive thoughts and behaviors.
   b. Relearn maladaptive behaviors that were acquired through improper learning.
   c. Facilitate personal growth and self-actualization through reflective listening and unconditional positive regard.
   d. Identify problem areas that are amenable to psychopharmacology.

4. Samantha has been feeling quite depressed lately and decides to go see a psychoanalyst. When she goes to her first session, she is told to say whatever comes to mind, no matter how crazy or embarrassing it may seem. This basic technique of psychoanalysis is known as
   a. free association.
   b. transference.
   c. word association.
   d. systematic desensitization.

5. Shelby goes into her therapist's office and spills all her current troubles. At the end of her monologue, the therapist says, "It sounds like you have a lot going on right now. You are having problems with your parents, your boyfriend, and at school, and you are unsure how to proceed." This is an example of the client-centered therapy technique of
   a. analysis of resistance.
   b. confronting irrational beliefs.
   c. unconditional positive regard.
   d. reflective listening.

6. Jerry is suffering from obsessions about germs and cleanliness and decides to seek out behavioral therapy. From his choice, it is obvious that Jerry believes his problem can be alleviated through
   a. uncovering unconscious feelings and drives that give rise to maladaptive thoughts and behaviors.
   b. unlearning maladaptive behaviors by the use of classical and operant conditioning.
   c. facilitating personal growth and self-actualization through reflective listening and unconditional positive regard.
   d. identifying problem areas that are amenable to psychopharmacology.

7. Joey is horrified by the idea of being in public. His therapist teaches him to pair relaxation with being in public. At first, Joey thinks about public places and relaxes. Then he steps outside and relaxes. Then he steps off his porch and relaxes. This goes on until Joey is able to go to the mall and stay without panicking. This treatment technique is called

   a. systematic desensitization.
   b. flooding.
   c. implosion.
   d. cathartic submersion.

8. Katie has been suffering from frequent panic attacks, so she goes to see a psychologist. The psychologist instructs her to hyperventilate, which causes her to panic. Then she teaches her to respond calmly to her panicked feelings. Soon Katie is able to calm herself when she feels the onset of panic. What type of therapy is the psychologist using to treat Katie?
   a. Aversion therapy.
   b. Cognitive therapy.
   c. Psychoanalytic therapy.
   d. Client-centered therapy.

9. Curly, Moe, Larry, and Shemp are in treatment to reduce their aggressive behaviors. The group setting provides an opportunity for members to improve their social skills, support one another, and learn from each others' experiences. The generic term for this treatment approach is
   a. interpersonal therapy.
   b. transpersonal therapy.
   c. group therapy.
   d. supportive therapy.

10. Carly and Gus are in therapy with the Whitaker family. They notice that as one child begins to improve her behavior, the other child becomes more disruptive. When both children are better, the mother and father begin to fight. Carly and Gus are trying to get the entire family to communicate and behave better. They are taking a(n) _____ approach to psychotherapy.
    a. dynamic
    b. supportive
    c. systems
    d. integrative

11. Benzodiazepines, such as Xanax and Ativan, increase the activity of y-aminobutyric acid (GABA) and are used in the treatment of
    a. depression.
    b. mood disorders.
    c. psychotic disorders.
    d. anxiety.

12. Christine's semester has been going downhill steadily. She is behind on all her course assignments and is having difficulty concentrating. Her physician decides to put her on antidepressants. Which of the following classes of medications is *not* a choice for her?
    a. MAO inhibitors.
    b. Tricyclics.
    c. Neuroleptics.
    d. SSRIs.

13. Carla has been depressed lately. Her boyfriend just broke up with her, and she is failing two of her classes. Her psychiatrist puts her on MAO inhibitors. Now Carla feels a lot better abut herself and is starting to pull up her grades. How do these pills work to improve Carla's mood?
    a. Increase the supply of melatonin and diethylamide.
    b. Increase her metabolism.
    c. Increase the supply of norepinephrine, serotonin, and dopamine.
    d. Increase the supply of GABA and endorphins.

14. Donny is a client at a day treatment facility for schizophrenics. When he takes his traditional antipsychotic medication (specifically chlorpromazine), his hallucinations are greatly reduced. This drug acts by
    a. blocking serotonin.
    b. releasing serotonin.
    c. blocking dopamine.
    d. releasing dopamine.

15. Most of the time Eileen is laughing, but she also has periods of wild mood swings that range from mania to depression. As she is diagnosed with bipolar disorder, which of the following medications is she most likely taking?
    a. Prozac.
    b. Librium.
    c. Tofranil.
    d. Lithium.

16. Kevin is worried about whether he will be wasting his money by seeking psychotherapy. Connie tells him that a recent study on psychotherapy by *Consumer Reports* found all *except* which of the following?
    a. Cognitive therapy was found superior to behavioral therapy as well as psychoanalysis.
    b. The majority of respondents felt that intervention had helped them.
    c. Those who sought help from mental health professionals reported more positive results than those who consulted with a family doctor.
    d. The longer the therapy, the greater was the reduction of psychiatric symptoms.

17. Dr. Freud is counseling a woman who has difficulty trusting men. She thinks they are all out to get her and will use her and toss her aside if she gives them the chance. Her therapist encourages her to open up to him and talk freely about her past experiences with men, including her father. What is Dr. Freud hoping to achieve by advising his patient to open up?
    a. Eclecticism.
    b. Conditional positive regard.
    c. Reciprocal determinism.
    d. Catharsis.

18. Manuel is afraid of heights. Because he lives in a small town, it is not easy to find a tall building to expose him to his fears. His therapist uses a computer to simulate for Manuel the experience of standing on the edge of a really tall building. His therapist has effectively created an exposure technique through the use of
    a. virtual environments.
    b. cybercasting.
    c. split reality.
    d. in vivo environments.

19. Which of the following is the most effective treatment for panic disorder with agoraphobia?
    a. Structured supportive therapy.
    b. Cognitive-behavioral therapy (CBT).
    c. Medication (e.g., imipramine).
    d. CBT and medication.

20. Steve decides to pursue behavioral therapy to treat his obsessive-compulsive disorder. From reading about empirically validated treatments, Steve knows that the two most important components of behavioral therapy for OCD are
    a. relaxation and confrontation.
    b. contingency and reinforcement.
    c. insight and action.
    d. exposure and response prevention.

21. For which of the following disorders is electroconvulsive therapy (ECT) most effective?
    a. Depression.
    b. Schizophrenia.
    c. Dissociative identity disorder.
    d. Obsessive-compulsive disorder.

22. TMS seems to be more effective for _____ depression, whereas ECT seems to be more effective for _____ depression.
    a. dysthymic; bipolar
    b. unipolar; bipolar
    c. nonpsychotic; psychotic
    d. manic; unipolar

23. Which of the following statements is *true* regarding the prognosis for schizophrenia?
    a. Those diagnosed with schizophrenia later in life tend to have a poorer prognosis than those who experience their first symptoms during childhood or adolescence.
    b. Men tend to have a better prognosis than women.
    c. Schizophrenia in developing countries is often not as severe as in developed countries.
    d. Supportive family networks tend to interfere with improvement in schizophrenic individuals.

24. Which of the following is *not* one of the stages of dialectical behavior therapy?

a. The therapist targets the client's most extreme and dysfunctional behaviors.

b. The therapist confronts the client's manipulations.

c. The therapist helps the client explore past traumatic experiences that may be at the root of emotional problems.

d. The therapist helps the patient develop self-respect and independent problem solving.

25. Keith is a 30-year-old male who is in prison for embezzlement. He has a lengthy criminal history and is diagnosed with antisocial personality disorder. The prognosis for Keith's improvement is
  a. poor.
  b. fair.
  c. guarded.
  d. good.

26. Which of the following therapies is most effective for children with autism?
  a. Supportive therapies.
  b. Structured therapies.
  c. Play therapy.
  d. Unstructured therapies.

27. The long-term prognosis for children with autism is
  a. poor.
  b. fair.
  c. guarded.
  d. good.

28. Which of the following therapies is most effective in the treatment of attention-deficit/hyperactivity disorder?
  a. Play therapy.
  b. Stimulant medication (e.g., Ritalin).
  c. Behavior modification.
  d. Stimulant medication plus behavioral therapy.

29. According to the surgeon general, what percentage of Americans have some form of diagnosable mental illness in a given year?
  a. 1%.
  b. 5%.
  c. 10%.
  d. 20%.

30. Sandi is interested in becoming a clinical psychologist. She is looking into graduate schools and notices that some offer a Ph.D. and some offer a Psy.D. What is the difference between the two clinical psychology degrees?
  a. Both degrees have training in psychotherapy; however, the Ph.D. degree has more training in psychological research.
  b. The Ph.D. offers training in prescribing medication; the Psy.D. offers more traditional psychotherapy training.
  c. The Ph.D. has more of an environmental focus; the Psy.D. has more of a medical/biological focus.
  d. Although the degrees have a different history, they are virtually identical in everyday practice.

31. Jerry, George, Elaine, and Kramer are seeing a psychologist in group therapy during their stay in prison. What are their chances of receiving medication from him to deal with their mental health issues?
  a. None—psychiatrists are the only mental health professionals allowed to prescribe medication.
  b. None—nurses and medical social workers are the only mental health professionals allowed to prescribe medication.
  c. Slim—only New Mexico has passed legislation to allow clinical psychologists to prescribe medication, provided they receive appropriate training.
  d. Fair—recently graduated psychologists in all 50 states have completed special training programs and are allowed to prescribe medication.

32. Kevin is having some psychological problems, but he is picky about the qualifications of his therapist. He looks in the yellow pages under the term *psychiatrists*. From our knowledge of therapist training we can tell him that
  a. we know nothing about these therapists' qualifications.
  b. we know that these therapists have at least a master's degree in a mental health field.
  c. we know that the therapists have a medical degree and a supervised residency.
  d. we know that these therapists have a graduate degree and a one-year internship in a mental health setting.

MATCHING QUESTIONS

Fill in the letter from Column B corresponding to the term that is most associated with the description presented in Column A.

COLUMN A

____ 1. Later adaptations of Freud's approaches.

____ 2. Therapy based on the theory that distorted thoughts can produce maladaptive behaviors and emotions.

____ 3. Class of psychotropic medication used to treat depression.

COLUMN B

A. Monoamine oxidase
B. Neuroleptics
C. Counseling psychologists
D. Clozapine
E. Tardive dykinesia
F. Unilateral ECT

____ 4. Enzyme that converts serotonin into another chemical form.

____ 5. Category of antidepressants named after their core molecular structure of three rings.

____ 6. Category of antidepressants that act by inhibiting the reuptake of serotonin.

____ 7. One of the most widely prescribed SSRIs.

____ 8. Drugs used to treat schizophrenia and other disorders that involve psychosis.

____ 9. Psychological practitioners with a doctoral degree from graduate training in psychology.

____ 10. Practitioners with an M.D. and three to four additional years of specialized training in residency.

____ 11. Practitioners with an M.S.W. followed by specialized training in mental health care.

____ 12. Practitioners with a bachelor's degree in nursing and special training in the care of mentally ill patients.

____ 13. Doctoral-level psychological practitioners that typically deal with problems of adjustment and life stress.

____ 14. Practitioners that have limited advanced training and usually work under supervision.

____ 15. Barlow's term for evidence-based psychotherapy.

____ 16. Better known as the antidepressant Wellbutrin.

____ 17. Shock therapy over only the brain hemisphere that is not dominant for language.

____ 18. Most effective treatment for bipolar disorder.

____ 19. First antipsychotic medication used in the treatment of schizophrenia.

G. Para professionals
H. Psychodynamic
I. Cognitive
J. Tricyclic
K. Psychological treatments
L. Lithium
M. Chlorpromazine
N. Psychiatrists
O. Antidepressant
P. Clinical psychologists
Q. Psychiatric social workers
R. Bupropion
S. Psychiatric nurses
T. Prozac
U. SSRI

____ 20. Side effect of anti-psychotics: involuntary movements of the lips, tongue, face, and legs.

____ 21. Newer antipsychotic drug; beneficial in treating both positive and negative symptoms of schizophrenia.

THOUGHT QUESTIONS

1. How would you know if you needed to seek professional psychological help? If you did, what type of mental health practitioner would you choose? Why? What type of therapy approach would you prefer?

2. Suppose a close friend or family member has an obvious psychological problem (e.g., eating disorder, drug/alcohol, personality disorder) yet refuses to seek psychological treatment. What would you do? What can you do?

APPLICATIONS

An Activity to Assess Media Presentations of Therapists

One truism of psychological practice is that many more individuals suffer from psychological disorders than seek treatment for them. This results in much unnecessary suffering. Psychological scientists have long researched variables that lead people to either seek or avoid treatment.

One variable that you can explore with your friends is popular media presentations of psychotherapists. Get your group together and identify as many psychotherapists as you can think of from television and the movies (e.g., Frasier and Niles Crane on *Frasier*). After you compile your list, determine whether these characters are generally positive representatives of the therapy profession or are more negative. What are some common personality characteristics that are attributed to therapists? Do you think these characters would make you more or less likely to seek psychological help?

For extra credit, identify what type of therapy each psychological practitioner is portraying.

An Activity to Explicate the Common Beneficial Factors in Psychotherapy

One area many students have trouble understanding is how verbal psychotherapy can be of help. After all, you do not have any surgical tools and are not distributing any mind-altering drugs. Gazzaniga and Heatherton identify several factors (e.g., caring therapist, confession) that are common across different types of therapies.

To understand this more, think of a time in your life when you were in particular distress and someone was helpful to you. What did he or she do? List as many specific factors as you can.

Look at your list, and then look at the list of common factors in psychotherapy. Do you see any similarities? Students often respond that the person listened to their thoughts and feelings or just stayed with them through the difficult times. Some provided good information, challenged them, or saw things from a different perspective. Caring, reflective listening, providing data, and reconceptualizing the problem are all characteristics of quality psychotherapy. Carl Rogers, the author of client-centered therapy, stated that therapeutic success was based on a congruent (i.e., real) therapist who exhibited empathy and unconditional positive regard toward the client. What qualities would you want in your psychotherapist?

WEB SITES

General Psychology Sites

www.apa.org
www.psycport.com
www.nmha.org

General Treatment Sites

www.nami.org
www.ai.ijs.si/eliza-cgi-bin/eliza_script
www.cognitivetherapy.com
www.apsa-co.org/ctf/pubinfo/efficacy.htm
www.nimh.nih.gov

Treatment for Eating Disorders

www.anad.org
www.something-fishy.org

ANSWER KEY

Fill-in-the-Blank Questions

1. Psychotherapy
2. Biological therapies
3. Psychopharmacology
4. Dream analysis
5. Insight
6. Client-centered therapy
7. Motivational interviewing
8. Behavior modification
9. Social skills training
10. Modeling
11. Interpersonal therapy
12. Exposure
13. Cognitive restructuring
14. Rational-emotive therapy
15. Cognitive-behavioral therapy
16. Negative expressed emotion
17. Psychotropic medications
18. Anti-anxiety drugs
19. Antipsychotics
20. Tardive dyskinesia
21. Clozapine
22. Anticonvulsants
23. Fear hierarchy
24. Imipramine
25. Clomipramine
26. Phototherapy
27. Transcranial magnetic stimulation
28. Lobotomy
29. Dialectical behavior therapy
30. Methylphenidate

Multiple-Choice Questions

1. d. According to a recent study, there are approximately 400 approaches to psychotherapy.

   Incorrect answers:
   a. According to a recent study, there are approximately 400 approaches to psychotherapy.
   b. According to a recent study, there are approximately 400 approaches to psychotherapy.
   c. According to a recent study, there are approximately 400 approaches to psychotherapy.

2. d. Today many practitioners use an eclectic mix of techniques based on what they believe is best for the client's particular condition.

   Incorrect answers:
   a. A cognitive-behavioral therapist uses a combination of cognitive and behavioral approaches.
   b. Today many practitioners use an eclectic mix of techniques based on what they believe is best for the client's particular condition.
   c. Today many practitioners use an eclectic mix of techniques based on what they believe is best for the client's particular condition.

3. a. Psychoanalytic treatment is based on uncovering unconscious feelings and drives believed to give rise to maladaptive thoughts and behaviors.

   Incorrect answers:
   b. Behavioral treatment is based on relearning maladaptive behaviors that were acquired through improper learning.
   c. Humanistic treatment is based on facilitating personal growth and self-actualization through reflective listening and unconditional positive regard.
   d. Biological treatment is based on identifying problem areas that are amenable to psychopharmacology.

4. a. Free association is the psychoanalytic technique in which the patient says whatever comes to mind.

    Incorrect answers:
    b. Transference is treating the therapist like some significant person from one's life.
    c. Word association is responding to different words.
    d. Systematic desensitization is an exposure technique that pairs the anxiety-producing stimulus with relaxation techniques.

5. d. Reflective listening is when the therapist repeats the client's concerns to help the person clarify his or her feelings.

    Incorrect answers:
    a. Analysis of resistance is when the therapist explores what the client withholds in the session.
    b. Confronting irrational beliefs is a technique of identifying and challenging maladaptive cognitions.
    c. Unconditional positive regard refers to treating clients as worthy regardless of their behavior.

6. b. The basic premise of behavioral therapy is that behavior is learned and therefore can be unlearned using the principles of classical and operant conditioning.

    Incorrect answers:
    a. The goal of psychoanalytic therapy is uncovering unconscious feelings and drives that give rise to maladaptive thoughts and behaviors.
    c. The goal of humanistic therapy is facilitating personal growth and self-actualization through reflective listening and unconditional positive regard.
    d. The goal of biological therapy is identifying problem areas that are amenable to psychopharmacology.

7. a. Systematic desensitization is an exposure technique that pairs the anxiety-producing stimulus with relaxation techniques.

    Incorrect answers:
    b. Flooding is an exposure technique that forces one to confront an anxiety-provoking stimulus without avoidance.
    c. Implosion is an exposure technique that forces one to confront an anxiety-producing stimulus without avoidance.
    d. Cathartic submersion is a made-up term.

8. b. Cognitive therapy is based on the theory that modifying maladaptive thought patterns via specific treatment strategies should eliminate the maladaptive behaviors and emotions.

    Incorrect answers:
    a. Aversion therapy is pairing a problem behavior with punishment.
    c. The goal of psychoanalytic therapy is uncovering unconscious feelings and drives that give rise to maladaptive thoughts and behaviors.
    d. The goal of client-centered therapy is facilitating personal growth and self-actualization through reflective listening and unconditional positive regard.

9. c. Group therapy provides an opportunity for members to improve their social skills and to learn from each others' experiences.

    Incorrect answers:
    a. Interpersonal therapy focuses on the interactions of members.
    b. Transpersonal therapy is a made-up term.
    d. Supportive therapy is a generic term for treatments that involve guiding the client through difficult situations.

10. c. According to a systems approach, an individual is part of a larger context, and any change in individual behavior will affect the entire family system.

    Incorrect answers:
    a. The goal of psychodynamic therapy is uncovering unconscious feelings and drives that give rise to maladaptive thoughts and behaviors.
    b. Supportive therapy is a generic term for treatments that involve guiding the client through difficult situations.
    d. Integrative therapy is another name for eclectic therapy borrowing the best techniques that fit the individual client.

11. d. Benzodiazepines, such as Xanax and Ativan, increase the activity of GABA and are used in the treatment of anxiety.

    Incorrect answers:
    a. Antidepressants are used in the treatment of depression.
    b. Antidepressants and lithium are used in the treatment of mood disorders
    c. Antipsychotics are used in the treatment of psychotic disorders.

12. c. Neuroleptics are antipsychotic medications.

    Incorrect answers:
    a. MAO inhibitors, tricyclics, and SSRIs are all treatments for depression.
    b. MAO inhibitors, tricyclics, and SSRIs are all treatments for depression.
    d. MAO inhibitors, tricyclics, and SSRIs are all treatments for depression.

13. c. MAO inhibitors work by increasing the supply of norepinephrine, serotonin, and dopamine.

    Incorrect answers:
    a. MAO inhibitors work by increasing the supply of norepinephrine, serotonin, and dopamine.
    b. MAO inhibitors work by increasing the supply of norepinephrine, serotonin, and dopamine.
    d. MAO inhibitors work by increasing the supply of norepinephrine, serotonin, and dopamine.

14. c. Traditional antipsychotics bind to dopamine receptors without activating them, which blocks the effects of dopamine.

    Incorrect answers:
    a. Traditional antipsychotics bind to dopamine receptors without activating them, which blocks the effects of dopamine.
    b. Traditional antipsychotics bind to dopamine receptors without activating them, which blocks the effects of dopamine.
    d. Traditional antipsychotics bind to dopamine receptors without activating them, which blocks the effects of dopamine.

15. d. Lithium is the most effective treatment for bipolar disorder, although the neural mechanisms of how it works are currently unknown.

    Incorrect answers:
    a. Prozac is an antidepressant.
    b. Librium is an antianxiety drug.
    c. Tofranil is an antidepressant.

16. a. The *Consumer Reports* study found that no specific type of therapy yielded more positive results than any other. The other statements are true.

    Incorrect answers:
    b. It is true that the majority of respondents felt that intervention had helped them.
    c. It is true that those who sought help from mental health professionals reported more positive results than those who consulted with a family doctor.
    d. It is true that the longer the therapy, the greater was the reduction of psychiatric symptoms.

17. d. Freud incorporated the term *catharsis* into his psychoanalytic approach to refer to the powerful emotional reactions and subsequent relief that would come from opening up and talking about unconscious material.

    Incorrect answers:
    a. Eclecticism is the use of the best techniques from varying approaches for each problem.
    b. Conditional positive regard is reward given only for particular behaviors.

c. Reciprocal determinism is the idea that the person, environment, and behavior are interrelated.

18. a. Virtual environments, sometimes called *virtual reality*, have computers simulate the environments and objects that are feared.

    Incorrect answers:
    b. Cybercasting is a made-up term.
    c. Split reality is a made-up term.
    d. In vivo environments would consist of actually facing the feared object.

19. d. For those who have panic disorder with agoraphobia, the combination of CBT and drugs is better than either treatment alone.

    Incorrect answers:
    a. For those who have panic disorder with agoraphobia, the combination of CBT and drugs is better than either treatment alone.
    b. For those who have panic disorder with agoraphobia, the combination of CBT and drugs is better than either treatment alone.
    c. For those who have panic disorder with agoraphobia, the combination of CBT and drugs is better than either treatment alone.

20. d. The two most important components of behavioral therapy for OCD are exposure and response prevention.

    Incorrect answers:
    a. The two most important components of behavioral therapy for OCD are exposure and response prevention.
    b. The two most important components of behavioral therapy for OCD are exposure and response prevention.
    c. The two most important components of behavioral therapy for OCD are exposure and response prevention.

21. a. ECT is the single most effective treatment for those who are severely depressed and do not respond to conventional treatments.

    Incorrect answers:
    b. ECT is the single most effective treatment for those who are severely depressed and do not respond to conventional treatments.
    c. ECT is the single most effective treatment for those who are severely depressed and do not respond to conventional treatments.
    d. ECT is the single most effective treatment for those who are severely depressed and do not respond to conventional treatments.

22. c. TMS seems to be more effective for nonpsychotic depression, whereas ECT seems to be more effective for psychotic depression.

    Incorrect answers:
    a. TMS seems to be more effective for nonpsychotic depression, whereas ECT seems to be more effective for psychotic depression.
    b. TMS seems to be more effective for nonpsychotic depression, whereas ECT seems to be more effective for psychotic depression.
    d. TMS seems to be more effective for nonpsychotic depression, whereas ECT seems to be more effective for psychotic depression.

23. c. Schizophrenia in developing countries is often not as severe as in developed countries.

    Incorrect answers:
    a. Those diagnosed with schizophrenia later in life tend to have a more favorable prognosis than those who experience their first symptoms during childhood or adolescence.
    b. Women tend to have a better prognosis than men.
    d. Supportive family networks tend to increase improvement in schizophrenic individuals.

24. c. Having the therapist confront the client's manipulations is not one of the stages of dialectical behavior therapy. The other statements are stages.

    Incorrect answers:
    a. Having the therapist target the client's most extreme and dysfunctional behaviors is a stage of DBT.
    c. Having the therapist help the client explore past traumatic experiences that may be at the root of emotional problems is a stage of DBT.
    d. Having the therapist help the patient develop self-respect and independent problem solving is a stage of DBT.

25. a. The prognosis for improvement in antisocial personality disorder is poor.

    Incorrect answers:
    b. The prognosis for improvement in antisocial personality disorder is poor.
    c. The prognosis for improvement in antisocial personality disorder is poor.
    d. The prognosis for improvement in antisocial personality disorder is poor.

26. b. Because generalization of skills must be explicitly taught, structured therapies are more effective for autistic children than unstructured interventions such as play therapy.

    Incorrect answers:
    a. Because generalization of skills must be explicitly taught, structured therapies are more effective for autistic children than unstructured interventions such as play therapy.
    c. Because generalization of skills must be explicitly taught, structured therapies are more effective for autistic children than unstructured interventions such as play therapy.
    d. Because generalization of skills must be explicitly taught, structured therapies are more effective for autistic children than unstructured interventions such as play therapy.

27. a. Despite a few reports of remarkable recovery from autism, the long-term prognosis is considered poor.

    Incorrect answers:
    b. Despite a few reports of remarkable recovery from autism, the long-term prognosis is considered poor.
    c. Despite a few reports of remarkable recovery from autism, the long-term prognosis is considered poor.
    d. Despite a few reports of remarkable recovery from autism, the long-term prognosis is considered poor.

28. d. Recent research has shown that medication plus behavioral therapy are more effective than either approach alone.

    Incorrect answers:
    a. Recent research has shown that medication plus behavioral therapy are more effective than either approach alone.
    b. Recent research has shown that medication plus behavioral therapy are more effective than either approach alone.
    c. Recent research has shown that medication plus behavioral therapy are more effective than either approach alone.

29. d. According to the surgeon general, one in five (20 percent) of Americans have some form of diagnosable mental illness in a given year.

    Incorrect answers:
    a. According to the surgeon general, one in five (20 percent) of Americans have some form of diagnosable mental illness in a given year.
    b. According to the surgeon general, one in five (20

percent) of Americans have some form of diagnosable mental illness in a given year.

    c. According to the surgeon general, one in five (20 percent) of Americans have some form of diagnosable mental illness in a given year.

30. a. Both degrees have training in psychotherapy; however, the Ph.D. degree has more training in psychological research.

Incorrect answers:

    b. Both degree programs have the potential for offering training in prescribing medication.

    c. Both degree programs have a fairly strong environmental focus.

    d. Degree recipients tend to work in fairly different clinical settings.

31. c. Their chances are slim—only New Mexico has passed legislation to allow clinical psychologists to prescribe medication, provided they receive appropriate training.

Incorrect answers:

    a. Their chances are slim—only New Mexico has passed legislation to allow clinical psychologists to prescribe medication, provided they receive appropriate training.

    b. Their chances are slim—only New Mexico has passed legislation to allow clinical psychologists to prescribe medication, provided they receive appropriate training.

    d. Their chances are slim—only New Mexico has passed legislation to allow clinical psychologists to prescribe medication, provided they receive appropriate training.

32. c. Psychiatrists have a medical degree and a supervised residency.

Incorrect answers:

    a. Psychiatrists have a medical degree and a supervised residency.

    b. Psychiatrists have a medical degree and a supervised residency.

    d. Psychiatrists have a medical degree and a supervised residency.

Matching Questions

1. H Psychodynamic
2. I Cognitive
3. O Antidepressant
4. A Monoamine oxidase
5. J Tricyclic
6. U SSRI
7. T Prozac
8. B Neuroleptics
9. P Clinical psychologists
10. N Psychiatrists
11. Q Psychiatric social workers
12. S Psychiatric nurses
13. C Counseling psychologists
14. G Paraprofessionals
15. K Psychological treatments
16. R Bupropion
17. F Unilateral ECT
18. L Lithium
19. M Chlorpromazine
20. E Tardive dyskinesia
21. D Clozapine

Thought Questions

1. Answers will vary. In seeking therapy, students should consider issues of personal discomfort as well as impairments in relationships, school, and work. When seeking a therapist, one will have to consider issues of costs as well as preferred approach. For example, psychiatrists will have more of a biological emphasis whereas psychologists will use more of an environmental approach. Personality issues will factor into one's preferred approach. Some individuals will prefer the directness of behavioral and cognitive approaches, while others will prefer the exploratory nature of psychoanalytic and humanistic approaches. Finally, some students my simply prefer the most effective, empirically validated treatment for their specific problem.

2. Answers will vary, but this is a common problem individuals face. On the whole, psychotherapy is based on a client who is in distress and is willing to make changes to alleviate that distress. This is much more difficult when the individual either does not recognize the issue or is unwilling to take steps to correct it. As an interested bystander, you can tactfully express your concerns to your friend or family member. If this does not work, you should consider involving other friends and family members both for feedback and support. You will want to be diplomatic about this because you want to continue to keep the lines of communication open and be available when needed. Immediately alienating the person generally is not beneficial. If the behavior continues or becomes more dangerous or life-threatening, then you and the other members of this person's social circle might consider an intervention where everyone gets together at one time in one place and expresses their concern. Again, be sure this is done in a caring rather

than punitive fashion, and have some concrete sources available for help. If the person becomes a danger to self or others, you can go to your local hospital to get him or her committed against his or her will. If you are totally stuck and afraid, call your local police and they will help you with options.

Remember that going through psychological problems with a friend or family member can be stressful for you. Consider getting your own sources of help including friend and family support groups. Research the disorder and support groups to see what is available in your community. You can also go to the sites for the American Psychological Association (www.apa.org) and National Alliance for the Mentally Ill (www.nami.org) for further information.

| Social Psychology

GUIDE TO THE READING

How Do We Know Ourselves?

The first section of the chapter introduces the discipline of social psychology—the study of how people influence other people's thoughts, feelings, and actions. Because we are social creatures, social psychology influences virtually every area of psychology. Interestingly, we tend to underestimate the importance of the social situation in explaining other people's behavior, a pervasive phenomenon known as the fundamental attribution error. The authors move on to explore the idea of self-concept, which is everything that you know about yourself. In addition, they comment on recent literature regarding self-esteem. This is the evaluative aspect of self-concept, referring to whether people view themselves as worthy or unworthy, good or bad. The idea that children should have a high self-esteem has reached nearly cult status in recent years, leading to unconditional acceptance of children by their parents. More recent research suggests this is a useful idea but only in the context of relatively strict parenting and clear limit setting. We seem to be preprogrammed to view ourselves in a favorable fashion. Most people view themselves as better than average in many domains. We maintain positive illusions, bask in the glow of reflected glory, and compare ourselves socially with those who we believe are deficient compared to us (downward social comparison). We also tend to take credit for successes ourselves but blame failures on outside factors (self-serving bias). These ego-defensive distortions appear to make us feel better and prevent rejection from the group.

How Do Attitudes Guide Behavior?

The next part of the chapter concerns social cognition as it relates to how we make sense of other people and our social situations. It seems that we are cognitive misers who make quick judgments about others based on limited information. Our evaluation of objects or ideas is known as an *attitude*, and it has affective, cognitive, and behavioral components. The mere exposure effect illustrates that our attitudes about an object or situation can improve simply through greater familiarity. Our implicit attitudes can influence us unconsciously, and those whose associated memories are easily accessible are more predictive of behavior.

One of the classic findings in social psychology was Leon Festinger's discovery that discrepancies between attitudes and behavior can lead to cognitive dissonance. Generally, individuals are motivated to reduce this dissonance by changing either their attitudes or their behavior. Many disciplines are interested in how attitudes can be changed through persuasion. We like to think of ourselves as rational decision makers, but there is a wealth of evidence to the contrary. Richard Petty and John Cacioppo's elaboration likelihood model indicated that there are two distinct ways by which persuasion leads to attitude change. The central route to persuasion is one that uses rational cognitive processes. The peripheral route to persuasion is one by which people minimally process the message and make decisions by numerous nonrational processes. The ways of influencing both routes continue to be investigated.

How Do We Form Our Impressions of Others?

The next section of the chapter looks at social cognition in terms of how we form attitudes about others. Individuals are highly sensitive to nonverbal behavior, and we often form impressions of others based on thin slices of behavior. We seem predisposed to making attributions or causal explanations about why events or actions occur. And rather than employing an objective evaluation, we tend to take shortcuts and attribute others' behaviors to personal traits but attribute our own behaviors more to situational factors (i.e., actor–observer discrepancy). These shortcuts continue in the arena of stereotypes, by which we organize social information about people based on their membership in certain groups. Although they are efficient, negative stereotypes can lead to harmful prejudices and dangerous discriminatory behavior. Fortunately, although the information processing that leads to these attitudes appears to be innate and based on historically adaptive ideas such as ingroups and outgroups, we can control our behavioral responses to some of our more pernicious stereotypes.

Research has indicated that cooperation with others, particularly in activities that have shared superordinate goals, can reduce the hostility between disparate groups. One educational application of this has been the jigsaw classroom, in which students work together in mixed-race or mixed-sex groups. The future of civilization may rest on how well we apply these ideas to broader races, nations, and cultures.

One precautionary note: It is tempting to believe that this portion of psychological science is just common sense—we all know how we deal with our friends and family. Actively fight that natural tendency. You will find that some of the research is actually counterintuitive (e.g., cognitive dissonance). Also, there are subtle distinctions among several of the social psychological terms. When answering the multiple-choice questions, be sure you know why the correct answer is accurate as well as why the wrong answers are incorrect.

How Do Others Influence Us?

Because groups are so important to us, they exert a powerful influence over our behavior. In fact, the power of social situations is much greater than most people believe, and individuals will often act in ways that greatly contradict their personal standards. The processes of social facilitation, social loafing, and deindividuation show how groups can influence individual behavior, sometime in dangerous ways. Groups can make terrible decisions, such as in the case of launching the space shuttle *Challenger*; thus it is necessary for individuals to understand the tendency toward group polarization and groupthink.

Individuals conform to social norms even when there may be obvious reasons not to do so. Those aware of strategies of social influence may use the techniques of foot in the door, door in the face, and lowballing to gain compliance. A rather frightening demonstration of the power of social influence was provided by Stanley Milgram's classic studies on obedience to authority. He showed that one can get others to engage in horrible, antisocial acts simply through the power of social context and by being insistent.

When Do We Harm or Help Others?

In the next section the authors present data from psychological science on when individuals are likely to harm or help others. Aggression—behavior intended to harm someone else—seems to be related to low levels of serotonin. It also stems from frustration and situations that elicit negative affect. Societal factors such as a culture of honor also can factor into displays of aggression. On the other side, humans engage in amazingly prosocial and altruistic acts. This is particularly evident when the person in need is a relative. Surprisingly, having more people around when in need does not increase your chances of getting help (bystander intervention effect) due to a diffusion of responsibility and fear of making social blunders.

What Determines the Quality of Relationships?

The final section of the chapter looks at the factors that influence some of our most critical social decisions—the choice of friends and relationship partners. These choices are affected by variables such as proximity, similarity, and physical attractiveness. Our society places a great emphasis on love, and a distinction is made between the intense longing of passionate love and the long-term commitment of companionate love. Divorce statistics indicate that making love last is a difficult proposition. Relationships are challenged by the fading of passion, jealousy from extramarital affairs, and maladaptive strategies for coping with conflict. Happy couples explain their partner's behavior through partner-enhancing attributions, but unhappy couples make distress-maintaining attributions.

FILL-IN-THE-BLANK QUESTIONS

1. _____ is concerned with how people influence other people's thoughts, feelings, and actions.

2. The sense of self as the object of attention is the psychological state known as _____.

3. The _____ is the cognitive aspect of the self-concept, consisting of an integrated set of memories, beliefs, and generalizations about the self.

4. People in collectivist cultures tend to have _____, in which their self-concepts are determined to a large extent by their social roles and personal relationships.

5. _____ is the evaluative aspect of the self-concept, referring to whether people perceive themselves to be worthy or unworthy, good or bad.

6. _____ means that parents should love their children no matter what their children do.

7. Self-esteem is a _____, an internal monitor of social acceptance or rejection.

8. _____ are overly favorable and unrealistic beliefs about oneself.

9. According to the theory of _____, people can feel threatened when someone close to them outperforms them on a task that is personally relevant.

10. _____ occurs when people evaluate their own actions, abilities, and beliefs by contrasting them with other people's.

11. The concept of _____ refers to the evaluation of an object, event, or idea.

12. _____ attitudes influence our feelings and behavior at an unconscious level.

13. The ease with which memories related to an attitude are retrieved is known as _____.

14. _____ causes a person to seek attitudinal information that supports his or her decision and avoid information suggesting it is a poor choice.

15. _____ is the act and conscious effort to change attitudes through the transmission of a message.

16. According to Petty and Cacioppo's _____, there are central and peripheral routes to persuasion.

17. In the _____ to persuasion, people minimally process the message.

18. _____ are people's causal explanations for why events or actions occur.

19. _____ are cognitive schemas that organize information about people on the basis of their membership in certain groups.

20. Stereotypes lead to an _____ in which people believe that a relationship exists when it actually does not.

21. A _____ is when people come to behave in ways that confirm their own or others' expectation.

22. _____ are shared goals that, because they require people to cooperate to succeed, reduce hostility between groups.

23. A _____ is a program in which students work together in mixed-race or mixed-sex groups in which each member of the group is an expert on one aspect of the assignment.

24. _____ is when people work less hard in a group because the efforts are pooled together so that no one individual is accountable for the group's outcome.

25. The finding that groups often make riskier decisions than do individuals is known as the _____.

26. _____ is the process in which groups tend to enhance the initial attitudes of members who already agree.

27. When people do things requested by others, they are exhibiting _____.

28. In the _____ effect, people are more likely to comply with a large and undesirable request if they have earlier agreed to a small request.

29. _____ is when people follow orders given by an authority.

30. According to the _____ model, frustration leads to aggression because it elicits negative affect.

MULTIPLE-CHOICE QUESTIONS

1. Kristen scurries into her general psychology professor's office late. Her hair is sticking up and her notebook has papers falling out in every direction. Before she can explain that her electricity went haywire, her professor assumes that she is disorganized and lazy. This is an example of a
   a. confirmation bias.
   b. self-fulfilling prophecy.
   c. fundamental attribution error.
   d. misattribution.

2. Stephanie and Said have just met at a party. Stephanie asks him to describe himself. Said states that he is a senior finance major, 22 years old, Moroccan, Muslim, a soccer player, shy, and optimistic. These things Said knows about himself are part of his
   a. minimal self.
   b. self-concept.
   c. self-recognition.
   d. reflected appraisal.

3. Woody is having a tough time in college. There is a substantial gap between how he sees himself and how he believes he ought to seem to others. According to Higgins's self-discrepancy theory, which of the following emotions is Woody most likely to experience?
   a. Disappointment.
   b. Frustration and helplessness.
   c. Sadness and depression.
   d. Anxiety and guilt.

4. Naomi is a normal individual. She can recognize herself in a photograph with her sisters, and she can also recognize herself in photos as a little girl. This self-recognition is associated with which of the following brain areas?
   a. Basal ganglia.
   b. Frontal lobes.
   c. Limbic system.
   d. Parietal lobe.

5. Jennifer is at a sorority mixer talking to friends. Although engaged in conversation, she hears her name mentioned in a discussion across the room. Her tendency to process information about herself despite distraction is known as
   a. shadowing.
   b. the cocktail party effect.
   c. prosopagnosia.
   d. selective consciousness.

6. Brandy has been encouraged by her parents to attend soccer camp. They want her to develop her skills enough that she will be selected for competitive leagues, even though it will mean leaving her friends behind on the community teams. Because of this influence, Brandy's self-concept will likely be characterized by
   a. independent self-construals.
   b. interdependent self-construals.
   c. collectivism.
   d. self-discrepancy.

7. Charles works hard at maintaining a positive public image. He does a lot of high-profile charity work, and he is careful not to lose his temper in public. He believes that other parents see him as a role model for their children. His views of what he thinks others believe about him are known as
   a. reflected appraisals.
   b. basked glory.
   c. the collective self.
   d. the minimal self.

8. Jeffrey flunked out of school, got caught cheating on his girlfriend, lost his job due to embezzlement, and was arrested for running a methamphetamine lab. That fact that his parents still love him demonstrates
   a. sociometry.
   b. the better-than-average effect.
   c. the self-enhancement motive.
   d. unconditional acceptance.

9. Raymond says to his brother Charlie, "I'm a very good driver," despite the fact that he is totally inept and has never driven before. This inflated view of the self is often referred to as
   a. delusional cognitions.
   b. the better-than-average effect.
   c. self-evaluative maintenance.
   d. downward social comparison.

10. Which of the following is *not* one of the domains of positive illusions?
    a. Overestimate one's skills, abilities, and competencies.
    b. Unrealistic perception of one's personal control over events.
    c. Unrealistically optimistic about one's personal future.
    d. Unconditional acceptance of other's misfortunes.

11. Tara and Lynn just finished a difficult psychology exam. Lynn is upset and expresses concern over several questions on which she felt she might have done poorly. Although Tara is mildly apprehensive about a couple of questions, she feels much better after hearing Lynn moan about her test disaster. Tara's reaction illustrates the working of
    a. upward social comparison.
    b. counterfactual thinking.
    c. self-serving bias.
    d. downward social comparison.

12. Jodie got her results for her two exams on the same day. She made an A on her psychology exam but received a D on her anthropology exam. She attributed her psychology grade to her hard work, but stated that her poor performance in anthropology was because her professor is a "stupid jerk who tested irrelevant information." Assuming the tests were roughly equal in difficulty, her attributions are an example of
    a. downward social comparison.
    b. upward social comparison.
    c. a self-serving bias.
    d. the better-than-average effect.

13. We tend to prefer photographs of ourselves with the image reversed, but we prefer photographs of friends as we see them because of
    a. the mere exposure effect.
    b. social exchange theory.
    c. need complementarity.
    d. attitude similarity.

14. Samantha and her boyfriend, Lance, decide to be participants on a couples reality television show. Before the show Samantha believes she is totally committed to Lance and will not give in to the temptations presented by the show's premise. However, after a few dream dates with a single guy on the show, Samantha gives in to temptation and cheats on Lance. Afterward she feels guilty about it and suddenly realizes that she is not as

in love with Lance as she thought she was. What do Samantha's latest realizations illustrate?

a. Social facilitation.
b. Implicit attitudes.
c. A consensus effect.
d. Cognitive dissonance.

15. Leon did an experiment with a group of graduate students who were music teachers. He paid one group of teachers $100 to try to convince an alleged school board member that music education was unimportant and the funding for it should be cut. He paid the other group $1 to accomplish the same task. He found that the group to which he paid $1 actually agreed with the message more because they had _____ for lying.

a. insufficient justification
b. postdecisional dissonance
c. implicit attitudes
d. selective exposure

16. Ozzy has free tickets to a baseball game and a rock concert. He really wants to attend both, but they are at the same time. He finally decides on the baseball game. He immediately focuses on the positive aspect of the baseball game (good weather, good pitching matchup) and the negative aspect of the rock concert (poor parking, hearing loss). Ozzy is motivated by

a. peripheral routes to persuasion.
b. elaboration likelihood.
c. effort justification.
d. postdecisional dissonance.

17. Rory is pledging a sorority on campus. As part of initiation, she is forced to wear silly clothes, sing silly songs, and disregard her personal hygiene for a couple of weeks. After acceptance, she tells her family it was all worth it because the ridicule brought her pledge class much closer together. Rory is engaging in the dissonance-reducing strategy of

a. selective exposure.
b. effort justification.
c. hazing denial.
d. elaboration likelihood.

18. Chris is a first-year student who has not had much luck with studying. After listening to a couple of lectures on memory and studying tips, he tells his psychology professor that he found the lecture and text material influential. He said that because of all these good suggestions, he was beginning to study more effectively. Chris's decision-making process is an example of using

a. the central route of persuasion.
b. the peripheral route of persuasion.

c. groupthink.
d. social facilitation.

19. Mario is a political candidate who is debating the merits of the death penalty. He decides to explain both sides of the argument and then focus on his position. This strategy is a better idea if his audience is

a. strongly supportive of him.
b. strongly supportive of the idea.
c. skeptical.
d. gullible.

20. A man robbed a convenience store with a gun, escaping with all the money in the register. During the investigation detectives came up with several possible reasons why the man robbed the store. One was that maybe the man was poor and needed money to feed his family. This explanation is an example of

a. a personal attribution.
b. a situational attribution.
c. the fundamental attribution error.
d. groupthink.

21. People often have difficulty accepting that celebrities have substantial drug and alcohol problems because their television characters are so nice and sweet. This expectation that behavior should correspond with beliefs and personality (even if acting) is known as the

a. actor–observer discrepancy.
b. intuitive cognitive system.
c. correspondence bias.
d. Hollywood effect.

22. Patty falls over a hole in the sidewalk and start cursing the slowness of the university's maintenance workers. However, she laughed at how clumsy one of her friends was when she fell over the exact same hole 30 minutes earlier. This tendency to focus on situational factors to explain your behavior but dispositional factors to explain the behavior of others is known as the

a. confirmation bias.
b. self-fulfilling prophecy.
c. actor–observer discrepancy.
d. misattribution principle.

23. Josh, a Euro-American, has negative feelings about Juo, an Asian-American. Josh has no reason for these feelings and actually has not even talked to Juo. He just dislikes him because he is from a different ethnic background. What are Josh's feelings called?

a. Prejudice.
b. Discrimination.
c. A stereotype.
d. A typology.

24. Since the terrorist attacks on September 11, 2001, some American citizens have taken out their fear and anger on people who look like they might be from the same ethnic group as the hijackers. This type of unjustifiable behavior is called
    a. prejudice.
    b. assimilation reaction.
    c. ethnic referencing.
    d. discrimination.

25. Following the terrorist attacks on September 11, 2001, some angry Americans have lumped together all people who look even vaguely "Middle Eastern" and believe they all are linked to terrorism in some way. The beliefs of these Americans illustrate
    a. social categorization.
    b. the outgroup homogeneity effect.
    c. social role typing.
    d. ingroup favoritism.

26. Sandy, Roxanne, and Carolyn are put into a group in their statistics class. Kristen, Lori, and Melinda are put into a different group. All six of these women were originally friends. However, since being put into opposing groups, they have become bitter toward those not in their group and will share notes and homework only with group members. Their reactions reflect
    a. egoistic realism.
    b. ingroup favoritism.
    c. outgroup homogeneity effect.
    d. social roles theory.

27. Kristen decided to try out for the university's gymnastics team. When she performed her routine in front of team members and the coach, she did well on an easy cartwheel. However, when she tried the difficult double-twisted flip, she fell over and lost her shoe. Kristen's performance was affected by
    a. social loafing.
    b. deindividuation.
    c. the bystander effect.
    d. social facilitation.

28. Brandy is at a music concert where she is surrounded by thousands of people. Although she is normally shy and afraid to express her feelings, she soon gets swept up in the madness around her. She joins the mosh pit and begins yelling, laughing, and dancing hysterically. Which of the following best explains her sudden loss of inhibition?
    a. Deindividuation.
    b. The bystander effect.
    c. Social facilitation.
    d. Emotional contagion.

29. The space shuttle *Challenger* was launched despite the fact that it was a cold morning and NASA had been warned about faulty O-rings on the solid-rocket booster. The term that describes this extreme form of group decision-making among NASA engineers is
    a. groupthink.
    b. deindividuation.
    c. conformity.
    d. conflict avoidance.

30. Dr. Smith, an American psychologist, went to a professional conference. When she greeted other psychologists, she politely said hello and firmly shook hands with them. What does Dr. Smith's behavior illustrate?
    a. Social schemas.
    b. Ingroup rules.
    c. Sanction norms.
    d. Social norms.

31. When Phoebe stopped by her friend Monica's new apartment, she noticed that the living room walls were covered by hideous orange wallpaper. However, the next day when Monica asked her group of friends if they liked her beautiful wallpaper, all the rest said yes, so Phoebe did too. Phoebe's statement is an example of
    a. social facilitation.
    b. groupthink.
    c. deindividuation.
    d. conformity.

32. Ginger is interested in buying a new evening dress. She tells her mother that she will need $300 to purchase it. After her mother goes through an emotional tirade, Ginger asks for $100 to purchase the dress (which is the amount she wanted all along) and her mother agrees. Ginger is engaging in the influence tactic of
    a. foot in the door.
    b. door in the face.
    c. lowballing.
    d. high rolling.

33. Pedro is shopping for a car. He finally finds one at a reasonable price with all the options he wants. He agrees to buy it from the salesperson. When he goes to sign the contract, he notices a number of extras have been added at his expense (e.g., pinstripes, floor mats, keys, undercoating). Pedro believes the salesperson is trying the tactic of
    a. high rolling.
    b. door in the face.
    c. options management.
    d. lowballing.

34. In the famous Milgram obedience study, approximately what proportion of volunteers were willing to deliver the highest level of shock (450 volts) to the innocent volunteer/confederate?
    a. None.
    b. One-fifth.
    c. One-third.
    d. Two-thirds.

35. Which of the following is *not* an example of aggression?
    a. Shelton breaks the leg of a pedestrian he does not see and backs over.
    b. Because of jealousy, Mara starts a vicious, untrue rumor about a girl who talks to her boyfriend.
    c. Mac pushes his professor down the stairs after getting frustrated in a psychology exam.
    d. After Elliot and his girlfriend break up, he goes for a walk and knocks over the little statues on everybody's lawns.

36. Lori, who was in a hurry to get to school so she could be on time for a big test, became angry because Kristen was driving like a snail in front of her. When then they stopped at a red light, Lori got out of her car and smashed Kristen's windshield. Lori's behavior can best be explained by
    a. social facilitation theory.
    b. the frustration-aggression hypothesis.
    c. the projection hypothesis.
    d. the bystander effect.

37. Jerry was involved in a train crash. Although numerous cars were on fire, he rushed back into the train to save as many others as possible. This providing of help without any apparent reward for doing so is known as
    a. inclusive fitness.
    b. altruism.
    c. hedonism.
    d. reciprocity.

38. Jen was leaving a house with friends after a night of partying. In the street, they see several groups and pairs of people staring at and discussing a scene involving a man repeatedly slapping a woman while yelling and cursing at her. Jen experiences the bystander intervention effect, so she
    a. ignores the scene and does not help the woman.
    b. ignores everyone standing around and runs to help the woman.
    c. immediately finds a phone and calls the police.
    d. rallies a bunch of other observers to help the woman.

39. Which of the following is *not* one of the reasons for the bystander intervention effect?
    a. Diffusion of responsibility.
    b. Fear of making social blunders.
    c. Personal anonymity.
    d. Low level of moral reasoning.

40. Norman found that his friends in college were the people in the dorms who lived near him. He saw them a lot and they began hanging out together. His situation illustrates the effects of _____ on friendship.
    a. matching
    b. proximity
    c. conditioned rewards
    d. propriety

41. Pam and Tommy have all the same interests. They both like wild parties, tattoos, constant stimulation, and loads of attention. Because of the effects of _____, they have become close friends.
    a. matching
    b. propinquity
    c. conditioned rewards
    d. similarity

42. When Lyle and Erik were facing charges in court, their attorney took great pains to ensure that they had fresh haircuts and were dressed as attractively as possible. Their attorney is using the _____ stereotype.
    a. door in the face
    b. what is beautiful is good
    c. birds of a feather flock together
    d. external similarity

43. Dennis decides to bring home some flowers to show his girlfriend, Carmen, how much he cares for her. When she sees the flowers, she flies into a rage accusing him of infidelity or doing something else that he is trying to atone for. Carmen is making _____ attributions.
    a. distress-maintaining
    b. partner-enhancing
    c. external
    d. socially destructive

MATCHING QUESTIONS

Fill in the letter from Column B corresponding to the term that is most associated with the description presented in Column A.

Column A		Column B
____	1. Theory that self-awareness leads people to act in accord with personal values and beliefs.	A. Implicit B. Outgroups C. Diffusion of responsibility

___ 2. Theory that self-esteem protects people from death anxiety.

___ 3. Comparing self with those who are superior.

___ 4. Attitudes of which we are aware and can report to other people.

___ 5. Attitudes that we don't even know or recognize.

___ 6. Facial expressions, gestures, walking style, fidgeting.

___ 7. Idea that victims must have done something to justify what happened to them.

___ 8. Refer to something within a person such as abilities, traits, moods, or effort.

___ 9. Those groups to which we belong.

___ 10. Those groups to which we do not belong.

___ 11. Belief system in which men are primed to protect reputations through physical aggression.

___ 12. Behavior in which one acts in ways that benefit others.

___ 13. People are altruistic toward those with whom they share genes.

___ 14. One helps nonrelatives because they can return the favor in the future.

___ 15. People expect that others around in emergency situations will also offer help.

___ 16. State of intense longing and sexual desire.

___ 17. Strong commitment to care for and support a partner that develops slowly over time.

___ 18. Attributions of happy couples in which bad outcomes are attributed to the situation.

___ 19. Type of couple in which partners value each other's opinions, even if they disagree.

D. Matching principle
E. Companionate love
F. Prosocial
G. Just world hypothesis
H. Objective self-awareness
I. Terror management
J. Nonverbal behavior
K. Ingroups
L. Validating
M. Partner-enhancing
N. Reciprocal helping
O. Kin selection
P. Upward social comparisons
Q. Explicit
R. Personal attributions
S. Culture of honor
T. Passionate love

___ 20. Finding that the most successful romantic couples tend to be most physically similar.

THOUGHT QUESTIONS

1. You have been brought in as a consultant to a school system that is experiencing considerable racial conflict and gang violence. Considering the research on stereotypes, prejudice, and discrimination, discuss how you might address these problems.

2. You are a psychotherapist at the university counseling center. The university has instituted a policy that all students who wish to get married can come in for four sessions of free prenuptial advice. Describe how you would assess which couples were at risk for problems and how you might help the couples with future difficulties.

APPLICATIONS

An Activity to Demonstrate the Power of the Situation and the Fundamental Attribution Error

One of our (BB, EAS) favorite videos to show in class is a 1962 clip from the old *Candid Camera* television show. The clip, called *Facing the Rear*, shows the *Candid Camera* staff purposefully facing the wrong way in an elevator. Time after time individuals come into the elevator and, going with the norm of the situation, face the wrong way also. As the clip continues riders will turn all the way around, remove their hats, and put their hats back on if the other members in the elevator do so.

You can do your own version demonstrating the power of the situation with games you probably played in adolescence. Get a group of friends together in a public place, then have everybody look up. Have someone record how long it is before most of the people around you are also looking up. Recreate the *Candid Camera* scenario and face the wrong way on the elevator. See what percentage of people comply with this subtle social norm. If you are really brave, rearrange the desks in one of your classrooms and see if people will comply with that seating arrangement. Make up your own scenarios to see if people (particularly students) will mindlessly comply with your prearranged conditions. Make predictions about the variables that will facilitate this compliant behavior.

This also is an excellent exercise to illustrate one of the major concepts of the chapter—the *fundamental attribution error*. We vastly overestimate the power of traits and personal variables in explaining behavior when many times the cause is the power of the situation.

An Activity to Assess Gender Differences in Friend Relationships

The text alludes to various types of relationships, including both friendships and romantic relationships. With current divorce statistics, people argue that you need to pay particular attention to your friends because partners may come and go. The text talks about several factors related to friend relationships, including similarity and physical attractiveness. Another variable that is interesting with regard to friendships is gender differences; that is, how do men and women differ with respect to friendship patterns?

Assemble your male and female psychology friends and ask them the following questions. Who (males or females) has more friendships? Who (males or females) has the better or closer friendships? What are the characteristics of these relationships? How are they similar? How are they different? The perspectives from each gender may surprise you.

Researchers have addressed these exact questions and have found that women have *more* and *better* friends. The idea of male bonding has generally been found to be a myth. Whereas women tend to talk and share with their friends, men tend to have *activity buddies*. That is, they might have their golf buddies, poker buddies, football buddies, and so on. However, often the conversation does not vary far from the activity at hand.

The other interesting finding in this area is that men and women are seldom friends with each other, particularly after the college years. Students always laugh when I (BB) ask whether it would be acceptable to go over to my girlfriend's house late at night to discuss problems with my wife. Apparently this is a major reason why women and men are not friends. It is feared that once intimate feelings are discussed, then romance and sexual feelings cannot be too far behind. Therefore, we immediately cut in half the pool of possible friends.

Think of the implications here. First, who is at greater risk in the breakup of a relationship? (Men are.) Women generally foresee this possibility and establish support networks with their female friends. Males tend to be quite clueless and unsupported at the termination of a relationship. What are the implications of having only same-sex friends? Are there other perspectives that you might learn about and could benefit from? Do you think the current generation will do better with these gender disparities in friendship than previous ones? Why or why not?

WEB SITES

www2.psy.ohio-state.edu/programs/social
www.shyness.com
http://counseling.uchicago.edu/resources/virtualpamphlets/
relationships.shtml
www.spsp.org

ANSWER KEY

Fill-in-the-Blank Questions

1. Social psychology
2. Self-awareness
3. Self-schema
4. Interdependent self-construals
5. Self-esteem
6. Unconditional acceptance
7. Sociometer
8. Positive illusions
9. Self-evaluative maintenance
10. Social comparison
11. Attitude
12. Implicit
13. Attitude accessibility
14. Postdecisional dissonance
15. Persuasion
16. Elaboration likelihood model
17. Peripheral route
18. Attributions
19. Stereotypes
20. Illusory correlation
21. Self-fulfilling prophecy
22. Superordinate goals
23. Jigsaw classroom
24. Social loafing
25. Risky-shift effect
26. Group polarization
27. Compliance
28. Foot-in-the-door
29. Obedience
30. Frustration-aggression

Multiple-Choice Questions

1. c. The fundamental attribution error is the tendency to overemphasize personal factors and underestimate situational factors in explaining behavior.

   Incorrect answers:
   a. Confirmation bias is a made-up term.
   b. A self-fulfilling prophecy is when people come to behave in ways that confirm their own or others' expectations.
   d. A misattribution is identifying the wrong cause for one's behavior.

2. b. Self-concept is the term for everything that you know about yourself.

   Incorrect answers:
   a. Minimal self is a made-up term.
   c. Self-recognition is being aware of and able to identify oneself.
   d. Reflected appraisals are based on how people believe others perceive them.

3. d. According to Higgins's self-discrepancy theory, anxiety and guilt result from gaps between how we see ourselves and how we believe we ought to seem to others.

   Incorrect answers:
   a. Discrepancies between how we see ourselves and how we would like to see ourselves can lead to disappointment, frustration, and depression.
   b. Discrepancies between how we see ourselves and how we would like to see ourselves can lead to disappointment, frustration, and depression.
   c. Discrepancies between how we see ourselves and how we would like to see ourselves can lead to disappointment, frustration, and depression.

4. b. Self-awareness is highly dependent on the normal development of the frontal lobes of the brain.

   Incorrect answers:
   a. The basal ganglia are support structures in the brain.
   c. The limbic system is involved in emotional understanding and expression.
   d. The parietal lobe integrates the functions of several sensory modalities.

5. b. The cocktail party effect is the tendency to process information about the self despite distractions.

   Incorrect answers:
   a. Shadowing is a term from auditory testing when a stimulus is played at minimally different times in each ear.
   c. Prosopagnosia is the inability to recognize faces or objects.
   d. Selective consciousness is a made-up term.

6. a. Those in individualistic cultures tend to have independent self-construals because they are encouraged to be self-reliant and pursue personal success, even at the expense of interpersonal relations.

   Incorrect answers:
   b. People in collectivist cultures tend to have interdependent self-construals, in which their self-concepts are determined by their social roles and personal relationships.
   c. People in collectivist cultures tend to have interdependent self-construals, in which their self-concepts are determined by their social roles and personal relationships.
   d. Self-discrepancy is Higgins's theory for the perceptions of the differences between what one is and what one would like to be or ought to be.

7. a. Reflected appraisals are based on how people believe others perceive them.

   Incorrect answers:
   b. Basking in reflected glory is the tendency to identify with a group when it is popular.
   c. The collective self emphasizes connections to family, social groups, and ethnic groups and conformity to societal norms and group cohesiveness.
   d. The minimal self is a made-up term.

8. d. Unconditional acceptance is when parents love their children no matter what they do.

   Incorrect answers:
   a. A sociometer is an internal monitor of social acceptance or rejection.
   b. The better-than-average effect refers to the tendency for people to describe themselves as above average in just about every possible way.
   c. The self-enhancement motive is when individuals are especially motivated to seek information that confirms their positive self-views.

9. b. The better-than-average effect refers to the tendency for people to describe themselves as above average in just about every possible way.

   Incorrect answers:
   a. Delusional cognitions is a made-up term.
   c. According to the theory of self-evaluative maintenance, people can feel threatened when someone close to them outperforms them on a task that is personally relevant.
   d. In downward social comparison, people contrast themselves with others who are deficient to them on relevant dimensions.

10. d. The three domains of positive illusions are overestimating one's skills, abilities, and competencies; unrealistic perception of one's personal control over events; and being unrealistically optimistic about one's personal future.

    Incorrect answers:
    a. The three domains of positive illusions are overestimating one's skills, abilities, and competencies; unrealistic perception of one's personal control over events; and being unrealistically optimistic about one's personal future.
    b. The three domains of positive illusions are overestimating one's skills, abilities, and competencies; unrealistic perception of one's personal control over events; and being unrealistically optimistic about one's personal future.
    c. The three domains of positive illusions are overestimating one's skills, abilities, and competencies;

unrealistic perception of one's personal control over events; and being unrealistically optimistic about one's personal future.

11. d. In downward social comparison, people contrast themselves with others who are deficient to them on relevant dimensions.

   Incorrect answers:
   a. People with low self-esteem tend to make upward social comparisons with those who are superior to them.
   b. In decision making, counterfactual thinking is the consideration of different hypothetical outcomes for events or decisions.
   c. The self-serving bias is the tendency to take credit for success but blame failure on outside factors.

12. c. The self-serving bias is the tendency to take credit for success but blame failure on outside factors.

   Incorrect answers:
   a. In downward social comparison, people contrast themselves with others who are deficient to them on relevant dimensions.
   b. People with low self-esteem tend to make upward social comparisons with those who are superior to them.
   d. The better-than-average effect refers to the tendency for people to describe themselves as above average in just about every possible way.

13. a. The mere exposure effect indicates that the greater exposure we have to an item, the more positive attitude we have toward the item.

   Incorrect answers:
   b. Social exchange theory states that if the rewards are greater than the costs in a relationship, the relationship endures.
   c. Need complementarity refers to attraction of individuals who are opposites in traits because their needs complement one another.
   d. Attitude similarity refers to the common occurrence that those who are attracted to each other have similar attitudes.

14. d. Cognitive dissonance states that when there is a contradiction between an attitude and behavior, people change either their attitude or the behavior.

   Incorrect answers:
   a. Social facilitation is when the mere presence of others enhances performance.
   b. Implicit attitudes influence our feelings and behavior at an unconscious level.
   c. A consensus is an agreement among individuals.

15. a. The $1 group had insufficient justification for lying; therefore, they had to change their attitude more to reduce their dissonance.

   Incorrect answers:
   b. Postdecisional dissonance motivates individuals to focus on the positive characteristics of their choice and the negative aspects of the choice not made.
   c. Implicit attitudes influence our feelings and behavior at an unconscious level.
   d. Selective exposure is a made-up term.

16. d. Postdecisional dissonance motivates individuals to focus on the positive characteristics of their choice and the negative aspects of the choice not made.

   Incorrect answers:
   a. In the peripheral route to persuasion, people minimally process the message.
   b. The elaboration likelihood model is a theory of how persuasive messages lead to attitude changes.
   c. Effort justification is when individuals resolve their dissonance by increasing the importance of the group and their commitment to it.

17. b. Effort justification is when individuals resolve their dissonance by increasing the importance of the group and their commitment to it.

   Incorrect answers:
   a. Selective exposure is a made-up term.
   c. Hazing denial is a made-up term.
   d. The elaboration likelihood model is a theory of how persuasive messages lead to attitude changes.

18. a. The central route to persuasion is one in which people pay attention to arguments, consider all the information, and use rational cognitive processes.

   Incorrect answers:
   b. In the peripheral route to persuasion, people minimally process the message.
   c. Groupthink is the extreme form of group polarization where group members conform to the initial attitudes of other members who already agree.
   d. Social facilitation is when the mere presence of others enhances performance.

19. c. Two-sided arguments tend to be more persuasive when the audience is skeptical.

   Incorrect answers:
   a. One-sided arguments are best if the audience is on the speaker's side or is gullible.
   b. One-sided arguments are best if the audience is on the speaker's side or is gullible.
   d. One-sided arguments are best if the audience is on the speaker's side or is gullible.

20. b. Situational or external attributions refer to outside events, such as the weather, luck, accidents, or the actions of other people that cause actions to occur.

    Incorrect answers:
    a. Personal attributions are explanations that refer to something within a person, such as abilities, traits, moods, or effort.
    c. The fundamental attribution error is the tendency to overemphasize personal factors and underestimate situational factors in explaining behavior.
    d. Groupthink is the extreme form of group polarization where group members conform to the initial attitudes of other members who already agree.

21. c. The correspondence bias is when we expect people's behavior to correspond with their beliefs and personality.

    Incorrect answers:
    a. In the actor–observer discrepancy, people are biased toward situational factors when explaining their own behavior but toward dispositional factors when explaining the behavior of others.
    b. The intuitive cognitive system is a made-up term.
    d. The Hollywood effect is a made-up term.

22. c. In the actor–observer discrepancy, people are biased toward situational factors when explaining their own behavior but toward dispositional factors when explaining the behavior of others.

    Incorrect answers:
    a. Confirmation bias is a made-up term.
    b. A self-fulfilling prophecy is when people come to behave in ways that confirm their own or others' expectations.
    d. The misattribution principle is a made-up term.

23. a. Prejudice refers to the affective or attitudinal responses associated with stereotypes, and it usually involves negative judgments about people on the basis of their group membership.

    Incorrect answers:
    b. Discrimination is the unjustified and inappropriate treatment of people due to prejudice.
    c. Stereotypes are cognitive schemas that allow for easy and efficient organization of information about people based on their membership in certain groups.
    d. Typology is a made-up term referring to particular types.

24. d. Discrimination is the unjustified and inappropriate treatment of people due to prejudice.

Incorrect answers:
a. Prejudice refers to the affective or attitudinal responses associated with stereotypes, and it usually involves negative judgments about people on the basis of their group membership.
b. Assimilation reaction is a made-up term.
c. Ethnic referencing is a made-up term.

25. b. In the outgroup homogeneity effect, individuals tend to view outgroup members as less varied than ingroup members.

    Incorrect answers:
    a. Social categorization is a made-up term.
    c. Social role typing is a made-up term.
    d. With ingroup favoritism, individuals are more likely to distribute resources to members of the ingroup than the outgroup.

26. b. With ingroup favoritism, individuals are more likely to distribute resources to members of the ingroup than the outgroup.

    Incorrect answers:
    a. Egoistic realism is a made-up term.
    c. In the outgroup homogeneity effect, individuals tend to view outgroup members as less varied than ingroup members.
    d. Social roles theory is a made-up term.

27. d. Social facilitation is when the presence of others influences performance; it can enhance performance for simple tasks but interfere with performance of complex tasks.

    Incorrect answers:
    a. Social loafing is when people work less hard when in a group than when working alone.
    b. Deindividuation occurs when people are not self-aware and, therefore, not paying attention to their personal standards.
    c. The bystander intervention effect refers to the failure to offer help by those who observe someone in need.

28. a. Deindividuation occurs when people are not self-aware and, therefore, not paying attention to their personal standards.

    Incorrect answers:
    b. The bystander intervention effect refers to the failure to offer help by those who observe someone in need.
    c. Social facilitation is when the presence of others influences performance; it can enhance the performance for simple tasks but interfere with performance on complex tasks.
    d. Emotional contagion is a made-up term.

29. a. Groupthink is the extreme form of group polarization where group members conform to the initial attitudes of other members who already agree.

    Incorrect answers:
    b. Deindividuation occurs when people are not self-aware and, therefore, not paying attention to their personal standards.
    c. Conformity is the altering of one's behavior or opinions to match those of others.
    d. Conflict avoidance is a made-up term.

30. d. Social norms are expected standards of conduct, such as behavior that is appropriate in a given situation.

    Incorrect answers:
    a. Social schemas is a made-up term.
    b. Ingroup rules is a made-up term.
    c. Sanction norms is a made-up term.

31. d. Conformity is the altering of one's behavior or opinions to match those of others.

    Incorrect answers:
    a. Social facilitation is when the presence of others influences performance; it can enhance performance for simple tasks but interfere with performance of complex tasks.
    b. Groupthink is the extreme form of group polarization where group members conform to the initial attitudes of other members who already agree.
    c. Deindividuation occurs when people are not self-aware and, therefore, not paying attention to their personal standards.

32. b. Door in the face is the influence technique in which people are more likely to agree to a small request after they have refused a large request because the second request seems modest in comparison and people want to seem reasonable.

    Incorrect answers:
    a. In the foot in the door effect, people are more likely to comply with a large and undesirable request if they have earlier agreed to a small request.
    c. Lowballing is the tactic of getting people to agree to a very low price and then adding additional costs.
    d. High rolling is a made-up term.

33. d. Lowballing is the tactic of getting people to agree to a very low price and then adding additional costs.

Incorrect answers:
a. High rolling is a made-up term.
b. Door in the face is the influence technique in which people are more likely to agree to a small request after they have refused a large request because the second request seems modest in comparison and people want to seem reasonable.
c. Options management is a made-up term.

34. d. Approximately two-thirds of volunteers were willing to deliver the highest level of shock.

Incorrect answers:
a. Approximately two-thirds of volunteers were willing to deliver the highest level of shock.
b. Approximately two-thirds of volunteers were willing to deliver the highest level of shock.
c. Approximately two-thirds of volunteers were willing to deliver the highest level of shock.

35. a. Aggression is any behavior or action that involves the intention to harm someone else.

Incorrect answers:
b. Aggression is any behavior or action that involves the intention to harm someone else.
c. Aggression is any behavior or action that involves the intention to harm someone else.
d. Aggression is any behavior or action that involves the intention to harm someone else.

36. b. The frustration-aggression hypothesis states that the more one's goals are blocked, the greater the frustration and thus the greater the aggression.

Incorrect answers:
a. Social facilitation is when the presence of others influences performance; it can enhance performance for simple tasks but interfere with performance of complex tasks.
c. The projection hypothesis is a made-up term.
d. The bystander intervention effect refers to the failure to offer help by those who observe someone in need.

37. b. Altruism is the providing of help without any apparent reward for doing so.

Incorrect answers:
a. Inclusive fitness is a made-up term.
c. Hedonism is acting in a way that maximizes pleasure and avoids pain.
d. Reciprocity is acting in a way to ensure rewards for self in the future.

38. a. The bystander intervention effect refers to the failure to offer help by those who observe someone in need.

    Incorrect answers:
    b. The bystander intervention effect refers to the failure to offer help by those who observe someone in need.
    c. The bystander intervention effect refers to the failure to offer help by those who observe someone in need.
    d. The bystander intervention effect refers to the failure to offer help by those who observe someone in need.

39. d. The bystander intervention effect is due to a diffusion of responsibility, fear of making social blunders, personal anonymity, and a cost–benefit trade-off.

    Incorrect answers:
    a. The bystander intervention effect is due to a diffusion of responsibility, fear of making social blunders, personal anonymity, and a cost–benefit trade-off.
    b. The bystander intervention effect is due to a diffusion of responsibility, fear of making social blunders, personal anonymity, and a cost–benefit trade-off.
    c. The bystander intervention effect is due to a diffusion of responsibility, fear of making social blunders, personal anonymity, and a cost–benefit trade-off.

40. b. The effects of proximity are that the more often people come into contact, the more likely they are to become friends.

    Incorrect answers:
    a. Matching is the principle that the most successful romantic couples also tend to be the most physically similar.
    c. The term *conditioned rewards* refers to the fact that we are attracted to individuals who are associated with rewards.
    d. Propriety is acting in a dignified and respectful manner.

41. d. People who are similar in attitudes, values, interests, backgrounds, and personalities tend to like each other.

    Incorrect answers:
    a. Matching is the principle that the most successful romantic couples also tend to be the most physically similar.
    b. The effects of proximity are that the more often

people come into contact, the more likely they are to become friends.
    c. The term *conditioned rewards* refers to the fact that we are attracted to individuals who are associated with rewards.

42. b. The "what is beautiful is good" stereotype relates to the finding that physically attractive people are judged to be less socially deviant and are given lighter sentences when convicted of crimes.

    Incorrect answers:
    a. Door in the face is the influence technique in which people are more likely to agree to a small request after they have refused a large request because the second request seems modest in comparison and people want to seem reasonable.
    c. "Birds of a feather flock together" refers to the fact that people are attracted to similar others.
    d. External similarity is a made-up term.

43. a. Unhappy couples make distress-maintaining attributions in which they view one another in the most negative way possible.

    Incorrect answers:
    b. Happy couples make partner-enhancing attributions in which they overlook bad behavior or respond constructively.
    c. External attributions are causal explanations aimed at environmental events.
    d. Socially destructive attributions is a made-up term.

Matching Questions

1. H Objective self-awareness
2. I Terror management
3. P Upward social comparisons
4. Q Explicit
5. A Implicit
6. J Nonverbal behavior
7. G Just world hypothesis
8. R Personal attributions
9. K Ingroups
10. B Outgroups
11. S Culture of honor
12. F Prosocial
13. O Kin selection
14. N Reciprocal helping
15. C Diffusion of responsibility
16. T Passionate love
17. E Companionate love
18. M Partner-enhancing
19. L Validating
20. D Matching principle

Thought Questions

1. Answers will vary but might include a discussion of the contact hypothesis or the idea that simply learning more about outgroups will lessen tension and hostility (it does not). Students might incorporate Sherif's ideas of disparate groups having shared superordinate goals and how this might be incorporated into school activities. In addition, they might propose a variation of Aronson's jigsaw classroom as a way of facilitating more positive attitudes toward other ethnicities. Finally, students might discuss how ingroup and outgroup formation seems to be a natural, and normally adaptive, process of social interaction.

2. Answers will vary. In terms of assessment, students might address the issues of proximity and similarity while taking into account the phenomenon of need complementarity. The couples could also be rated on Sternberg's three components of love: passion, intimacy, and commitment. One also could relate the differences between passionate and companionate love and the toxicity of extramarital affairs.

   In terms of treatment, the therapist could attempt to alter Gottman's four interpersonal styles that lead to marital discord: being overly critical, holding the partner in contempt, being defensive, and mentally withdrawing from the relationship. One could also try to help the couple make partner-enhancing attributions as opposed to distress-maintaining attributions.